ERIC WARBURG

ERIC WARBURG

A TRANSATLANTIC LIFE

JEANETTE ERAZO
HEUFELDER

Translated by Peter Lewis

Contents

Introduction

Eric Warburg was a banker all his life, just as his grandfather, father, brothers, and generations of male members of his extensive family had been before him. And yet his name is primarily associated with his role as a transatlantic networker during the early years of the Federal Republic of Germany; in 1952 he played a key part in two private initiatives on both sides of the Atlantic that were designed to forge closer ties between the newly created state occupying the western part of pre-war Germany and the United States of America. The American Council on Germany (ACG), which he was instrumental in forming in the USA, served the purpose of promoting dialogue between German and American business groups. Its German sister organisation was intended, under the name *Atlantik-Brücke* (Atlantic Bridge), to set transatlantic exchange in motion from its base in Hamburg. Eric Warburg provided the *Atlantik-Brücke* with a range and quality of contacts in the US establishment that existed nowhere else in Germany at this time, seven years after the collapse of the Nazi regime.

Born the son of Max Warburg in 1900 into the banking dynasty M. M. Warburg, which since the late nineteenth century had had ties to the United States, Eric Warburg saw German–American relations as a natural element of his life right from childhood. His family had been involved in forming transnationally oriented think-tanks once before, in the period immediately after the First World War. Paul Warburg was an initiator of the Council on Foreign Relations, which came into being in New York in 1921, and he and his brother Max Warburg were also involved in the simultaneous creation of the Hamburg Institute for Foreign Policy. Both these institutes were established with the purpose of formulating foreign policy concepts promoting the cause of international peace, initiatives that were meant to give Germany and Europe as a whole greater democratic stability in the aftermath of the Great War.

Yet in order to understand what impelled Eric Warburg – a Jewish returning emigrant who had stayed on in Germany for several years after 1933 and had experienced persecution, expropriation, and expulsion at first hand – to provide the representatives of German elites with a transatlantic lobbying instrument so soon after the end of the Second World War, which had been so traumatic not just for European Jews but for the Jewish people in general, it is not sufficient simply to point to the biographical fact that it was wholly consistent with the bourgeois-liberal self-image of the Warburg family that it should get involved in the founding of 'societies'.

Eric Warburg was born at the very start of the twentieth century, the great political upheavals of which took him on an odyssey with an uncertain outcome. When the career in banking in Germany that had been mapped out for him came to an abrupt end after the National Socialists seized power in 1933, he remained in the country to help his father in his endeavours to facilitate an orderly emigration for German Jews. In 1938 he emigrated himself, took US citizenship, decided to adopt the English form of his forename 'Erich', and enlisted in the US military to fight the Nazis. After the war he went back to his native city of Hamburg, but was unsure whether he ought to live permanently in Germany with his Jewish wife and children so soon after the end of the Nazi period. At least the active involvement of the USA in the post-war order in Europe gave him grounds for optimism.

Eric Warburg's memoirs appeared at the beginning of the 1980s and were intended solely for his friends and family. In them he recounted episodes from his childhood, youth, and his parental home; wrote about friends, family, and the years he spent in the USA; and did not omit the war years and the post-war period. Yet he disclosed virtually nothing about his own role during this time. The caution that made him deem it inadvisable to make any great fuss about himself obeyed a principle of his father's: Max Warburg believed that it was imperative for a person to champion a cause that they thought was right and urgent, but that that cause had to speak for itself and require no explanation, or rather the explanations had to be delivered 'neutrally'. Every other course of action he deemed 'inappropriate'.[1] Max Warburg instilled this principle into his son in 1935, in the Germany of the Nazi period, for obvious reasons. Eric Warburg internalised this attitude to such an extent that he even published his memoirs only privately – out of the public eye, so to speak – and mentioned nothing in them that he thought might potentially compromise their private character. His friend Nina Grunenberg, who worked as a journalist on the newspaper *Die Zeit*, expressed her astonishment to him that he had glossed over a number of important chapters in his life 'with a sense of decorum' that left many questions unanswered. She was not alone in believing that discretion had its limits in this regard.[2] For in order to understand why he alone, out of all his family, was the only one to return to Germany after 1945, and why he felt so responsible for fostering and maintaining German–American relations that he espoused this cause with every fibre of his being over the ensuing decades, it is essential that we learn more about his life between the First World War and the beginnings of the Federal Republic than he himself was prepared to divulge. It is the aim of this present book to fulfil that task. Against the historical background, it describes Eric Warburg's emergence from the looming shadow of the preceding generations of Warburgs, repurposing their liberal values to form the core of his own Atlanticist agenda.

*

The Warburg Cultural Studies Library, a greatly revered institution in academic circles, which Aby Warburg famously established in Hamburg with the funds that his brothers amassed from their banking activities, could only be saved from destruction after 1933 by being moved abroad. A heated dispute flared up between the German and the American branches of the Warburg family over its future location. Felix Warburg wanted to bring the library to America, but his nephew Eric insisted upon London and won the day. The strong characters of the Warburg family did not shy away from confrontation, though always retained their keen sense of irony in the process – a fact attested to not least by the motto that Eric Warburg applied to himself and likeminded family members: 'All the good guys are on our side!'[3] This phrase, which he was wont to weave into debates on matters of fundamental principle, became something of a dictum within his family. His fierce commitment to the cause of goodness is fitting as the motto of a staunch defender of democracy, whose views were shaped equally by the liberal atmosphere of the 1920s and his experience of the overthrow of democracy. Before his death in 1990, he witnessed the end of the Cold War.

I

The Setting

In 1897, the banker Moritz M. Warburg acquired the Kösterberg, a plot of land on a hillside overlooking the River Elbe on the western fringes of the Hamburg suburb of Blankenese. Its grounds were home to a former hostelry that the family dubbed Noah's Ark because it looked as though it had been 'washed up on the banks of the Elbe after the Flood'.[1] Not far from the Ark, Moritz Warburg had a white villa built for himself and his wife, with ample room to put up their grown-up sons and daughters when they descended on the Kösterberg with their families at weekends. When Moritz Warburg bought the plot above the Elbe, two of his five sons, Felix and Paul, had just married into the New York banking house of Kuhn, Loeb & Co., which had been founded in 1867 by German–Jewish emigrants. Paul got to know his future wife, Nina Loeb, the daughter of the bank's founder Solomon Loeb, at his brother Felix's wedding in 1895. On that day, Felix was marrying Frieda Schiff, the daughter of Jakob Schiff, whose first job had been as an apprentice at M. M. Warburg in Hamburg and who in 1885 succeeded both Abraham Klein and Solomon Loeb as director of the bank they had founded. On his visits back home, Paul – who had had been permanently resident in New York since 1902 with his wife and two children, James and Bettina – stayed at the Ark, which had in the meantime likewise been refurbished as a private residence, while Felix, who settled in the USA immediately after getting married, occasionally dispatched his children to stay with his relatives on the Kösterberg in Hamburg during the long holidays. When Moritz M. Warburg died in 1910, his son Max and his wife Alice were already living on the family estate above the Elbe. The couple had another villa built in the grounds, using the red bricks that would come to typify buildings of this period in Hamburg. Fritz, the youngest of the five brothers, took over his parents' house and spent the summers there with his family. Only for Aby, the oldest, was the Kösterberg no longer a central focal point. After a long period of research in Florence devoted to his study of the Renaissance, Aby returned to Hamburg with his wife Mary in 1902 and began assembling his famous cultural studies library. In 1909 he bought the property at Heilwigstraße 114 that would, over time, become a magnet for art and cultural historians from all over Europe. It was within this family milieu on the Kösterberg, which was characterised by scholarliness, commercial acumen, and a liberal cosmopolitan outlook, that Erich Warburg, the only son of the Hamburg banker Max Warburg, grew up with his four younger sisters.

*

In his biography of the Warburg dynasty, Ron Chernow paints a very positive picture of the young Erich. Reputedly, the author reports, Erich was convivial, friendly, at ease with himself and others, and down-to-earth; someone who did not take himself too seriously and who was always game for a laugh. From his very first day at school, he compensated for the fact that he was raised among a gaggle of sisters by having a classmate, Wolfgang Rittmeister, take the place of the brother he never had. As far as Erich's relationship with his father was concerned, he was forever trying to please him. Conversely, Max Warburg found his son endearing but was doubtful whether he possessed the qualities that made for a good banker.[2] Erich's four sisters – Lola, Renate, Anita, and Gisela – were all younger than him and not subject to the pressure of expectation that weighed heavily upon the sole male heir, who was supposed to further expand the transatlantic links to Kuhn, Loeb & Co. in the next generation. Thanks to Jakob Schiff's investments in the expanding railroad-construction sector, the New York banking house had developed into a significant American financial institution.

*

Around the turn of the twentieth century, Kuhn, Loeb & Co. was the only Jewish banking operation that could seriously compete with John Pierpont Morgan, unquestionably the most influential banker in the history of the USA, whose financial institution was the epitome of a WASP (White Anglo-Saxon Protestant) firm. This strict division into WASP and Jewish banking houses also extended to their employees, though relationships with individual clients and businesses were not affected.[3] Thus, even at the time of Jakob Schiff, the banking house of Kuhn, Loeb & Co. received legal advice from a WASP law firm: Cravath, Henderson & de Gersdorff – Cravath for short – was one of the first major legal practices in New York to specialise in commercial law.[4] The institution of the large law firm was one of the innovations introduced at the start of the American century.[5] For, as a result of the great socioeconomic transformation of the USA that took place at the turn of the nineteenth to the twentieth century, within a short space of time commercial and corporate legal consultancy became too complex and large an area to continue to be left to individual lawyers – as it had been up until then. Paul D. Cravath had begun practising as a lawyer in New York in the 1880s. On being appointed head of the firm in 1906, he immediately transformed the business by turning it into a 'law factory'. Places on the conveyor belt were reserved for young lawyers who proceeded, working in a team, to reassemble legal problems that had been broken down into their individual components. In 1903 the firm took occupancy of a large suite of offices at 52 William Street in Lower Manhattan, situated within the newly built Kuhn–Loeb Building, a move that made communication with the important Cravath client far easier.

*

Even at the end of the nineteenth century – when the stream of investment capital still flowed from Europe to America, funding modern infrastructure projects and the construction of entire cities – US entrepreneurs and financial investors had a clear conception of the economic dependencies that existed between America and the old continent. Yet a political mission only grew out of this after the outbreak of the First World War, when the USA changed within just a few short years from being a debtor country to the largest creditor nation on earth. American steel producers, who were still struggling with a recession in 1914, switched to the manufacture of armaments. Between 1914 and 1917, J. P. Morgan alone provided England and France with loans running into billions of dollars in order to finance the war effort, and this money duly flowed back into the USA in the form of arms purchases. Steadily increasing investment in Europe brought with it a growing interest on the part of US investors in American foreign policy. Positions that could be defined as 'internationalist' began to make themselves apparent. As early as four months before the outbreak of the war, in an interview with *The New York Times* Jakob Schiff warned about the consequences of a protracted conflict – and about either Germany or England achieving an outright victory. He regarded the European standpoints in this war as all being wrong, since they jeopardised the American position and the possibility of a stable European peace order in equal measure.[6] In believing this, he was an early adopter of a position that was sympathetic to the new 'internationalist' trend in US foreign policy, which identified a clear link between peace and a stable democratic order in Europe on the one hand and a leading role for America on the other. Even so, he kept his distance from the group of Atlanticists that was beginning to form within this tendency, who as soon as war broke out in Europe called for the USA to intervene in a manner that was commensurate with its democratic leadership role, and in 1915 launched a campaign which they dubbed the Preparedness Movement. Its motto was: 'Anyone who wants peace should prepare for war.'[7] And, in the view of that group of New York investment bankers, politicians, and commercial lawyers who now linked the upholding of American values like freedom and democracy with the military defence of the USA, the nation was decidedly *un*prepared.[8] The instigators of the Preparedness Movement, who also counted Paul Cravath among their number, donated funds to raise an army of volunteers. Their historical models for this were the Rough Riders, a volunteer regiment led by General Leonard Wood and the future US president Theodore Roosevelt during the Spanish–American War of 1898. This unit had been the only one of three American volunteer units to play an active role in combat on the island of Cuba. Because the preparedness campaign was totally at odds with the official policy of neutrality adopted by President Woodrow Wilson, Schiff found himself unable to support it. Schiff's reticence can be explained through his consistently firm compliance with the policies of his adopted country; he would never have taken the liberty of criticising it openly. And after Woodrow Wilson changed course and the United States entered the war, he continued to remain in step with the official line, despite the fact that a large part of his family was still living in Germany.[9]

*

Erich graduated from secondary school in Hamburg in the spring of 1918 and immediately signed up for military service, convinced as he was that his year of school graduates would still be required to fight if victory was to be achieved.[10] 'Uncle Aby' was the first family member he told about his enlistment. 'My military service is now a done deal,' he wrote.[11] There was now nothing to stop him, he went on, from being drafted into the Third Guards Field Artillery Regiment. Aby Warburg could sympathise with his nephew's patriotic zeal. He had found his own army days, which were by now a good quarter of a century ago, a positively liberating experience. It gave him a sense of belonging, even though this was illusory: as a German Jew he would have been disbarred from a full-time career in the military. Yet whereas he was able to simply 'play at being a soldier in peacetime', his nephew was now serving in a hot war.[12] In the final phase of the conflict,

Erich was in danger of losing his life, or possibly his 'idealism', which in the opinion of his uncle was more pronounced in Erich than it was in all his other nieces and nephews.[13] This concern for Erich's idealism came from the fact that Jewish men, despite laying down their lives in their thousands on the battlefield for Germany, were as a matter of principle commonly suspected of disloyalty toward the Fatherland on account of their membership of a community that transcended nationality. Like so many Jews who had volunteered for active service, at the beginning of the war Aby Warburg had still entertained the illusion that they might now be recognised as full members of German society. Too old himself to serve in the conflict, in late 1914 he brought out a new Italian magazine, *La Rivista Illustrata*, which had the stated aim of convincing his intermittent adopted homeland of the 'intrinsic need to become involved in this conflict'[14] – for Italy was still undecided over which side it should enter the Great War on.[15] In fact, Austria-Hungary and Germany had been Italy's partners in a military alliance since the formation of the Triple Alliance in 1882. Yet when Italy threw in its lot with the Entente powers of Great Britain and France in May 1915, Aby Warburg recognised how futile his endeavours were and ceased publication of *La Rivista Illustrata*.[16] At the outset of the war, Germany was confident of a swift victory. When this did not eventuate, the military authorities and the right-wing press were quick to scapegoat the Jews. In 1916, the German Popular Party (*Deutschvölkische Partei*) successfully enacted its policy of requiring that the Prussian War Ministry conduct a statistical census of 'all Jewish military personnel at the front, behind the lines, and in the reserves'. This so-called 'Jewish census' was designed to corroborate the propaganda that was being spread about 'Jewish shirkers', 'black marketeers', and 'war profiteers', though a subsequent enquiry held in 1922 found that the percentage of Jews called up for active service matched that of conscripted non-Jews among the populace.[17] Aby Warburg was deeply traumatised by the slanders that his brothers, above all, were subjected to. For while the right-wing press laid the blame for America's entry into the war in 1917 at their door, in actual fact the contribution made by Max and Fritz in terms of financial and economic policy was of incalculable value to the 'German cause'.[18] The patriotic stance of the Warburgs during the war was not restricted to the voluntary enlistment for front-line service of family members of fighting age, and the German Empire profited from the Hamburg banking house's connections to international market players. It was only thanks to the agency of the Warburg bankers that Germany was able to secure urgently needed currency to the tune of 3 billion Reichsmarks through the sale of German bonds in Scandinavia. For the duration of the war Fritz Warburg had relocated to Stockholm with the express intention of forging closer links with companies with which the banking house had long collaborated, and on which the continuing supply of iron ore to the German munitions industry depended.[19] During the period of American neutrality, before the USA itself became a combatant nation in April 1917, when the German Empire could hardly obtain any credit due to the influence that British banks could bring to bear in the United States, Max Warburg was able to win neutral banks like the Java Bank of Batavia round to the idea that they should not issue bonds in the Netherlands but instead place them with Kuhn, Loeb & Co. in New York, which explains why numerous banking transactions conducted by German firms took place in the Far East and South East Asia during the First World War.[20] The fact that the family was then suspected and openly accused of acting 'solely in the interests of International Jewry' drove Aby Warburg to the brink of despair.[21] As the war dragged on, his situation grew markedly worse; in November 1918, under the pressure of Germany's imminent defeat, he suffered a nervous breakdown. In his medical report, his doctor, the Hamburg neurologist Heinrich Embden, drew a clear connection between the catastrophe suffered by the Fatherland and Aby Warburg's own personal mental collapse, which led to his first spell of treatment as an inpatient at a Hamburg clinic.[22]

*

The American branch of the Warburg family also felt at first hand the impact of a public mood that was now increasingly nationalistically minded and hostile to anything German. After Germany's invasion of neutral Belgium at the start of the war, but at the very latest since the sinking of the passenger liner *Lusitania* by a U-boat of the German Imperial Navy on 7 May 1915, the USA was gripped by a wave of indignation. Thanks to his exposed position, Paul Warburg in particular became the target of anti-German hostility. Since 1913 he had occupied the post of vice-chairman of the US central bank the Federal Reserve, having been instrumental in its founding – on his arrival in New York in 1902 he had been so appalled by the chaotic state of the US banking sector that he lobbied hard for the establishment of a central banking system along European lines.[23] After war broke out in Europe, he adopted much the same attitude toward events as Jakob Schiff – and that of many other loyal US citizens who happened to be of German–Jewish descent. At the very start of the war, long before the USA entered the fray, Paul Warburg

15

had left his shares in the Hamburg family bank to his brother Felix, in order to avoid any suspicion of a conflict of interests. Nonetheless, so much hostility was directed at him during the war that he voluntarily stepped down from the board of the Federal Reserve in August 1918.

*

As for his nephew, Aby Warburg's fears proved unfounded. The overwhelming public atmosphere of anti-Semitism did not trigger any disillusionment in Erich. Even after Germany's final defeat, which was sealed by the Armistice of November 1918, he retained his idealism; attacks by right-wing elements, who blamed the Jews for Germany's defeat, left little impression on him, nor did he shed any tears for Germany's crumbling monarchy. But the chaos on the streets in the weeks that followed, and the lack of any political leadership while Germany was being provisionally governed by a deeply divided council of people's representatives, marked him for life. For the climate of political uncertainty was exploited equally by right-wing insurrectionists, leftwing Spartacists, and Bolsheviks. And so, rather than immediately stripping off his uniform on the day of Germany's defeat and, like other sons of the bourgeoisie of his generation, joining the ranks of the workers' and peasants' revolutionary councils, on 24 December 1918, six weeks after the cessation of regular hostilities, Erich Warburg found himself in the ranks of the Third Guards Cavalry Regiment battling against revolutionary forces of the People's Marine Division, who had barricaded themselves in Berlin's City Palace.[24] This 'Christmas Offensive' was Erich's only taste of action. From his point of view, it had to do with defending a democracy that was still very much in its infancy.

*

On November 16, a week after the collapse of the monarchy, an appeal was circulated in the press calling on Germans to 'exorcise ... the tendency to resort to force' in foreign policy and to prepare for a 'tough battle to assert our rights through legal means'.[25] The signatories of this appeal were all employees of the Foreign Ministry, who had come together under the leadership of Kurt Riezler, the head of the newly formed Germany bureau. They called themselves the November 16th Society after the date of their public appeal. En bloc, they joined the left-liberal German Democratic Party (*Deutsche Demokratische Partei*; DDP), which had only recently been launched. Other members of the DDP from the very beginning included Theodor Heuss and Count Harry Kessler, joint editors-in-chief of the magazine *Die Deutsche Nation* (*The German Nation*), who attempted to influence how German foreign policy was perceived abroad through the means of journalism.[26] The DDP was a meeting ground for people who over the course of the war had changed their views and who had subsequently thrown their weight behind attempts to negotiate an equitable peace. As is well known, though, the German generals had done nothing to initiate such a peace settlement. Admittedly, the last German chancellor under the monarchy, Max von Baden, did try to exert some influence to this end over the peace negotiations. At this time, his advisor Kurt Hahn founded a 'Working Group for Law Politics' headed by the sociologist and economist Max Weber. Its brief was to devise legal arguments that could be used at the Versailles Peace Conference to refute the idea that Germany bore sole responsibility for the war. The desired goal was to achieve not a 'peace through coercion' but rather – taking its cue from the 'peace without victory' envisaged in President Wilson's peace plan – a 'peace under the law'.[27] However, the Kaiser's abdication and the change of regime had come too late to have any real impact on the peace talks. Germany's sole responsibility for the outbreak of the war, and all the associated consequences, were enshrined in the Peace of Versailles, which was signed in June 1919 and entered into force in January 1920. In the weeks leading up to the signing, Carl Melchior and the German Finance Commission had drawn up an alternative draft linking reparations payments to Germany's economic capacity, but to no avail.[28] Melchior, who attended the peace talks as head of the German Finance Commission, was a co-shareholder in the M. M. Warburg banking house. Acting initially as a legal advisor to the bank, at the time when the United States entered the war in April 1917 he took over Felix Warburg's shares when they became enemy assets, and in doing so became the first shareholder in the bank who was not part of the Warburg family. At the Versailles peace negotiations, Carl Melchior quit the German delegation twelve days before the treaty was signed in protest at the unachievable peace conditions, which were based on Article 231 – a key clause in establishing German war guilt – which stated that Germany was responsible for all the losses and damages sustained by the Allied governments as a result of a war that had been forced upon them. Like Melchior, the British economist John Maynard Keynes, who attended the peace talks as a British negotiator, saw himself obliged to quit his post and walk out of the proceedings.

*

The total sum owing in reparations was to be determined over the following two years by a reparations commission that was convened for this sole purpose. One member of this commission was a young lawyer by the name of John Foster Dulles, who accompanied the American delegation to Paris on the recommendation of his uncle, US secretary of state Robert Lansing. It was on his advice that Article 231 of the Versailles Treaty, commonly referred to as the 'war guilt clause' and the prime cause of German indignation, was included in the final settlement, as a way of ensuring that the reparations were organised on the basis of universally binding law rather than allowing them, as had previously been the case, to be brokered *in camera* by diplomats, to the exclusion of all public scrutiny. Following the principle of the oblivion clause, they tended to adhere to the notion of 'beneficial forgetting'.[29] John Foster Dulles, who over three decades and another world war later would himself become US secretary of state under President Dwight Eisenhower, strove to find a compromise formula in the peace negotiations. On the one hand, the German government would have to agree that Germany should be liable for reparations covering the total cost of the war. On the other, Allied governments would have to accept that the German administration's capacity to pay the reparations owing was limited. The first part of this compromise was incorporated into Article 231. The second part, however, which was split off from the first and included in Article 232 instead, played no further role in the ensuing wranglings, since Article 231 was perceived by Germany as a war guilt clause and, in conjunction with the claim made by the Allied governments that Germany bore moral responsibility for starting the war, had a fatal effect on public opinion in Germany.[30] Max Weber, who had joined the German delegation attending the Versailles peace talks as an expert on the question of war guilt, responded there and then to Article 231 by issuing the so-called 'professorial memorandum', a position statement he authored jointly with the jurist Albrecht Mendelssohn Bartholdy, the historian Hans Delbrück, and the former general and latterly pacifist Maximilian von Montgelas, who took a stand against the Allied contention that Germany was solely to blame for the war, a thesis that was advanced to justify the harsh peace terms. On the periphery of the peace negotiations, this 'committee of four' devised the idea of a peace research unit that would examine the causes of the First World War and issue guidelines for a democratically legitimised foreign policy. The first fruit of this idea was the Peace Treaties Archive, for which Paul Warburg put Noah's Ark – as his house on the Kösterberg was still known by the family – at the disposal of Mendelssohn Bartholdy, who had been appointed to the chair of foreign law and international private law at the University of Hamburg in 1920. On the Warburg estate in the Hamburg suburb of Blankenese, the future director of the Institute for Foreign Policy embarked on his work reappraising all diplomatic files from the German Foreign Office relating to the lead-up to the First World War from the founding of the Second German Empire in 1871. Together with the orientalist Johannes Lepsius and the historian Friedrich Thimme, he published the documents under the title *The Grand Politics of the European Cabinets 1871–1914*, in forty volumes. Commissioned by the German Foreign Office, this work was published with the intention of refuting the accusation of war guilt contained in the Versailles Treaty with documentary evidence.[31]

*

Among the Atlanticists in the USA there was sympathy for the German efforts to use targeted lobbying to exert influence on how German foreign policy was perceived abroad, and accordingly Albrecht Mendelssohn Bartholdy was invited to deliver lectures at Yale.[32] The fear was that, if Germany was not given the chance to recover economically, further unrest would erupt again among the populace and place peace in jeopardy once more in Central Europe.[33] As long as the USA did not refocus on its foreign affairs role as international peacekeeper, then in the view of the Atlanticists, who thought in terms of *realpolitik*, the greatest threat came from Soviet communism. From an internationalist perspective, Wilson's idea of a League of Nations was a first step in the right direction. Nevertheless, the ideology of the Atlanticists differed in one important respect from the idealism of the US president: in their eyes, America's military might and economic strength was a far more important factor for the functioning of democracies than the global promotion of liberal ideals and values.[34] Consequently, they believed that even in a body like the League of Nations, where all nations were on an equal footing in formal legal terms, the role of global peacekeeper would necessarily have to devolve to the USA. The Atlanticists' aspirations did not materialise, for in 1920 Warren G. Harding won the US presidential election with the promise to return to 'normality'. For the citizens of the United States, this meant an isolationist stance that kept their country out of the European political arena. The ratification of the Treaty of Versailles, of which Wilson's League of Nations was an integral part, was rejected by the new US Senate on the grounds that the USA would incur too extensive international commitments if it were to be a signatory. The USA preferred to conclude a peace deal with Germany in a separate agreement. The Berlin Treaty, which was signed in August 1921, provided for the establishment of a Mixed Claims Commission. A joint

German–American court of arbitration would rule on the claims of American firms and individuals who had suffered harm as a result of German military action.

*

This return to an inward-looking tendency on the part of US politics also spelt the end of a project by a group of British and American economists, who had got together on the fringes of the Paris Peace Conference and come up with the idea of a joint British–US institute for foreign relations designed to furnish the governments of both countries with foreign policy expertise. In place of a transnational institute, what emerged from this initiative were two independent institutes: in Britain the Royal Institute of International Affairs, commonly referred to as Chatham House; and in the USA the Council on Foreign Relations, which oriented itself towards Woodrow Wilson's foreign policy programme.[35] Once again, Paul Warburg was on the founding committee of this latter institution. As a currency expert, he took the view that there was an urgent necessity after the war for an institution that could plan transnational strategies for political action. In April 1921, the Allied reparations commission had set German reparations debt at 132 billion gold marks and at the same time presented the German government with an unworkable repayment plan in the form of an ultimatum. While the Harding administration, which did not prioritise foreign affairs, made no comment on this development, Atlanticists on the Council on Foreign Relations argued for a revision of the Versailles Treaty in the name of 'common sense', since otherwise, in light of the challenge represented by communism, the capitalist economic system and the fledgling liberal democracy that had been established in Germany would be jeopardised.[36] The Atlanticists would stand by this fundamental conviction in the decades that followed, yet in its early years the Council on Foreign Relations had little in common with the highly politically influential think-tank of the 1940s. Rather, it resembled an exclusive gentlemen's club where the financial elite who had financed the First World War met, and were now using their connections to convince politicians that economic and social chaos in Germany would in the long term also endanger the prosperity and the security of the USA. Yet such ideas fell on deaf ears in the political sphere; America was too preoccupied with its own affairs.

2

Becoming a Warburg Banker

At that time, Erich Warburg was already in his second year of training to become a banker; the individual stages of this apprenticeship had taken him from Berlin to Frankfurt am Main and Lübeck. He lived a very independent life and was especially adept at making friends. Most of his friends came from his family environment. He was particularly drawn to Kurt Hahn, at whose instigation the 'Working Group for Law Politics' had been set up. The Warburg and Hahn families already had a longstanding business relationship through their common shareholding in the Lübeck blast furnace plant. Together with the Berlin iron-ore trading company Rawack & Grünefeld, which was owned by the Eisner family, the Hahns, whose main facility was the Hahn Works, a steelworks and rolling mill at Duisburg in the Ruhr, had an 80 per cent holding in the Lübeck blast furnaces. The remaining 20 per cent was divided between the Metallgesellschaft company and M. M. Warburg. When Lola Warburg, Erich's sister, married Kurt Hahn's younger brother Rudolf in 1920, family connections blossomed alongside the existing commercial ties. Erich Warburg learnt from the example of Kurt Hahn that an individual who could make things happen and set innovations in motion did not necessarily have to be someone in an official position formally charged with those responsibilities.[1]

The Working Group for Law Politics was based on personal contacts that Hahn had been busy making from 1914 onwards at the international peace conferences in The Hague, a process best described as 'networking'. His participation in the peace conferences was on his own initiative. He wanted to sound out the chances of peace talks between the Germans and the British.[2] At the time, he was working in the Central Office of the Foreign Service, a newly established department attached to the Foreign Office. His specific remit was to analyse every article on Germany that appeared in the English-language press. After the outcome of the Versailles negotiations, the concept of revision became for him less a battle-cry and more a key element of the politics of rapprochement, as a way of creating a lasting peace and an indispensable prerequisite for stable democratic conditions in the young Weimar Republic. He shared this liberal-conservative viewpoint with Max Warburg but also with members of the left-liberal DDP. For example, dedication to the cause of revising the Versailles Treaty through the politics of rapprochement was a common aim shared by all the members of the editorial board of the magazine *Die Deutsche Nation*, under the leadership of Count Harry Kessler and Theodor Heuss. The Institute for Foreign Policy, which received financial support from Max and Paul Warburg, also took the same political line. The founding of the Society of Friends of the United States in 1929 in Hamburg, at the instigation of Albrecht Mendelssohn Bartholdy, was one practical manifestation of this trend. Members of the society's executive board included the lawyer Kurt Sieveking, the legal scholar Magdalene Schoch, who was Mendelssohn Bartholdy's assistant at the Institute for Foreign Policy, and Erich Warburg.[3] The society saw itself as a 'goodwill envoy between the USA and Germany'. And indeed, this mission statement was also the subtitle of the *Hamburg–Amerika Post*, the dual-language journal of the society edited by Magdalene Schoch.

*

By 1923, around the time when the peace archive was relocated from the Ark to occupy premises of its own, Kurt Hahn was already in Salem. He had concluded from the failure of Max von Baden's chancellorship and the collapse of the monarchy and society that the state of the young Weimar Republic could only be improved if a new, intellectually more enlightened generation took over the reins of power in the country. Accordingly, he switched his field of activity from politics to education and in 1920 opened a rural school at Linzgau on Lake Constance, which was housed in the former imperial abbey of Salem, part of the estate of the Margraviate of Baden. Reformist educational theories lay behind the concept of this institution, but it was also inspired by ideas that its Anglophile founder, who had himself studied at Oxford, gleaned from the English public-school system. The intellectual superstructure of the enterprise was provided by Plato's *Republic*. Hahn had studied this work at the suggestion of Leonard Nelson, a philosopher who taught at the University of Göttingen and a childhood friend. Immediately after completing his studies in Oxford, Hahn had attended a seminar run by Nelson on the Ancient Greek philosopher, whose theory of human education now served as a model for his pedagogical concept of the formation of character.[4]

*

In the meantime Erich Warburg continued with his course of training to become a banker. His apprenticeship, which had begun at the Disconto-Gesellschaft Bank in Berlin and continued at the banking house of J. Dreyfus & Co. in Frankfurt, led to his third position working at the Lübeck blast furnace. Erich Warburg served a six-month internship there, returning to Hamburg in March 1921 where he worked for a further six months as a trainee at the bank owned by his family. These were the typical stages of apprenticeship for a trainee Warburg banker, which everyone in the family went through. But in Erich's case, a yearning to make his own way in the world persisted. Erich enquired of his uncle Aby what lectures would suit him, in order to ensure that the few he could attend would be the right ones for him.[5] On Aby's advice, while still undergoing his training in Berlin, in his free time he attended lectures given by the art historian Adolph Goldschmidt, a friend of his uncle. During his internship in the Lübeck works, he lodged with Carl Georg Heise, a former student of Aby Warburg who in the meantime had been appointed director of the St. Anne's Museum in Lübeck, and became friends with him. In the summer of 1921 Erich announced that he wanted to suspend his apprenticeship as a banker in order to study for a year in Göttingen under Leonard Nelson.[6] Kurt Hahn may well have given him a glowing account of attending Nelson's lectures on Plato, and told him that Nelson's ideas on moral philosophy and jurisprudence were born of a profound sense of justice.[7]

*

When Max Warburg learned of his son's intention to go and study in Göttingen, without further ado he presented him with a stark choice: either study at the university or train to be a banker. Combining the two was not an option. By contrast, Aby Warburg could well understand the dilemma in which his nephew found himself. In their family, anyone who had thus far sought to discover where they belonged in the world had in the process been left in no doubt about the limited opportunities that came with ploughing one's own furrow. He too, the oldest of the five Warburg brothers, had not felt the urge to go into banking. At the age of thirteen he had made a pact with Max, his younger brother by one year: he, Aby, would gladly cede leadership of their father's bank to him. In return, Max would bear the cost of the books that Aby assembled to create his library. Aby Warburg had studied art history and archaeology in Bonn in the face of the family's objections. But Erich was far too self-effacing to claim that he possessed any such extraordinary talent that would justify disappointing his father. He chose not to rebel, but instead to continue his apprenticeship at the bank.

While Erich was getting a taste of hands-on business experience in Lübeck, two of his cousins had arrived at the Kösterberg, who themselves were working as trainees at M. M. Warburg: Frederick, from New York, was the eldest of Felix Warburg's sons, just three years older than Erich. Siegmund came from Reutlingen in Württemberg, where another branch of the Warburg family lived. Max Warburg was beside himself with joy. He spoke to Aby about having an 'embarras de richesses', giving him hope that he could gradually hand over banking duties to the next generation.[8] Siegmund displayed particular flair as a banker. He was far more strongly attracted to a life in the banking business than Max's own son. All the same, it was naturally enough Erich whom Max Warburg wished to see carry the history of the Hamburg banking house on into the fifth generation. In 1922, his son travelled to London in the company of his two cousins, where the next phase in their training awaited them; a posting as an internee at N. M. Rothschild & Sons was already a firm fixture in the family's own training programme. Max Warburg himself had also practised here as a banking apprentice in 1890, at the same age as his son was now.

*

The acceptance by the German parliament of the repayment plan put forward by the inter-Allied reparations commission on 10 May 1921 marked the beginning of a 'policy of appeasement' that stirred up the vehement opposition of right-wing and nationalist forces within Germany; ultimately this backlash was to cost the lives of finance minister Matthias Erzberger and foreign secretary Walther Rathenau. Carl Melchior, who was repeatedly asked by the German government to take part in negotiations concerning the question of reparations, incurred the wrath of right-wing radicals, as did Max Warburg, who was vilified on political pamphlets as an 'emperor behind the scenes', a war profiteer, and the chief architect of Germany's defeat.[9] When the paramilitary group Organisation Consul, an offshoot of the ultra-right Freikorps, murdered foreign minister Walther Rathenau on 24 June 1922, Max Warburg was warned by the chief of police in Hamburg that the hit list of this terror organisation also included him.[10] On the strength of this, he went into hiding for several months, including a spell staying with his two brothers in the USA.[11] There, in his brother Felix's house in New York, he received a visit in November 1922 from the Hamburg judge Wilhelm Kiesselbach, whom the German government had dispatched to the city as a member of the three-man American–German Arbitration Commission. Accompanying Kiesselbach, an entire staff of lawyers from the German Foreign Office set up camp in Washington that same month. Max Warburg arranged things so that immediately after his arrival Kiesselbach could confer undisturbed with his brother Paul, who gave the German commissioner a great deal of useful and helpful information for his forthcoming work with the Americans.[12] Max Warburg himself avoided making any official appearances in front of the Mixed Claims Commission. The anti-Semitism that was assuming ever more threatening dimensions in Germany suggested to him that he should keep a low profile. He was happy enough, he said, 'to work away on the quiet or even just to be able to offer advice'.[13] When the people who had planned Rathenau's murder were arrested at the end of 1922, he returned to Germany.[14]

*

In 1923, Erich was still living in London, where Albrecht von Bernstorff had just taken up his post as an ambassadorial councillor at the German Embassy. Before the USA entered the Great War in April 1917, Albrecht's uncle Johann Heinrich von Bernstorff had been German ambassador in Washington DC. And like his uncle, Albrecht was one of the founding members of the DDP. From the early 1920s Erich was among a group of friends who made a regular pilgrimage to Lake Schaal, some 50 kilometres east of Hamburg, where Bernstorff would receive them at his Stintenburg estate. When Bernstorff arrived in London in 1923, Erich began to pay him frequent visits at the German Embassy residence on Carlton House Terrace in London.[15] However, it was not long until he had to move on to his next training location, which took him across to the other side of the Atlantic – to the banking houses owned by his relatives in New York.

*

The initial impulse to use the American capital market after the First World War to finance German industry once again came from Max Warburg's brothers in New York. Thanks to their family connections, the necessary basis of trust for credit and shareholding structures had remained intact throughout the war years.[16] Three years after stepping down from the board of the Federal Reserve, in 1921 Paul Warburg founded the International Acceptance Bank, which as its name suggested extended a form of acceptance credit that was specially geared towards foreign trade, where the bank stood surety with its creditworthiness for payment of the bills of exchange it issued. Paul Warburg conceived his bank with the explicit aim of contributing to the financing of European reconstruction, in the realm of reorganisation and rationalisation measures – in particular to the benefit of German industry.[17] In the process he cooperated with stockholders and banking houses on both sides of the Atlantic. One of the early recipients of credit from his bank was the Ballestrem concern in Upper Silesia, which owned the Schaffgot works, the Ballestrem mines, and the manufacturing businesses established by Count Carl Lazarus Henckel von Donnersmarck.[18] At the beginning of the 1920s, these were badly hit both by hyperinflation and by the division of Upper Silesia into a German and a Polish sector. This turmoil brought a string of reorganisations of ownership structures in the iron-ore smelting and pig-iron reprocessing industries.[19]

The New York banking houses of the two American Warburg brothers Felix and Paul were to be the crowning conclusion to Erich's banking apprenticeship. There he would receive a final polishing and be transformed into a fully fledged Warburg banker. Aby Warburg, who was still mindful of his nephew's plan to study, asked his brother whether Erich's apprenticeship period could possibly be shortened. But Max Warburg wouldn't hear of it. 'Just as you are very concerned to ensure that your son Max Adolf completes all his courses of study in the approved manner, so too must I insist that Erich finishes his banking apprenticeship properly.'[20] Max Warburg even planned to extend his son's sojourn in America beyond the customary one year because, he reasoned, the necessary know-how for a banker of the next generation could not be acquired in Germany in 1923, ravaged as it was that year by hyperinflation. In the meantime, in their bank they had taken to paying their employees their salaries on a daily basis one hour before the current dollar exchange rate was announced and let them clock off from work immediately thereafter so that they could quickly go and buy in provisions. For as soon as the exchange rate was announced, prices instantly skyrocketed again by several billion Reichsmarks. The situation turned commercial logic on its head. Whereas their bank had 174 employees in 1919, by 1923 that figure had risen to 505, since the work for clerks in the bookkeeping department increased in inverse proportion to the hourly loss in the purchasing power of the Reichsmark. By November 1923 one US dollar was worth a staggering 4.2 billion Reichsmarks.[21] 'As paradoxical as it may sound,' wrote Max Warburg to his brother in December of that year, 'I could almost believe that all those who have not lived through these past few years will be spared from drawing false conclusions about the future.'[22] Erich, his father maintained, would surely need to stay in America until the end of 1924. 'And not just in New York either, but in the West as well.'[23] This would only serve to do him good in other respects too. One could see, he said, from the example of Frederick, the son of his brother Felix, the beneficial results of a change of scenery when that involved escaping from the customary hustle and bustle. He had always thought that Frederick lived too easy-going a life at his brother's house in New York. But in Hamburg, as he confided in Aby, Frederick had become 'an ambitious, serious young man.'[24] Max Warburg was certain: in America, Erich would undergo a similar transformation and return as a mature banker to Germany. According to his father's plans, Erich would learn his profession both with Paul at the Acceptance Bank and with Felix at the banking house of Kuhn, Loeb & Co. As Erich later noted: 'Very wisely, however, my father apprenticed me first to my uncle Paul M. Warburg. A much calmer atmosphere – involving a lot of reading, discussion, and philosophising – prevailed at his banking house than at my uncle Felix's. And alongside the work, my lodging arrangement, staying for a time with one uncle and then with the other, was a great experience for me.'[25] On weekdays he lived in New York, while on the weekends he went to stay at Woodlands, the American equivalent of the Kösterberg: a family estate of enormous proportions near White Plains. In Hamburg Erich had introduced his American cousin to his friends, and now Frederick returned the favour by introducing his German cousin to his circle of American acquaintances. Over games of tennis at Woodlands, Erich Warburg got to know the young up-and-coming legal and financial elite of New York. A frequent invitee among the guests was a young lawyer who had recently joined the team at the Cravath practice: John McCloy, known to his friends as 'Jack'. He had already shown a great sense of timing in applying to Cravath's in 1924, right at the very beginning of the boom in securities resulting from the opening up of the European market to US capital investment.

*

In 1924 the USA had abandoned its policy of staying aloof from any solution to the question of reparations payments. The preamble to this decision was when Germany had to default on its repayments in October 1923. Even so, the USA made its involvement contingent upon the search for a solution being conducted by a commission staffed by international finance experts. For in the meantime, US producers and consumers alike had come to feel the downside of a protectionist policy. The new import tariffs that were enacted, or more accurately raised, in 1922 seriously hampered the ability of European nations to pay off the burden of debt arising from the war, which amounted to a total of 12.5 billion dollars, to their American creditor banks. In their turn those institutions, having come under pressure from the lack of credit repayments and correspondingly increased equity costs, now raised their lending rates, which had a chilling effect on domestic economic growth and consumer confidence in the USA.[26] In order not to have to abandon its protectionist course, the US administration left the task of saving Europe financially to private US capital. The basis for the reorganisation of German reparations payments was the report issued by the committee bearing the name of its chairman, the financial expert Charles Dawes. Implementation of the Dawes Plan[27] in August 1924 saw reparations linked to German economic strength – just as Carl Melchior and John Maynard Keynes had advocated at the Versailles Peace Negotiations. In addition, a loan to the value of 800 million gold marks was provided at international stock markets; this was designed to improve Germany's conditions for payment. Moreover, the US government facilitated the provision of short-term credit on favourable terms as a way of helping Allied debtor countries to settle their burden of debt with US creditors. Kuhn, Loeb & Co. traded in government bonds from Czechoslovakia and the Netherlands, the American financier William M. Blair marketed bonds issued by the Kingdom of Norway, and so on and so forth.[28] Alongside the 800 million gold marks loaned under the Dawes Plan, Germany alone received additional credit to the tune of 21 billion gold marks from American banks and export firms.[29] But because this was, for the most part, short-term credit that had to be extended on a monthly basis, while longer-term credit continued to be hard to come by on the capital market, Felix Warburg (Kuhn, Loeb & Co.) and Paul Warburg (International Acceptance Bank) in conjunction with other American banks founded the American and Continental Corporation (A & CC), which was the first US financial institution to extend medium-term loans to German industrial concerns.[30] On the German side, the private banking houses of M. M. Warburg, Oppenheim, A. Levy & Co., J. H. Stein, and Deutsche Bank formed a syndicate that sounded out the credit requirements of German industrial firms and passed on this information to A & CC. Examples of companies that received credit from A & CC include Köln Rottweil AG/Dynamit AG, IG Farben, the Deutsche Maschinengesellschaft in Duisburg, Deutsche Kabelwerke in Berlin, and the Mannesmannröhrenwerke in Düsseldorf.[31]

Erich spent a portion of his free time in the USA following in
the footsteps of his uncle. After coming to New York almost
thirty years earlier in 1896 for his brother Felix's wedding,
when the ceremony was over Aby Warburg had set off on an
extended trip to the US Southwest. The time he spent living
among the Hopi people of New Mexico was reflected in his
later account of their 'snake ritual', which draws a connection between the symbolic–graphic transformation of a Hopi
creation myth into ritualistic dance and the origins of the
formation of symbols in European culture.[32] Like his uncle,
Erich now embarked on a journey to the western USA. In
his case, however, it took him further north to the state of
Oregon, to the vicinity of the Blue Mountains, where Erich
attended a traditional pow-wow of the Umatilla people. This,
though, marked the end of the tenuous parallels between the
trips on which the uncle and nephew, each in his own way, had
a brief encounter with the world of Native American peoples.
For Erich, following the destiny his father had in mind for his
offspring, applied to work in a bank on the US west coast, in
the city of Portland. And yet the fact that he stayed there for
much longer than planned, enjoyed the easy-going course of
events, was content with the 150 dollars a month he earned,
formed pleasant friendships, and met an American girlfriend –
all of this a far cry from the world of the Warburgs – no longer
chimed in with the career his father envisaged for his son.
When Erich had entered the USA two years before, immigration officials at Ellis Island had not bothered interviewing
him but simply included him in the immigration quota just
in case he changed his mind and decided to stay on in the
United States. For people who, like Erich, had a confident air

about them went down well in America.[33] And indeed, Erich Warburg already appeared to be relishing the idea of staying in Portland for an indefinite period and relinquishing his place in the Hamburg bank to his talented cousin Siegmund when a letter arrived from his uncle, reminding him that obligations elsewhere awaited him.[34] Paul Warburg knew that his nephew could be swayed by sound arguments and so painted a picture that he thought would appeal to Erich. He compared Erich's stay in Portland to a bath full of water that was very comfortable to luxuriate in just as long as the water stayed warm. But in the interim the water had gone completely cold. Even so, Paul said, Erich couldn't summon up the energy to pull the plug and get out and dry himself. 'I've often thought that someone should come over to Portland and drain the water for you!' he wrote.[35] With the best will in the world, Paul Warburg could not figure out either why his nephew wanted to spend months in a backwater like Portland when there was so much going on in the wider world at that time that one could learn from. To bring him to his senses, he chided him that he could never retrospectively experience the things he was missing right now. Erich had no answer to such an appealingly phrased wake-up call, and duly returned to New York. The year in Portland remained a rite of passage marking the transition to a new phase in his life.

*

What now followed was a final internship in the American and Continental Corporation. Erich's duties included a briefing twice a week by the bank's lawyers on the agreements that had been negotiated with contractual partners. A & CC were advised by the law firm Sullivan & Cromwell, whose senior partner, John Foster Dulles, had returned to his chosen profession after his first foray into foreign affairs at the conclusion of the Paris Peace Conference. By the time Erich came back from Portland, John Foster's younger brother Allen Welsh had also started working at Sullivan & Cromwell as an associate.[36] At the age of thirty-three, Allen Welsh Dulles could already boast a truly impressive professional résumé, which he owed in large part, like his brother before him, to his family's close ties to the secretary of state, Robert Lansing. Lansing had also included his younger nephew in the US delegation that attended the Paris Peace Conference; by May 1919 the younger Dulles brother had a position at the legation in Prague, and in October of that year transferred to the US embassy in Berlin. By August 1920 Allen Welsh Dulles was working in the State Department in Washington. Just two months later he went to join the American High Commission in Constantinople. And finally, in 1922, he was appointed chief of the Near East division at the Department of State.[37] Latterly, however, when his diplomatic career stalled, the younger Dulles began studying for a law degree; he calculated that his elder brother John Foster would be able to secure him a position at Sullivan & Cromwell. His plan duly paid off. By 1926 he had also been invited to sit on the Council on Foreign Relations, and in the following year he would be offered one of the directors' posts on this body, the first time since the founding of the CFR six years earlier that a new director had been appointed. In his briefings at Sullivan & Cromwell, Erich Warburg sat opposite someone who had never entertained so much as a scintilla of self-doubt. Erich, who himself was blessed with an ample measure of charm, regarded this talent as the only thing that made life bearable for those who possessed it, no matter whether they were rich or poor. But in Allen

Welsh Dulles, charm was mixed with extrovert upper-class affectation and a propensity for ruthlessness. The young Warburg was uncertain what to make of this. Nevertheless, after returning to Hamburg he maintained contact with the young American, for in 1927 Sullivan & Cromwell opened two offices in Germany, one in Frankfurt and the other at the Hotel Esplanade in Berlin.[38]

*

During Erich Warburg's three-year absence, in 1926 a library building had arisen at Heilwigstraße 116 in Hamburg, right next to the house where Aby Warburg lived; the clinker facade of the new building was embellished with the initials of the Warburg Cultural Studies Library: KBW (*Kulturwissenschaftliche Bibliothek Warburg*). This brand-new exterior made the institutional nature of the library clearly visible to the outside world. Professors from the University of Hamburg organised seminars on art history and cultural affairs there. Twenty years earlier Aby and Max Warburg had fought to establish this university and in 1907 laid its groundwork with the founding of the Hamburg Scientific Foundation.[39] In 1911 a new lecture hall was built on the Moorweide. In 1919 Hamburg University began its programme of teaching and research activities, of which in a wider sense the library in the Heilwigstraße also formed part. A board of trustees oversaw the university's publications, its academic syllabus, and its financial provisions; this body was made up of Aby Warburg and his four brothers, who financed the construction and upkeep of the library, together with an interdisciplinary panel of academic advisors. A number of illustrious names sat on this panel, among them the art historian Edgar Wind, Erwin

Panofsky, head of the art history department at Hamburg University, and Ernst Cassirer, who had held the professorship at the philosophical faculty ever since its inception. In 1913 the art historian Fritz Saxl moved from Vienna to Hamburg and, at the age of twenty-three, began work as Aby Warburg's research assistant. From 1921 to 1924, during Aby Warburg's stay at the Bellevue Sanatorium, the clinic run by the psychiatrist Ludwig Binswanger in Kreuzlingen on Lake Constance, Saxl and Gertrud Bing developed the library into a research institute.[40] Since receiving her doctorate in 1922, Bing, who had studied under Cassirer, had also been a member of the Warburg staff.

*

Together with his cousin Max Adolf, Aby Warburg's son, Erich represented the next generation on the board of trustees.[41] When it came to decisions, the family always had one more vote than the panel of academic advisors and members of staff. In addition, Erich promoted the work of contemporary artists who had gained the recognition of his uncle. He was one of the first patrons of the photographer Albert Renger-Patzsch, who became famous as a member of the *Neue Sachlichkeit* (New Objectivity) movement. He was introduced to Renger-Patzsch by Carl Georg Heise, his former host during his internship in Lübeck. Erich Warburg commissioned the photographer to create a series of images of the Kösterberg. While these photos were intended as gifts and as postcards for private use, for his next commission Renger-Patzsch developed the Kösterberg portfolio into the 'Hamburg' book, which was conceived as a multilingual promotional volume showing Hamburg as a 'city on the up and up'.[42]

The relationship between the nephew and his uncle, who had a reputation for being difficult, was frank and open. For instance, Erich once asked Aby Warburg if Kurt Hahn could use the auditorium at the museum to deliver a lecture. His brother-in-law wanted to present the work of the Salem boarding school to interested parents and pupils. Aby Warburg felt as though he had been railroaded. 'Just this once, but never again,' he chided his nephew. 'You know there's no one from the younger generation I'd rather support in his voluntary cultural work than you, but that's why you should pay special attention when I say no. You're not capable of appreciating like I can the dangers arising from a misuse of the KBW as an institute.'[43] Erich Warburg's 'voluntary cultural work' would remain only a sideline, for since returning from America in 1926 he had been working full-time at the family bank in Hamburg. Primarily in order to please his father, he had come to terms with life as a banker. The lessons he had learned about the American banking mentality over the preceding years spent in the States he now applied to family bank, which at this time was providing German industry within a new influx of American capital. The many firms to receive loans from M. M. Warburg included the Berlin Elevated and Underground Railway company, the Weserthal Electricity Works, the German Knitting Machine company in Chemnitz, and the Charlotte Mine in Silesia, to name just a few.[44] The best years of the Weimar Republic were based on loans like these. German industry used part of the money on advertising campaigns designed to boost their export business. To this end, in 1922 the Imperial German Industry Federation and a number of steel and iron producers had banded together to form the

WPG (*Wirtschaftspolitische Gesellschaft*, or the Economic Society), which was aimed at promoting the image of German industry through the creation of information offices abroad. And because the WPG followed the policy guidelines laid down by the German government, the Foreign Office could dispose of the material that industry supplied to the information bureaux as it saw fit.[45] At the German Embassy in London, Albrecht von Bernstorff was instrumental in setting up a whole series of such offices, and in so doing serving the political interests of both the German Foreign Office and the commercial interests of Germany's export industry. In order for the WPG to preserve an outward appearance of independence, Bernstorff sought out private individuals to support the expansion of the information offices with donations. In this way, he could make a credible case for telling the British press that the funds did not come from the German Foreign Office. In the case of the Ruhr Information Office, Erich Warburg was enlisted as a benefactor in 1927.[46]

*

In 1928, the Bank of the Manhattan Company in New York, which specialised in financing industry, announced a merger with the International Acceptance Bank. In March of the following year it increased its capital to 22.5 million dollars and bought up the entire stock of shares in the Acceptance Bank. The banking house of M. M. Warburg in Hamburg profited from this growth in bank lending, and this is what may have induced Max Warburg to extend credit of more than 19 million Reichsmarks to Rudolf Karstadt AG.[47] Erich, whom M. M. Warburg had in the meantime authorised to be a procurator, was shocked at the size of this loan. Since 1927, Karstadt had been constructing Europe's largest and most modern department store on Hermannplatz in Berlin. Some 37,000 square metres of retail space were to be created over nine floors, yet the massive expansion of the Karstadt business was entirely financed by foreign capital. When Erich tried to find out more from his father about the planned investment, he was referred to 'Uncle Fritz', who sat on the Karstadt board. Yet his uncle took the view that Hermann Rudolf Münchmeyer, chairman of the board at Karstadt AG, would be better placed to tell Erich what was going on. Münchmeyer, who sat on several committees of the chamber of commerce as well as on the standing committee of the German Association of Chambers of Industry and Commerce, the central committee of the German State Bank, and on the boards of numerous companies, simply informed Erich that Erich's father had virtually press-ganged him into sitting on the Karstadt board of directors and that, in consequence, he had 'precious little' to say about the company.[48] The young Warburg was referred to Herman Schöndorff, the CEO of Karstadt. Schöndorff had previously incorporated his own bedding company into Karstadt AG, and this only served to make Erich even more uneasy. He had heard that department stores which produced their own goods were twice as vulnerable in the event of an economic crisis. He started to get the feeling that his father may have made a big mistake in extending credit to Karstadt. And because he had no desire to share in the risk their bank had taken, he told his father he would have to resign.[49] His father would have none of it. The bank's future director couldn't just quit like any other employee. Besides, Max assured him, in view of the economic upswing in recent years, he was absolutely confident that the loan would be repaid. The demand for foreign capital would remain at the current level for some considerable time yet.

Instead of releasing his son from his responsibility, in January 1929 he made him a bank partner by assigning to him a 9 per cent stakeholding, the standard share for a junior partner at the bank. Alongside Erich, Ernst Spiegelberg also became a new co-partner of the bank, only the second outsider to do so. At the same time Spiegelberg was also promoted to director of the newly opened Amsterdam subsidiary Warburg & Co.[50] Erich's cousin Siegmund was appointed to the vacant position of head of the Berlin branch, and by dint of this new position he too became a junior partner with a 9 per cent share allocation like Erich. In addition to the three newcomers, the only other bank partners were Max Warburg, the principal shareholder, his youngest brother Fritz, their cousin Aby S. Warburg from the Alsterufer line of the family[51] – not to be confused with Aby M. Warburg, the art historian from the Mittelburg Warburg line – and finally Carl Melchior, hitherto the only non-family member among the Warburg partners. Yet in the 1920s Carl Melchior's advice was repeatedly sought by successive German governments. Ever since Germany had been accepted into the League of Nations in 1926, he had been the German representative on its finance committee; while retaining this post in 1929 he also took part in the negotiations surrounding the Young Plan, a final reparations treaty that was scheduled to supplant the Dawes Plan in 1930. Spending most of his time shuttling between Paris and Geneva, his visits to Hamburg were only sporadic, which was why Ernst Spiegelberg was now added to the circle of partners.

*

However optimistic Max Warburg may have been about the economic mood in Germany, the country's financial lifeblood was provided by the New York Stock Exchange. Credit for speculative trading was easy to come by, and shares were priced according to the expected profits and increasingly traded well above market value. For a long time Paul Warburg had been warning about the consequences of the market overheating. He had learned about his brother's Karstadt loan too late, otherwise he would presumably have tried to stop it. The new Karstadt store opened its doors on Hermannplatz on 21 June 1929, and the Amsterdam subsidiary of the Hamburg Warburg Bank began operations in September – as did Alfabet, the Warburg holding company, through which the bank held 21 per cent of Karstadt stock.[52]

One month later came the Wall Street Crash, which triggered the collapse of the international credit system. Stockbrokers terminated loans to their clients and demanded immediate payment for shares; in a panic, shareholders sold at any price. Banks ran out of money. They found themselves unable to settle the loans which they themselves had borrowed from other banks, and went bankrupt by the dozen. The Federal Reserve Board, the body that was actually entrusted with banking supervision, had looked on helplessly as share prices spiralled out of control.

*

Two days after the Wall Street Crash, on 26 October 1929, Aby Warburg died. Friends, companions, co-workers, and academic colleagues bade him farewell at his graveside. Ernst Cassirer, who had meanwhile become dean of the philosophical faculty, recalled intellectual and scientific milestones in the career of this great cultural historian. Erich spoke a few words on behalf of the family. When he had returned from

America three years before, his uncle had asked him to name something that distinguished Germany from the United States. Something that could not be copied or transplanted. The only thing Erich could think of was the kind of research that he, Aby, was engaged in. That might well, he said, be the only remaining advantage that the old world had over the new.[53] In his eulogy, he said how lucky the family had been to come under the influence of Aby's ideas. Aby had discovered and disclosed to his family the similarities between their own situation as bankers in Hamburg in the twentieth century and that of the mercantile elite in Florence during the Renaissance. Just as the merchants of Florence had commissioned artworks that drew upon the cultural legacy of antiquity, so they, the Warburgs in modern Hamburg, were using their bank's profits equally advantageously to lend artistic and cultural heft to capitalism – firstly by building a library and secondly by promoting research in the arts.[54] Aby Warburg died at a moment when the market crash and the banking crisis rendered the model of the library as a 'branch of the banking house' null and void.[55] Yet his personality, Erich declared at his uncle's graveside, would live on in them all, 'leading us by example and inspiring us now more than ever.'[56]

*

After 'Black Friday' in October 1929, credit in Germany dried up overnight. In the USA, German securities were liquidated. As a result, banks in Germany collapsed like punctured balloons, with no bank being spared – not even M. M. Warburg. Without the Kara Corporation, through which Felix and Paul Warburg channelled financial aid totalling 32 million gold marks to their beleaguered brother, the banking house would not have withstood the crisis of 1931.[57] The name of this corporation was inspired by Dostoevsky's novel *The Brothers Karamazov*.[58] In their choice of name, the New York Warburg brothers demonstrated that they had not lost their sense of irony, though Max Warburg could not hope that they would henceforth allow him to act with such uncontrolled licence as they had done before. For a long time Felix and Paul had been taking a far more realistic view of the situation than him, and they could only see light at the end of the tunnel if M. M. Warburg was to merge with a larger bank. Max was not prepared to do this. Paul was too close to him to pressurise him against his will. Accordingly, Felix hit upon the idea of sending Paul's son to Hamburg. James 'Jimmy' Warburg, an economist and Harvard graduate, had himself been working in the banking sector since 1919. Although he was born in Hamburg in 1896, he grew up in the USA and so did not have the same emotional tie to the Hamburg family bank as his father. He was not dazzled by his Hamburg uncle's charm but judged according to the facts and spoke his mind bluntly: Uncle Max had squandered the trust of his American relatives with the Karstadt credit fiasco.[59] By the time Jimmy departed again for New York, Max Warburg knew that his brothers in New York would have a say in all future decisions taken by the Hamburg firm. At the end of this nerve-wracking year, Paul Warburg suffered a stroke from which he never recovered. He died in January 1932. After his death, the family discovered that he had used more than half of his fortune to save his brother's bank. The playful literary allusion in the name of the Kara Corporation now seemed grotesquely out of place in the light of this painful encounter with reality.

*

The fate of the KBW was now shackled to that of the bank, and even in this deepest of banking crises, Paul Warburg had not left the library in the lurch. Jimmy and his sister Bettina would now take their father's place on the board of trustees. However, there was no expectation that he would also continue Paul's generous patronage.[60] He regarded the library as one of those cost-producing factors that had played a part in the death of his father.[61] In practical terms, since Aby Warburg's death, work in the library had been restricted to dealing with his estate, a task for which Gertrud Bing was principally responsible.[62] During the banking crisis the institution's already reduced budget suffered a further drastic cut, with periodical and book orders being cancelled and the salaries of staff reduced. Henceforth, it seemed, financial constraints would become the key factor in all its academic work. Blank cheques of the kind that the brothers had issued when Aby Warburg was still alive were no longer on the agenda. But what sources of funding beyond the family were there to be tapped in the crisis year of 1932, with economic activity at rock bottom, work desperately hard to come by, and most people simply doing what they could to survive? In times like these who could possibly support a cultural studies institution that had once been financially cosseted, especially with rumours already circulating that even Hamburg University might fall victim to cost-cutting in the political budget for education and culture? If the university sector ground to a halt as a result of the crisis, then the rationale for the library would evaporate too. In view of this bleak prospect, Max Warburg began to think about moving the library abroad. Fritz Saxl, who had been head librarian since Aby Warburg's death, suggested Rome as an alternative site. Indeed, in the final year of his life Aby Warburg, dismayed at Hamburg's

49

educational-research policy, had himself mooted Rome as a possible venue. There were already academic institutions there in the shape of the Bibliotheca Hertziana and the German Archaeological Institute, whose interdisciplinary work paralleled that of the Warburg Library. Max Warburg liked the idea, but the rest of the family were not so keen. Aby's widow Mary Warburg and her three children were opposed to the library leaving Hamburg.[63] As for the Rome plan, no firm decision had yet been reached, Mary wrote to her youngest daughter Frede in February 1932. For, she continued, even if Uncle Max were to welcome the plan, Erich and Fritz would use their veto.[64] Aby Warburg had once told his nephew that he should really sit up and take notice when he said no, on the occasion when Erich had wanted to use the KBW auditorium to hold a lecture given by Kurt Hahn. Now it was Erich's turn to put his foot down in protest at the way people were trying to reach a quick decision of the future of the KBW by pointing a gun at one another's heads. In his opinion, there was absolutely no need for this; the Karstadt reorganisation was well underway and in addition, together with the American Warburgs, M. M. Warburg now owned 36 per cent of the shares in the Berlin department-store company. The Berlin private bank, which numbered among Germany's most major banks, had weathered the banking crisis well.[65] Erich Warburg did not think that the library project in Hamburg was in any serious danger. Over the years the American Warburgs had simply invested far too much money in the Hamburg library to see it uprooted. If they were to take such a step, he argued, the banking crisis would wipe out the intellectual capital of their bank as well as its financial assets. And the Fascists were already in power in Italy.

3

Years On Standby

On 30 January 1933 Paul von Hindenburg, president of the Reich, appointed the leader of the National Socialist German Workers' Party (NSDAP), Adolf Hitler, as chancellor of Germany. His party's manifesto openly threatened German Jews with repressive measures, while in his 1925 programmatic tract *Mein Kampf* Hitler had written about a 'Jewish world conspiracy' and called for Jews to be exterminated. However, Erich Warburg and his friends, along with many Jews not only in Hamburg but throughout Germany, believed that things were not as bad as they seemed. In what would be the final federal election, held on 5 March 1933, the NSDAP secured 38.7 per cent of the vote in Hamburg, around 5 per cent below their average polling in the country at large. Erich's circle of friends told themselves that the electoral success of the National Socialists was the result of the enormous pressure that was being exerted on Germany from abroad. Kurt Hahn even went so far as to remark that if the Nazis didn't already exist, then they would have to be invented in order to consolidate the centre ground of politics.[1] For him and for Erich Warburg, the reasons for Hitler's victory lay in the Versailles Peace Treaty and the policies pursued by the Allies since the end of the war, but also in the fact that the USA had presided over a process of impoverishment of large sectors

of the populace in the final years of the Weimar Republic.[2]
Even this analysis was testament to the pernicious effect of the
destructive propaganda that radical right-wing and nationalist forces had spent many years spreading. According to this
viewpoint, Versailles and the policy of appeasement adopted
by governments of the republic were to blame for Germany's
parlous state. This totally ignored the fact that the Lausanne
Conference in the summer of 1932 had actually resulted in
all German reparations payments being written off. The
Allied powers had not even insisted on exacting the remaining repayment sum of 3 billion gold marks, with the result
that, of the 132 billion gold marks originally stipulated as
reparations in London in 1921, between that date and 1932
only 70 billion were actually repaid. The success of German
foreign policy in this regard during the Weimar Republic was
due in no small part to the efforts of Carl Melchior, who in
April 1930 had taken over the post of acting chairman of the
supervisory board of the Bank for International Settlements,
which had been founded in the context of the Young Plan. In
this capacity he made a major contribution to easing the economic burden on Germany. Yet all this remained hidden to
the general public. Such decisive, positive measures aimed at
bringing about an economic recovery in Germany no longer
had any effect against the sheer weight of the destructive
forces that were unleashed at this moment.

*

On 11 March, just a few days after the election, the headmas-
ter of the Salem boarding school, Kurt Hahn, was one of the
first to be arrested. In September 1932, outraged at the murder
of a communist worker by members of the Nazi paramilitary

Sturmabteilung (SA), Hahn had sent a circular letter to the school's alumni in which he demanded, if they were active members of either the SA or the SS, that they 'sever their allegiance either to Hitler or to Salem'. Although Hahn was released from custody just five days later, after numerous representations on his behalf, he was banned from resuming his post at Salem.[3] What had happened to Hahn in these very first days of repression set alarm bells ringing among the academics of the KBW. The question of relocating the library, which had been deferred only the year before, now reared its head once more under conditions that had grown ominously worse. Unlike the lobbying for Rome that had occurred the previous year, now the initiative within the family came from Erich and Fritz Warburg. This time, both assured Fritz Saxl, who was already in contact with universities and scholars abroad, of their full support in searching for a new location; they agreed that he should be given a completely free hand in his endeavours. However, because Max Warburg also had a say in the matter of the library, with the backing of his uncle and Fritz Saxl Erich now set about impressing upon his father why none of them believed it was right to wait any longer before moving the library's holdings out of the country.[4] This time, though, it was Max Warburg who warned against any precipitate solution. It might be the case, he argued, that they were dealing with a crisis that would soon blow over, a storm that Germany could weather.

Then came 1 April, the day of the 'Jewish boycott': a blockade of Jewish-owned businesses, followed a week later by the expulsion of all Jewish academics from German universities. Anyone who had not, like Fritz Saxl, already renounced his professorial chair, summarily lost it on this day, with the passing of the 'Law for the Restoration of the Professional

53

Civil Service', which was aimed at rooting out all social groups whom the National Socialists hated. Carl Melchior resigned his post on the supervisory board at the Bank for International Settlements.

*

Anyone who encountered Erich Warburg after the events that saw his friends forcibly excluded from their middle-class lives found him a completely changed man. James McDonald, an American friend of the family, recorded in his diary: 'No longer is he the carefree, optimistic young man who was so sure of his own future and that of his people in the Reich.'[5] McDonald was a journalist and head of the Foreign Policy Association in the USA, a society founded in 1918 that made it its mission to inform the American public about developments relating to foreign affairs. He had been visiting Germany every year since 1919 and had gained access to the most diverse of circles, interviewing politicians of all persuasions, employers, workers, policemen, trade unionists, and political activists – indeed, practically anyone who could help him gauge the political situation in Germany. Hardly any doors remained closed to him. Over the years, he formed friendships with a number of his interlocutors – for instance with the Warburgs on both sides of the Atlantic. Still reeling under the impact of the repressive measures of the preceding few weeks, Erich Warburg asked McDonald how he rated the prospects for Jewish businessmen in Germany. McDonald's answer was that he should abandon any illusions and sell his business as quickly as he could.[6] Early on he recognised that Hitler would carry out his threatened extermination of the Jews, having interviewed the NSDAP leader in the

Chancellery on 8 April 1933.[7] Yet Erich Warburg could not imagine things getting any worse than they already were. His family was part of a long-established German–Jewish upper middle class. Despite having spent some of his formative years in the United States, Germany was the only civilisation and nation he felt he belonged to. He did not have another homeland. Notwithstanding all the legal discrimination that had been enacted and the anti-Semitic abuses that had already occurred, he hoped that his father was right and, now that the National Socialists had the responsibility of governing, people like Hjalmar Schacht would ultimately prevail in their ranks, someone whom he regarded as a moderate economic politician and who had just been reappointed as president of the Reichsbank. Schacht had held this post once before, from 1923 to 1930, and after stepping down had made overtures to the National Socialists. Yet for that reason alone he was 'no friend of the Warburgs', as Erich Warburg explained to McDonald. For all his relative moderation, there was every reason to fear that he would try to do them serious harm.[8] Other people whom Schacht found more acceptable would thus have to bring their influence to bear to improve the lot of Jews in Germany. In Warburg's view, McDonald could assist in this matter, since with his slim, tall figure and blond hair he perfectly fitted the image that the Nazis had of an 'Aryan'.[9] Yet McDonald had already conducted an interview with Hjalmar Schacht on 1 April, and had not come away with the impression that he was particularly concerned by how events in Germany were being viewed abroad. During their discussion Schacht had put it on record that the '[National Socialist] movement' had initially had his sympathy, then his support, and now it was triumphant.[10] McDonald thought that John Foster Dulles would be the ideal person to impress upon

Schacht that anti-Semitic actions like those of 1 April would harm international trade and business links with the German Empire.[11] After all, it was the Sullivan & Cromwell branch in Berlin that negotiated contracts with American companies for German clients, agreements from which Germany greatly profited. And indeed, a few days after his discussion with Erich Warburg, McDonald asked John Foster Dulles if he could come to Germany.[12] Dulles, however, had sympathies with fascist administrations. Regimes 'that maintained order and disciplined themselves economically' fascinated him. In his eyes, Hitler was doing Germany and the world good. He regarded him first and foremost as an ally in the fight against Bolshevism.[13] In 1934 he brokered a deal for IG Farben with the International Nickel Company, a client of Sullivan & Cromwell, which gave the German company access to raw materials from the world's largest nickel producer and required that payment for only half of the total cost be made in foreign currency, an arrangement that greatly facilitated German rearmament. In the German branch of Sullivan & Cromwell, all official correspondence ended with the salutation 'Heil Hitler'.[14] For the office manager there was Heinrich F. Albert, who had formerly been state secretary in the cabinet of Wilhelm Cuno, the seventh chancellor of the Weimar Republic. In the First World War, the German Ministry of the Interior had sent Albert to the United States as an advisor on economic matters arising during mobilisation and the war itself.[15] He was a commercial attaché and at the same time an agent of the German emperor. He was unmasked in 1915 in the 'Briefcase Affair', so called because a federal agent of the US Secret Service took a briefcase containing documents from him while he was riding on the New York elevated railway system.[16] In the weeks that followed, leading American newspapers ran stories almost daily, containing embarrassing revelations for Germany about its US embassy's sabotage activities, payments to *agents provocateurs* to organise strikes, the creation of dummy and shell companies, and the falsification of passports used by reserve officers of ethnic German origin to travel on British merchant ships across the Atlantic to the European theatre of war. However, it was Albert's intimate knowledge of the German economy that secured him his position at the Berlin branch of Sullivan & Cromwell.

*

The book burnings announced for 15 May 1933 as a further action 'against the un-German spirit' now led even Max Warburg to the conclusion that the Warburg library would no longer be safe in Germany. In August 1929, just two months before Aby Warburg's death, he and his four brothers had reached a contractual agreement whereby each of them was entitled to a fifth of the plot at Heilwigstraße 116, the library built on it, and the library's holdings.[17] On 6 May 1933, Fritz and Max Warburg transferred half of their library shares (covering the land, the building, and the collections) to their American co-owners. This step immediately ensured that three-fifths of the Warburg library was now American-owned.[18] Yet while Max and Fritz Warburg transferred half of their shares in the library, they did not not cede half of their voting rights. Each of the five parties continued to have a vote in decisions.[19] In order to prevent Aby's heirs and the two American parties from banding together when it came to the upcoming decision on what to do about the library, Max and Fritz agreed with Aby's heirs 'that, insofar as a decision about the dissolution, relocation, or significant restructuring of the library depends upon the vote of the heirs, this vote shall only be cast in agreement with Mr. Erich M. Warburg should it run counter to the concerted wishes of Messrs. Max M. Warburg and Dr. F. M. Warburg.'[20] This somewhat legalistically formulated agreement basically meant that an American solution reached in conjunction with Aby's joint heirs against the votes cast by Max and Fritz Warburg could only be implemented if Erich was also in agreement with it. In the event of disagreement on the German side of the family, the outcome of the decision now rested on his vote.

*

Once the family had settled these internal matters, on 8 May Erich informed the American consul general in Berlin, George Messersmith, that the nationwide 'book burning' that was due to take place on 15 May put American property in jeopardy. As a result the KBW was immediately placed under the protection of the American consular authorities. Anyone attempting to clear or close the institute would be answerable to the US consulates general in Berlin and Hamburg.[21] The latter moved into premises on one floor of the Warburg Bank building on Ferdinandstraße in Hamburg. And the Swedish and Danish consulates were housed in Fritz Warburg's private dwelling.[22] As it happened, when book burnings took place in Hamburg on 15 May there was no need to make use of the US consul general's promise of protection. Even so, by this time Fritz Saxl had already informed the art historians who belonged to the Warburg circle that the whole family had in the meantime concluded that the most sensible course of action would be to move the library abroad as quickly as possible. Naturally enough, he made no mention of the fact that this was now their firm plan. The codeword used for this in correspondence between those in the know was 'catalogue'. Saxl took the opportunity of a supposedly planned publication of a catalogue as a pretext to confer with his colleagues about giving him free rein to 'start looking around for co-workers and printing options.'[23] Because Max Warburg was being shadowed by the Gestapo, the correspondence was increasingly conducted via the bank's Amsterdam subsidiary, which became ever more important for maintaining their connections to the outside world.[24] A rescue plan was now devised in the innermost circle, with the aim of avoiding paying the 'Reich Flight Tax'. On no account should the Foreign Exchange Board get wind of the fact that the family was making arrangements to transfer 60,000 books and 25,000 photographs abroad.

*

Albrecht von Bernstorff was the next of Erich Warburg's friends to be put out of action by the German authorities. Bernstorff, who in January had celebrated ten years' service at the German Embassy in London, wrote to a female friend just a few days after the National Socialists took office: 'One can only blush with shame that people like this have bamboozled our poor nation.'[25] In conversation, he made no secret of his deep aversion to the new rulers of Germany, but was adamant that he wasn't about to cede his position voluntarily to the Nazis. He therefore had no other option but to 'get himself fired'.[26] In the second half of May 1933 he spent a few days at the Stintenhof estate in the company of his closest friends, the British author Enid Bagnold and Erich Warburg. While he was there, the chief ideologue of the National Socialist party, Alfred Rosenberg, arrived in London.[27] Rosenberg, the head of the NSDAP Office of Foreign Affairs, had learned of Bernstorff's hostile stance. When Bernstorff returned to London in June, he was relieved of his post at the embassy and sent on leave. Friends advised him to remain abroad. Instead he went back to Germany in order to be at the scene of the action and even sought another position in the Foreign Service.[28]

*

The Warburgs too planned on staying in Germany. Only the library would be relocated abroad. The family, on the other hand, became ever more intensively involved in developing Jewish self-help organisations. In 1933 Fritz Warburg took over chairmanship of the Israelite Hospital, a cause that the family had been supporting for decades; Max Warburg for his part became president of the German Jewish Benevolent Society (*Hilfsverein der Deutschen Juden*), an organisation originally founded by their father with the purpose of improving the lot of Jews in Eastern Europe. In September 1933 the Reich Deputation of German Jews (*Reichsvertretung der Deutschen Juden*) was founded as an umbrella organisation representing all Jewish groups in Germany.

At the same time, however, German Jews were being systematically excluded from commercial life. Max Warburg had to relinquish the many seats on boards and the honorary posts he held. Of all businesses, the department store Karstadt, which had ridden out world economic crises and banking collapses unscathed with the help of credit from the Warburgs,[29] was the first German firm to dismiss all of its

Jewish co-workers, in March 1933. Pressure was also brought to bear on Warburg. The bank was forced to sell, at a fraction of its actual value, its 21 per cent stake in Karstadt, which it held through its Amsterdam holding company.[30] In just a year the banking house lost 70 per cent of its asset value as well as three-fifths of its business clients.[31] A subsequent modest increase in client numbers was explained by the fact that the banking house began to specialise in liquidations and matters pertaining to emigration and foreign currency, and in this way acquired a new customer base of Jewish employers and businessmen.

The hurdles that Jews wanting to leave Germany had to clear were set ever higher. The National Socialists turned measures that had been introduced in the era of emergency legislation – such as the controls imposed on foreign exchange in 1931, which by means of blocked accounts and the Reich Flight Tax were aimed at making it more difficult to export foreign currency and thereby stabilising the Reichsbank, which had been weakened by the world economic and banking crisis – into a systematically conducted looting by the state of its Jewish citizens. The Reich Flight Tax, which in 1931 had only been levied on people taking more than 200,000 Reichsmarks out of the country, was now to be paid as a matter of course by all Jewish emigrants, regardless of the amounts of savings they were transferring abroad. They were also significantly hampered in taking their money abroad by the so-called Dego Levy set by the Deutsche Golddiskontbank, a tax that was deducted from assets that they had been forced to deposit in blocked accounts. From as early as 1934, only cash sums could be taken abroad, and these were not permitted to exceed 10 Reichsmarks. Thus overburdened with taxes, the emigrants were left with very little of the money they had saved up.[32]

In 1933 Max Warburg drew up plans that were designed to improve the expatriation conditions for Jews wanting to emigrate. The solution for him lay in an orderly emigration process on the basis of a clearing system, which provided for different forms of capital transfer. Yet in each case this was predicated upon cooperation with the German government authorities, which was unacceptable to the majority of representatives of Jewish organisations. Chaim Weizmann was one exception. The president of the Zionist Organization did not in principle rule out cooperating with any one side. As long as it served the cause of establishing a Jewish state in Palestine, he was willing to negotiate with the British, with Arab leaders, and even with the National Socialist authorities. In 1929, Weizmann established the Jewish Agency in Palestine, which also courted non-Zionists and alongside Albert Einstein was able to secure the support of Felix Warburg. By this stage, the Kuhn–Loeb banker had been resident in New York for almost four decades, where in his role as a philanthropist and patron of the arts, he was a focal point of Jewish social life. Felix Warburg was even-handed in his support of non-Jewish and Jewish institutions in New York, irrespective of their outlook and religion.[33] Similarly long was the list of organisations he was instrumental in founding and the number of projects to which he lent his backing. After 1933, the non-Zionist American Jewish Joint Distribution Committee, which he had founded in 1914 and which he himself chaired for eighteen years, took on particular significance. The 'Joint' became the largest and most important Jewish aid organisation worldwide working to save European Jews.

*

On 25 August 1933 the Jewish Agency for Palestine and the Zionist Federation of Germany signed an accord with the German Reichsbank, the German Ministry of Economics, and the German Foreign Office that bore the name of the Hebrew term for 'transfer': the Haavara Agreement. It henceforth formed the framework within which the Foreign Exchange Board would authorise future transfers of Jewish assets to British Mandatory Palestine: to begin with, up to a maximum of 50,000 Reichsmarks (less the Reich Flight Tax and the Dego Levy). Because the Jewish side was in no position to be able to choose its own negotiating partners, in the summer of 1933 Max Warburg, though not himself among the signatories to this transfer agreement, set up the Palestine Trust Corporation (*Palästina-Treuhandstelle*, or Paltreu for short) in Berlin to advise German Jews. Its partner bank was A. E. Wassermann. The Trust liquidated the assets of Jewish emigrants, remitted the fees to the Golddiskontbank and the Treasury, and transferred the capital released for export to a special Haavara account at the Reichsbank. On their arrival in Tel Aviv, the Haavara emigrants were paid the funds owed to them in Palestine Pounds by the Anglo-Palestine Bank, minus a deduction for the cost of an entry visa. These funds had been paid in by Israeli importers who did business with German exporters. In turn, their invoices were settled from the Haavara credit deposited by the Reichsbank. Although this arrangement meant that no foreign exchange fees were deducted, the German authorities only entered into this deal with the Zionists because it circumvented the international boycott of German goods.[34] The Zionist contractual partners agreed to this because the enterprise of building a Jewish state in Palestine was mainly focussed on destitute immigrants from Eastern Europe and hence, for any influx of capital, it was dependent upon other sources – such as well-off Jewish emigrants to Palestine from Germany. In the summer of 1933, the city councillor of Tel Aviv responsible for cultural affairs, Shoshana Persitz, heard about the planned relocation of the Warburg Library. She established contact with Fritz Saxl and indicated to him that Tel Aviv would be interested in hosting the library. Erich warned the head librarian: 'Hands off Frau Persiz (or whatever the woman's name is) … take it from me … don't have anything to do with Zionists or the *Magen David*.'[35] If Zionists became involved in the library transfer, he said, it would run the risk of becoming a bargaining chip in the Haavara Agreement.

*

The library was also a major subject of discussion among the Warburg family on the other side of the Atlantic. Because the American stakeholders, as a result of Max and Fritz Warburg's share transfer, now owned three-fifths of the shares in the library, it seemed to Felix Warburg that an American solution was more likely than a European one, not least because the centre of non-Zionist Jewish life had since the beginning of the twentieth century shifted to the USA. In August 1933 he had a discussion with Abraham Flexner about the library. Flexner was the founding director of the Institute for Advanced Study at Princeton, where many academics who had fled Germany were already researching and teaching: the most famous of them was Albert Einstein. The founding of this private institute at Princeton in 1930 had come about as the result of a donation by Louis Bamberger, a businessman from Newark, New Jersey. Felix Warburg entertained the idea of the Bamberger Foundation also playing a role in the expansion of the Warburg Library. 'But,' Felix Warburg told Flexner, 'the people in Hamburg continue to take the view that Hitler's pathological behaviour is curable.'[36] What Felix Warburg still did not know was that the 'people in Hamburg', as he called his German relatives, were already involved in transfer discussions with the Academic Assistance Council (AAC), an extramural rescue initiative launched by William Beveridge, the director of the London School of Economics. British academics had come together to form the Society for the Protection of Science and Learning, and in the AAC helped procure research assignments for German colleagues who had been prevented from continuing their teaching and research by the 'Law for the Restoration of the Professional Civil Service' and who had sought refuge in Britain.[37]

*

In July 1933, Fritz Saxl travelled to the Dutch city of Leiden, where Johan Huizinga, an art historian and rector of the University of Leiden, had offered the Warburg Library premises in a former orphanage.[38] Because Saxl was already aware of the initiative by British academics, he went on to London directly afterwards and got in touch with the instigators of the AAC.[39] The prerequisite for a residence permit was, Saxl learnt, an official invitation from either of the major universities of Oxford or London. During subsequent discussions with university representatives he got the impression that such an invitation would be easier to come by in London than in Oxford. London was *the* international university in England, he enthused to the Warburgs: 'The scope for action here, with the British Museum and all the collections of the Empire at our disposal, would be ... extraordinary.'[40] In a sense, the library would develop here into the 'academy' for 'the good European' that Aby Warburg had always envisaged.[41] And yet, Saxl went on to say straight afterwards, damping down his own enthusiasm, if the negotiations in London led nowhere, then the only remaining possibility in Europe was the Netherlands. This would certainly have the advantage that the library could continue to teach and publish in German. 'However,' he conceded, 'the Dutch don't see any possibility of being able to take on financial responsibility for the library, so this would be the most costly option for the family.'[42] Yet for the Warburgs the Netherlands was ruled out of being an alternative location for a different reason: in April an incident had occurred at an international student convention at Leiden University. Huizinga had discovered from the press that Johann von Leers, the head of the German delegation, was the author of strident anti-Semitic publications, and promptly barred him from the convention. In retaliation, the rector of Leiden University had meanwhile been declared *persona non grata* at German universities.[43] If the KBW was associated with the name Huizinga in future, this would only make the more than difficult position the Warburgs already found themselves in in Nazi Germany even more problematic.

*

Under the impact of the library's imminent destruction through National Socialist book burnings, the Academic Assistance Council took on its case. In July, William G. Constable and C. S. Gibson set off for Hamburg. Constable was the first director of the Courtauld Institute of Art, while Gibson, a scientist who worked at Guy's Hospital, was the honorary secretary of the AAC.[44] The two men wanted to get an overview of the books in Hamburg and confer with the library's employees. In spite of their precarious situation, Gertrud Bing – together with the librarian Hans Meier and the bookbinder Otto Fein – was adamant that they would not be travelling to London 'in an individual capacity, only in concert with the Library.'[45] And they categorically rejected the suggestion that was made to store the books in a warehouse.[46] After Denison Ross, director of the London School of Oriental Languages, had also visited Hamburg and convinced himself that the KBW, which had been closed to the public from 1 October 1933, satisfied the criteria of a university research institution, the University of London, following his recommendation, duly issued a formal invitation to the Library's employees to come to London. In addition, Ross had a meeting with Lord Lee of Fareham, a politician and noted art collector who sat on the administrative board of the recently opened Courtauld Institute. Samuel Courtauld, after whom the gallery was named, had made his fortune in the manufacture of textiles; as a patron of the arts, he had set himself the goal of establishing art history on the university curriculum in Britain. In discussion with Lord Lee, Ross quickly realised that the young Courtauld Institute could only profit from the presence of the Warburg Library.

*

In the final week of October Erich Warburg arrived in London, where Fritz Saxl had in the meantime strengthened his contacts with Constable and Ross.[47] Warburg and Saxl accepted an invitation from Lord Lee to visit him at White Lodge, his castle-like mansion in Richmond Park. Lee had asked them to come and see him in order to give them good news: a friend of his, who wished to remain anonymous, was prepared to support the Library in London with a grant of £3,000 annually.[48] He did not need to divulge the name of the noble donor. From the sheer amount involved they knew that it could only be Samuel Courtauld. At White Lodge, the library representatives and Lord Lee now set about planning how things should proceed. The crucial question was how the library could be relocated overseas without arousing the rapacious greed of the German Foreign Exchange Board. The whole affair could not come across as a rescue mission on the part of the AAC by virtue of it having declared the book transfer to be of a permanent and final nature. Instead the solution lay in establishing it as a loan arrangement restricted in the first instance to a period of three years. After the three years had elapsed, an extension would be considered. Officially, Lord Lee introduced himself to them as a representative of a circle of individuals with an interest in the history of art, who wanted to facilitate the continued use of the resources of the closed library in Hamburg by students of art history in Great Britain.[49] Accordingly, in his formal written request to Max M. Warburg, chairman of the Hamburg Library Committee, Lee stuck punctiliously to the formulation of a 'loan arrangement limited to three years'. For his part Erich Warburg assured him just a few days after their visit to White Lodge that, subject to consultation with the family, the expectation was that the library would remain in London after the initial three-year period had expired. For the generous offer of the anonymous donor was based on the assumption that the lending arrangement would become a permanent endowment. The American Warburgs announced that they would contribute $2,000 annually to the London library budget.[50]

Immediately after returning to Hamburg, Erich Warburg attempted to brief the city senator Wilhelm von Allwörden, who was responsible for cultural affairs, about the request from London. However, he only managed to gain an audience with Allwörden's secretary, to whom he conveyed the news that the Library's board of trustees thought it right to accept the invitation from Britain so long as a resumption of academic work in Hamburg was out of the question.[51] Senator Allwörden, who had joined the Nazi Party as early as 1926, informed Erich Warburg through his secretary a few days later that he had no intention of taking the slightest cognisance of a matter that had been arranged behind his back.[52] But transferring the library to Britain without official authorisation was unthinkable. The Warburgs therefore turned to an agency that had been set up the previous month by the Ministry for Propaganda under Joseph Goebbels: the Bureau for National Tradition, Church, and Art, which in Hamburg was headed by Baron Wilhelm Kleinschmit von Lengefeld. Kleinschmit, a private lecturer in English with a keen interest in art, was registered as a reader at the KBW.[53] Max Warburg outlined the situation to him and reiterated that it was a loan arrangement: 'We have been at pains to stress that things aren't set in stone.'[54] To back up his words, it was envisaged that a portion of the books would remain in Hamburg – the astronomical collection, for example, which was on loan to the Planetarium, and a special war library that Aby Warburg had assembled during the First World War. 'In addition,' Max Warburg told Kleinschmit, 'Dr. Paul Ruben, another former library employee, will be placed at the public's disposal in order to have any books they require and that aren't needed in London sent back to Hamburg.' And they did indeed fully intend to continue to lend out books that had been saved and taken to London in Germany via the Prussian State Library. The philologist Paul Ruben had been one of Aby Warburg's closest friends since adolescence and as the executor of his will, he stayed on in Germany as the representative of the KBW and made sure that no books went missing.[55] Max Warburg gave an undertaking to Kleinschmit 'that the work in London will be carried out with an absolute minimum of publicity.'[56]

*

In London, the Library was to be housed on the ground floor of Thames House, a recently completed office complex on the Millbank Road in Westminster, where Lord Lee also had his office. Because there was initially still plenty of vacant space in the building, which was located a little way out of central London on the banks of the Thames, Lord Lee was able to negotiate a very favourable rent for the Library.[57] After the British domestic security agency MI5 had given the green light, having found nothing adverse in its files about the library and its four staff, the Home Office issued residence permits. This now meant that, from the British side, nothing now stood in the way of the transfer.[58] Neither would the German agencies involved create any 'official problems', Kleinschmit assured them. He made every effort to personally ensure that the German newspapers reported nothing about the Library's departure, so as to avoid any 'unwelcome commentary'.[59] At this stage, the Nazi policy of *Gleichschaltung* (enforced uniformity) had still not taken hold of the authorities in Hamburg that were answerable to the Propaganda Ministry. Erich Warburg subsequently came to believe that the German

70

authorities had only issued an export licence because 'at that stage the National Socialists were still concerned to demonstrate to the British in particular that their regime wasn't all that bad.'[60] And in his view, their main motivation for that was to profit from the generous lines of credit that British banks made available to the Warburg banking house.[61]

*

The library had still not left Hamburg when *The New York Times*, under the headline 'Hamburg Will Lose Warburg Library' reported on the upcoming transfer of the Warburg Library to London. Erich Warburg lost no time in issuing a correction. It was, he let it be known, not a permanent loss but merely a loan limited to three years.[62] He himself could not be present when, on 12 December, the freighter *Hermia*, with 531 crates of books on board, set sail for England from Hamburg docks. For once all the necessary arrangements had been made in Hamburg and work had begun packing all the books into crates in the Heilwigstraße. Erich Warburg himself took passage on a steamer bound for New York. The library's employees took delivery of the books in London later in December, while in New York Erich presented an emigration plan to the Joint Distribution Committee. Erich had travelled to New York without Max Warburg in order to avoid, as Max rather crudely put it, 'having two of us gnawing at the same bone.'[63] This construction immediately gives the impression that Erich had gone there as his father's emissary. Although that wasn't entirely incorrect, Erich himself saw his role since the Nazis seized power as one of standing supportively by his father's side. Since he and Max fundamentally saw eye to eye on the question of emigration, it was immediately apparent how much of Erich's own take on things had shaped his father's plans. In all likelihood his fingerprints can be identified on the plan that he presented to the Joint in late December. It was directed at young people from assimilated families who, like himself, had grown up in a symbiosis of Judaism and German nationalist sentiment.[64] For these young people, their affiliation to Judaism was a given, though within this self-evident fact a specifically 'Jewish consciousness' tended to play something of a subordinate part. As Erich saw it, the Reich Deputation of German Jews ought to offer these young people, who did not share the Zionists' viewpoint regarding the founding of a nation-state of Israel in Palestine, a different emigration option. For the Zionists, Jewish emigration was only conceivable in the form of the *aliyah*, the immigration of diaspora Jews to the Palestine region. Although his father was working with the Jewish Agency on the transfer of assets to Palestine under the Haavara Agreement, in his ideological stance Erich himself was a world away from the Zionists who set the tone in Germany. In his view, assimilated Jews who had lived in Germany for centuries were heavily discriminated against by the Zionist associations in favour of Eastern European Jews who had only arrived in the country very recently. He was particularly incensed that war veterans, whom he called 'Jewish combatants', and who in many cases had suffered lifelong damage as a result of the First World War, got no help from the Zionists, even though the German authorities were denying them their rights.[65]

*

At this stage there was still widespread optimism that Jews would be granted asylum in many destination countries. On

16 October 1933 the League of Nations appointed a high commission for refugees from Germany, with a brief to ascertain which countries would be able to offer the refugees work.[66] Out of consideration for Germany, which at the time was still a member of the League of Nations, the commission was designated an autonomous body.[67] James McDonald was elected as the high commissioner. Its separateness from the League of Nations was also underlined geographically, with the seat of the new organisation being established not in Geneva but instead in London.[68] McDonald's role was akin to that of Herbert Hoover in the Commission for Relief in Belgium (CRB), which in the First World War organised an aid fund, with the support of the Allied governments, to provision Belgium, which was cut off from food supplies; this comparison is all the more apposite because, like Hoover, McDonald engaged in negotiations with foreign governments without any clearly defined status.[69]

*

When Erich Warburg met McDonald in New York at the end of December 1933, he told him that their emigration plan would be accepted by the Joint.[70] For, Erich assured, they were sticking to the guidelines which stipulated that aid money should under no circumstances earn the German Reich anything in foreign exchange commissions. Just a few days later, Erich Warburg was even able to report to the high commissioner for refugees that their scheme for an educational fund was now 'well under way':[71] the vocational schools of the Reich Deputation would henceforth offer young people a focused practical education that would put them in a position to carve out new existences for themselves even at destinations that were not, like Palestine, linked to the project of a nationally defined Judaism. To this end, Max and Erich Warburg had created a clearing system that channelled the liquidated assets into two relief funds which were entirely independent of one another: the financial means which were made available to the Reich Deputation for the training of young emigrants came from the young people's parents.[72] The layout that was necessary in order to get hold of affidavits, passports, visas, and boat tickets would later be reimbursed to the Joint by the emigrants once they had found work, in the currency of their destination countries. These funds would then be made available to the next wave of emigrants.

*

The other reason for the trip that Erich Warburg made to New York in late 1933 was the long-overdue discussion with his relatives there. 'Young Master Erich' would need to 'redefine their relationship' according to Fritz Saxl, who openly welcomed Erich's visit. In Saxl's view, since the death of his father Paul in 1932, James Warburg in particular had displayed an 'extraordinary degree of bitterness and mistrust'.[73] But at this juncture Erich Warburg had less of an axe to grind with his cousin than with his uncle. From the very outset, Felix Warburg had been greatly troubled by the fact that his German relatives did not, 'for political reasons', want to contractually commit to London for any more than three years, and had left it open what was to happen to the library thereafter.[74] Consequently, he was absolutely delighted when his efforts in the matter of the library finally bore fruit in November, with the University of New York expressing a serious interest in hosting the institution. On hearing this, he wanted to halt the negotiations with

London immediately and instead have the library shipped to New York, where he believed the books would find an ideal new home in the town house of his deceased brother Paul. Because Erich at that point was still on the high seas, Max wired his brother in New York to tell him that it was too late to pull out of the contract now without a loss of reputation.[75] And quite apart from that, he went on, from an academic point of view too London made sense as a location, because collaboration with scholars from the Warburg circle could be resumed there; many of them were already in the country and surviving by working on research projects that had been arranged through the AAC.[76] And so, once he disembarked in New York, Erich Warburg's most urgent task was to explain their dilemma to the chancellor of New York University and tell him that, in view of the acute danger that their library had found itself in in Hamburg, they had been forced to reach a quick decision. By way of consolation, he said that they could discuss a possible relocation of the library to New York in two years' time. After Erich had also been given a very sympathetic hearing by the chancellor of the New York Library, even Felix Warburg had no choice but to accept the decision. However, he insisted that, where the American side of the family was concerned, London could only ever be considered an interim solution born of the urgency of the situation. At the same time, though, he assured his nephew that he would abide by his part of the financial agreement over the next three years. This would mean that US$2,000 would be transferred annually from America to London. Meanwhile, the German side intended to contribute 10,000 Reichsmarks, or around £1,000 Sterling. But because these latter funds, which were deposited in a frozen Reichsmark account, were subject to foreign exchange control, only a fraction of that sum could be remitted to London. Accordingly, provisions were made to use the money in Germany to acquire books and produce in-house publications for the library. Yet this still did not fully provide for the salaries of the library staff. Fritz Saxl sensed that, in view of the financial provisions for their library, they would continue to be on thin ice, even in London. The search for further sponsors would probably turn out to be far more difficult in England than in New York. Yet Erich Warburg was convinced that these were nothing more than teething problems that they would have to contend with even in the event that they relocated the library to New York.[77] At times like these, Fritz Saxl was in the habit of calling him an 'incorrigible optimist'. But Erich Warburg believed that he had long since ceased to be any such thing. By now he had a very clear-eyed view of things.[78]

*

Thanks to the immigration authority official on Ellis Island, who on Erich's first visit to the United States in 1923 had played the role of destiny and unsolicitedly included him in the immigration quota, Erich Warburg could now have simply remained in New York.[79] Yet in spite of the very threatening situation, even at this stage he still believed that all the present hardships in Germany could ultimately be endured.[80] On 30 December, when he was still in New York, news reached him of Carl Melchior's death. After stepping down from his post as chairman of the Bank for International Settlements, Melchior had become involved, as they all had, in the Jewish Self-Help Organization and participated in the founding in Berlin of the Central Committee for Aid and Development, where – despite his terminal illness – he worked from April 1933 right up to the day he succumbed to a fatal stroke. With Melchior's death, Erich Warburg lost an important confidant whom he had known since boyhood, a sympathetic interlocutor who, when he was struggling to find his own niche in a family that was not exactly short on charismatic figures, always 'took him seriously' – something he could not say of his own father. There were many occasions on which Melchior's understatement and the calm, logical way he dissected Erich's questions had guided him back onto the path that his father had foreseen for him, without Erich even realising it. The term 'betrayal' hadn't even been in Carl Melchior's vocabulary according to Erich Warburg. He had used the word only once, in 1929, in connection with the Young Conference, when the president of the Reichsbank, Hjalmar Schacht, and Albert Vögler – with Carl Melchior and Ludwig Kastl as members of the German negotiating delegation – had tried to ensure that the Young Plan failed. 'Tenaciously and always with a firm guiding hand, he spent so many long years of his life, in the war and during peacetime and the interminable reparations talks, negotiating with the enemy. But it was the betrayal he suffered from within his own ranks that quite literally broke his heart.'[81]

*

In 1926 Aby Warburg had designed a postage stamp that paid homage to the idea of a united Europe, as a symbol of transnationalism.[82] Interlibrary lending, which could be interpreted as a variant of Aby Warburg's symbolic aspiration, took the place of 'supranational commonalities, at a time when Germany was already in the grip of nationalistic sentiments that negated any notion of common ground across national borders.'[83] In the prevailing circumstances, the whole concept of an interlibrary loan service represented a subtle form of resistance against the nationalistic culture war being waged by the National Socialists. All the same, the service was at great pains not to draw attention to itself. The political dimension of its cultural studies mission was only committed to paper *expressis verbis* on one occasion – namely in the introduction to the *Kulturwissenschaftliche Bibliographie zum Nachleben der Antike* (*A Bibliography on the Survival of the Classics*) written by the art historian Edgar Wind, which appeared in late 1934 as the first publication of the Warburg Institute Library, now located in London. Wind put his finger on the political aspect of the library's preoccupation with the ancient world, seemingly far removed from the present day, when he cited the existential threat faced by its cohort of academics. For this group of scholars represented an alternative to the political present inasmuch as, in contemporary Germany, the driving forces behind the Enlightenment – *humanitas* and *ratio* – were now being dismissed as 'relics of an "outdated" tradition' in an attempt to 'return cultural life to a state of health', in other words 'back to common-sense basics'.[84] Max Warburg was critical of this introduction by the art historian Wind, who by then was already living in exile, calling it 'inappropriate in the current climate'. If a bibliography of this kind was going to be published, he claimed, then it should either speak for itself and require no introduction or instead 'a fundamentally more neutral introduction would have been in order.' Erich, who represented the German side of the Warburg family on the London committee of the Warburg Institute, should, Max said, have paid closer attention to what was being published in their name from the safety of far-off England.[85] For alongside the Jewish academics Walter Schmitz and Lotte Labowsky – who from Germany commissioned all the contributions for inclusion in this work, which was copyedited in London but published and printed by Teubner in Leipzig – a whole string of other Jewish authors who were still living in Germany were involved in preparing entries for this extensive volume, including Paul Ruben, Hans Liebeschütz, Elsbeth Jaffé, and Richard Salomon.[86] These individuals now became the focus of a witchhunt, triggered by a hostile review of the book which appeared in the Nazi newspaper *Völkischer Beobachter*.[87] Granted, there was no question in Max Warburg's mind that they should nonetheless continue to publish. But so long as part of the Warburg circle remained in Germany, he expected their colleagues in the United Kingdom to show more restraint.[88]

*

Max Warburg himself was kept under surveillance by the Gestapo wherever he went. Every acquaintance he met in public was photographed and put under pressure. As far as his own future was concerned, Max took a pessimistic view. Every day he didn't know what to expect, he confided to James McDonald. He might get lucky and be left in peace, or under the pretext of having allegedly committed an offence he could be arrested and sent straight to a concentration camp.[89] In September 1933, James McDonald had been given access to the Dachau camp. On the whitewashed walls of the prisoners' mess hall, caricature portraits of the great 'traitors' of Germany had been painted. Included in this gallery of the so-called 'November criminals' (a reference to democratic politicians who had signed the Armistice of November 1918 with the Allies, and their confederates), alongside politicians like Walther Rathenau, Gustav Stresemann, Friedrich Ebert,

Rudolf Breitscheid, and Philipp Scheidemann, there was a picture of Max Warburg. He was the only one in this 'rogues' gallery' at Dachau who was still living in Germany.[90]

*

After the attacks in the *Völkischer Beobachter*, Felix Warburg again pressed for the library to be moved to New York. He found it unbearable to see all the trouble his relatives were put to as a result of the interlibrary loan arrangement. Mary Warburg died in Hamburg in May 1934. Felix Warburg took the death of his sister-in-law as an opportunity to pass his shares in the library building at Heilwigstraße in Hamburg to his heirs. He no doubt assumed that his heirs would transfer their shares in the library's holdings to him in return, and thought that his brothers Fritz and Max might also use this occasion to divest themselves of their remaining shares.[91] Yet on the German side, such decisions could only be taken on the basis of a majority vote. And Erich made it abundantly clear what he thought about his uncle's suggestion: 'What Felix is proposing here is naturally out of the question'.[92] However, the Bamberger Foundation declared its willingness to donate a million dollars for the upkeep of the library and its further expansion into a research institute. The plan was to turn Paul Warburg's mansion at 17 East 80th Street in Manhattan into the Aby and Paul Warburg Memorial, commemorating the life and work of both brothers. Max Warburg, though, did not consider this a great idea. For Paul, he said, 'had never had an especially practical interest in the library; he had often said that he found the work it did too cerebral and not useful enough, and that in truth he had always paid over the large donations he made somewhat reluctantly, purely out of love for Aby, and also because I had personally and repeatedly asked for them – Renovating Paul's house now for the library in memory of Paul and Aby would give a false impression of both brothers' activities. The memorial that Paul richly deserved should be housed at the Federal Reserve Board in New York or Washington, dedicated either to him alone or to him and the other founders of the system, since his work was unquestionably of extraordinary historical significance for America.'[93] Yet considering everything that Felix and Paul had done for the KBW, the New York family had every reason to expect that their wishes would be respected. And so Max Warburg informed the London committee of the Friends of the Warburg Library of the decision of the American branch of the family to transfer the library to the United States after three years.

*

Erich felt as though he had been snubbed. He could scarcely believe the predicament in which his uncle's decision placed him and the people in London. Lord Lee had only just sent London University a memorandum containing pleas by eminent British academics to integrate the library more fully into the university, also with regard to its physical location. Academic interest in the enterprise had grown considerably in the interim, and the idea was that the library should be accommodated rent-free in one of the university's own build-ings. However, after Lord Lee learnt of the latest twist in the family saga, he put all his efforts on hold. 'You could not have chosen a less auspicious moment to inform our British friends about the change of mind on your side,' Erich wrote reproachfully to his cousin Edward, the youngest of Felix

Warburg's four sons, who represented the American side of the family on the Warburg committee in London. 'You can imagine that Lord Lee almost fell off his chair ... when he learned of the sums being bandied about by the Bamberg Foundation.'[94] Edward was the patron of the first Stravinsky Festival in the Metropolitan Opera House and a supporter of the American Ballet, from which the New York City Ballet later evolved. In the same year as the library transfer, he joined the board of trustees of the Museum of Modern Art. New York was the centre of his world; a world in which donations in the millions were not so alien as they were in the context of a library that had just been saved from destruction by the Nazis. The point that no one in London really understood was this: why would those in New York initially give them hope that the library could stay in London for the long term, yet only twelve months later perform a complete about-face and announce that they would be transferring the library to New York after three years? Lord Lee invited the London friends of the Warburg Library, including the dean of the university, to White Lodge and informed them – in the presence of Erich Warburg and Fritz Saxl – about the latest developments. Naturally enough, everyone wanted to know what would happen to the library now. Erich could only repeat what he had told his uncle: namely that it would be impossible to reach a decision before the three-year period had elapsed, that is by the end of 1936.[95] Although Lord Lee 'remained of course the very model of politeness', Erich found the situation deeply shameful and humiliating. Writing to his cousin, he announced that he was speaking now not just as a family member but also as a Jew: 'We shouldn't allow anything to happen that could be used to stigmatise us.'[96]

Max Warburg had once confided in James McDonald that he would no longer be able to live in Germany if legislation turned the Jews into second-class citizens.[97] When, on the evening of 15 September 1935 the German parliament unanimously adopted the racial laws that had been announced at the Nazi Party Rally in Nuremberg that very same day, the limit of what was bearable was finally reached. Erich Warburg urged his father to close the banking house so that the National Socialists could not continue to profit from their good name abroad. Max Warburg was well aware that it benefitted the Nazis ('For the present, we are useful to them because we can help them'[98]) but as long as that remained the case, he believed it was his duty to leave no stone unturned in trying to make the situation of Jews in Germany more bearable. Eight lawyers were employed at the bank to help interpret the mass of new laws and regulations pertaining to the Jews. That was the crucial thing, since all possible loopholes had not yet been closed.[99] Max Warburg fancied that 'a kind of accord' might be reached between German–Jewish representatives and the German government, an agreement that would on the one hand properly regulate emigration while at the same time safeguard the rights of those Jews who remained in Germany.[100] He set much store by his 'direct line' to Hjalmar Schacht. Certainly, he realised that Schacht had 'no political conscience'.[101] He had placed himself at Hitler's service and contributed significantly to his early economic successes. But as the Reich economic minister, Schacht must have had an interest in US firms on the international market continuing to do business with the German Empire. And it was here that the mood had shifted in the meantime.

Unlike John Foster Dulles, who got on famously with Hjalmar Schacht, Foster's younger brother Allen was horrified by the 'dark mood in Berlin' which he encountered on his visits to the capital. Accordingly, in the late summer of 1935 he urged his fellow partners at Sullivan & Cromwell in New York to close their Berlin office and end all cooperation with German firms.[102] By contrast, during this period the Warburg bank gained a new colleague: Kurt Sieveking, formerly an employee of the American bureau at the German Foreign Office and a close friend of Erich Warburg, resigned his position at a Hamburg law firm and applied for a job as a legal advisor at the Warburg Bank. In making this move, Sieveking, who would later become mayor of Hamburg, exhibited the same courage as Albrecht von Bernstorff, who, after the Foreign Office had placed him in temporary retirement in November 1933, had become a partner in the Jewish banking house of A. E. Wassermann.

*

On the very first day the Nuremberg Laws came into force in Germany, Erich and his father finally resolved the question of where the library would be located. In view of the latest political developments there was no longer any question of repatriating the books to Germany, and a transfer of the library to America would have to be registered with the Foreign Exchange Board and the Reichsbank. But if they managed things 'adeptly and without much fuss', they could simply inform the local agency chief Baron Kleinschmit that they had extended the agreement with the British 'by five, ten or even twenty years'.[103] From an economic point of view as well, England had the edge over the USA. The library was – and in this they had come to share Saxl's view – primarily a research tool for European scholars, with a 'pronouncedly German' working method that was by no means moribund, merely dormant, and which, quite unlike outside Europe, could be put into effect once more within Europe 'in consultation with existing academics of the old school.' This would also be in the spirit of Aby, 'who always wished to see his library preserved for the "good European".'[104] But in order for the library to really thrive in England, the question of its location now needed to be settled; the interest of the British had waned noticeably since they had learned that there was no unanimity in the family over where the library should be sited.[105] The London friends on the Warburg committee expected them to leave the library *in situ* in England. If they cancelled that arrangement, then, as ungrateful refugees whom the British had been the only ones to help in a time of need, they would also be exposed to an anti-Semitically charged backlash. To be sure, the New York family might expect their wishes to be respected; however, these could not be allowed to run counter to the interests of the library or to disregard the special situation in which the family in Germany found itself. As a conceivable solution Max Warburg began to entertain the idea of a dual-site institution, something he had toyed with long before. In this scheme, he envisaged building a second library in New York, which would collaborate with the London library.[106] But Erich was sceptical from the outset. He doubted whether the 'extraordinary budget' needed to put such an 'audacious plan' into action could ever be raised. They had all too easily overlooked the fact 'that there is only a finite sum in total available in the world for academic purposes,'

Erich told his father, 'and that the KBW, which you know I have always been a staunch supporter of, should not be *over-estimated* in this regard.'[107]

*

In November 1935, in response to the passing of the Nuremberg Laws, a group of British Zionists and non-Zionists, many of them prominent figures, came together in London. In the presence of the League of Nations High Commissioner for Refugees, work began under extreme pressure on an emigration programme, the cost of which would be borne by Jewish organisations and financially powerful individuals.[108] At this point McDonald was already planning to resign from his post as high commissioner, since the latest political developments in Germany had shown that the possibilities of dialogue, as envisaged by the high commissioner's role, had turned out to be totally futile.

A first meeting was held at the Rothschild Bank building in New Court, and a second at the home of Walter Samuel, the 2nd Viscount Bearsted. Two different emigration plans were on the table. One was an emigration scheme funded through loans and credit that was proposed by the store owner Simon Marks, and which continued to see Palestine as the destination.[109] The other was Max Warburg's plan for emigration with a non-Zionist agenda, based on capital transfer and to destinations other than Palestine. Max had already unveiled his plan in September at the nineteenth Zionist Congress in Lucerne and so incurred the wrath of Chaim Weizmann, who was re-elected at the congress as president of both the World Zionist Organization and the Jewish Agency. Weizmann was opposed to putting the emphasis of emigration on wealthy

German Jews, and saw the desperate plight of some 3.5 million Jews in Poland as far more urgent.[110] He further believed that anyone who was not prepared to play a part in the Jewish reconstruction work in Palestine had no right to support from the Jewish community. Back in London, therefore, Weizmann threw his weight behind Simon Marks' scheme for an *aliyah* facilitated through loans and credit.[111] Lionel de Rothschild, on the other hand, endorsed Max Warburg's emigration plan.

Erich Warburg also travelled to London to be at the second meeting at Walter Samuel's house on 21 November 1935. Together with Salomon Adler-Rudel, the secretary-general of the Reich Deputation of German Jews, he endeavoured to dispel the misconception that the two schemes were in competition with one another. He assured James McDonald that his father was anxious to put the Marks plan into action, with some minor changes, as soon as possible.[112]

*

After the gathering in London – in close consultation with the Deputation – had settled on a combination of the Warburg and the Marks plan, albeit only as the basis for further discussions, a small delegation from London embarked for America in February 1936. There, in New York, the combined Warburg–Marks plan that had been worked out in England was roundly rejected by Jewish groups: their verdict was that 'Marks' was merely the packaging, while the content was 'Warburg'. Protest came from the American League for the Defense of Jewish Rights, the US association that was calling for a boycott of German goods and services, and whose president Samuel Untermyer knew how to make his voice heard. The American Jewish Congress and the Jewish Labor

Committee also turned down the Jewish–British scheme.[113] Plans in which an organised emigration could only be realised through cooperation with the National Socialist authorities were deemed to be out of the question.[114] The accusation was levelled at Max Warburg that his primary concern was to save German exports.[115] Instead of extending his hand to the Hitler regime, his critics argued, he would be better placed finding solutions that chimed in with the boycott movement.[116] The general impression was that he wasn't distancing himself sufficiently from Hitler's regime. Never had Max Warburg felt so disheartened by the USA.[117] His brother Felix, who in his heart of hearts sympathised with the boycott movement, only remained publicly neutral on the subject out of consideration for his German relatives.[118] He tried to get Samuel Untermyer to appreciate his brother's position.[119] Max, he explained, had taken it as read 'that he owed it to his coreligionists who could not emigrate and get their wealth out of the country to try his best with people like Schacht to obtain some concessions.'[120] All this did was earn him a reproach for being an appeaser in the *New Republic*, the organ of the Zionists.[121]

*

Against the background of this escalating debate within the Jewish community concerning questions of an organised emigration, the controversy within the Warburg family about the site of the library entered a decisive phase. Fundamentally, Felix Warburg too now regarded an extension of the contract with London University as a possibility, but he also picked up on the idea that his brother had mooted of a dual-site institution. Admittedly, his vision was rather of a kind of transatlantic interlibrary loan arrangement, with London sending books to the USA.[122] Erich was intent on having the academics explain to his uncle the many reasons why this was a bad idea.[123] Erwin Panofsky complied with Erich's request and set out the problems associated with an internationalisation of the library in the manner that Felix Warburg had suggested: if books were constantly being lent out, the efficacy of the library as a research tool would be compromised and the institution would be forced to contend with problems of a very practical nature that might potentially destroy Aby Warburg's life's work.[124] Gertrud Bing also weighed in on Panofsky's side: the really special thing about this library, she wrote, was not the sheer number of books it housed but the way in which its holdings were compiled. If they were divided into subject areas, then the collection would disintegrate into a series of ordinary specialist libraries. And if the books were organised according to era, then it would no longer be possible to study the lines of tradition that led from Antiquity through the Middle Ages and up to the Modern Period, and which constituted the true theme of the collection. Fritz Saxl, however, was able to find something positive in Felix's idea: 'I get the sense that this is the first time we've had a suggestion from over there that accords in principle with our own aims.' At least, he stated, 'Mr. Felix' seemed to have partially come round to the idea of the library remaining in London. 'And I would find it very regrettable if the primitive form in which the thought was first couched were to be made the reason for abandoning it entirely.' For, Saxl maintained, exchange arrangements with America would be of immense importance for the library's own development.[125] But Bing too found an internationalisation of the institute conceivable, 'and furthermore on so broad a basis that it would be precisely American students who regarded the library as their own exchange institution.'[126] She backed Panofsky's suggestion of further expanding the library's photocopying service. In this way they could supply American institutions with copies of books that did not exist in the United States.[127]

Felix Warburg blew his top at this suggestion: such a plan was wholly unacceptable, while the notion that Percy Strauss, the Trustee of New York University, would agree to a collaboration on the basis of a few photocopies was absurd. The time was ripe for the KBW to become resident in the United States! Aby Warburg's 'good European', who had been championing the cause of enlightenment ever since the Renaissance – well, that precisely described the hordes of academically highly qualified emigrants who had taken refuge in the States. They included many scholars who had worked with the KBW for years. After all, even Erwin Panofsky, the head of the art history faculty at Hamburg University, had emigrated to the USA in 1933. Without more ado, Felix Warburg dispatched a telegram: 'The American Warburgs intend to transfer the library to America in the future. If that is impossible at the present time, then we find ourselves compelled to withdraw financial support from the library until such a plan becomes feasible.'[128] Frieda Warburg supported her husband's decision. She had no sympathy for her nephew's attitude – on an earlier occasion she had reproachfully described him, with regard to Germany, as 'almost assimilated'. She could not understand why he and his father did not finally make a clean break with Nazi Germany.[129] Aby Warburg's former student Carl Georg Heise, however, strengthened Erich's resolve: 'I'm convinced that everything that you've done so far has been in the spirit of your uncle Aby, and that the rift in this matter with some of your American relatives will simply have to be taken on the chin if need be in the interest of a fruitful continued existence of the library.'[130] As an observer of the family dispute, Panofsky summarised the location question by saying that it all depended on 'whether one believes in Europe in the near future or not.'[131] The other family members were very hesitant to get involved in the argument. As the American representative of the second generation, James Warburg had never identified with the library project to the same extent as the German side of the family. His sister Bettina showed some sympathy for the predicament of the German family members, as did her mother Nina Warburg. Given the great dedication that the circle of supporters in London had shown in accommodating the library and its members of staff in the British capital, the two women deemed it inappropriate to talk of London merely as an interim solution.[132]

*

At least Erich was able to take something positive from his uncle's telegram. They now had a clear direction of travel.[133] In withdrawing his funding, 'Uncle Felix' had effectively left the decision in their hands. But he needed to realise that 'If our British friends have to shoulder the financial burden alone, then in return they will surely demand an extension of our arrangement beyond the three years so far agreed. The library will have to stay in London for many years to come.'[134] Felix Warburg pricked up his ears at this. It was clearly their intention now, in concert with the group around Lord Lee, to come to a permanent London solution. Prior to this, all Erich had ever done was reiterate that they couldn't come to any decisions that exceeded the agreed three-year loan period. Felix Warburg had apparently imagined that they might come up with the idea of sending the books back to Germany. He asked his nephew to hold off making a definitive commitment. But Max Warburg had had enough. He had, he told his brother, sent so many letters and telegrams that he felt utterly drained and couldn't put forward any new arguments. They couldn't delay coming to a decision about the library any longer. Quite understandably, he said, Lord Lee was breathing down their necks.[135]

*

In February 1936 Max and Erich informed Lord Lee that the family had decided that the library would remain in London. Lord Lee wanted to consult the committee members and then let the Warburgs know how things should proceed. In March a crisis meeting was held; the only information Gertrud Bing could elicit was that there was no possibility of further financing for the present.[136] Funds should already have been applied for in December. Because of the long delay, they were now earmarked for the following years. The limbo in which they had found themselves for years and the enduring uncertainty frayed the nerves of the library staff. Gertrud Bing turned to Erich Warburg. She and Fritz Saxl believed that it would make a good impression 'if an attempt was made from our side to make up the shortfall left by the Americans, or at least some of it.' She would have explained this situation to his father, Gertrud Bing went on, 'but the sad fact is that your father now takes the view that he is unable to do anything for us, because he will need to exploit his connections to realise his other plans, which involve incomparably large sums of money.' She summoned up her courage and asked: 'Could we ask you to discuss the matter with him one last time?'[137]

*

Max Warburg collected donations for the *Allgemeine Treuhand* fund (Altreu for short). Unlike Paltreu, this fund for destitute emigrants was not focussed on Palestine. But he had disengaged his emigration plan from any idea of capital transfer and adopted Simon Marks' approach of funding emigration through loans and credit. The sums that built up in the Altreu fund came from emigrants who had left their capital behind in blocked Reichsmark accounts and transferred this to the Reich Deputation. Warburg & Co., the banking house in Amsterdam, became an important outpost in the clearing system, since it was there that the emigrants reclaimed the savings they had left behind converted into foreign currency. The Altreu fund also held 600,000 Reichsmarks from the personal assets of the Warburgs. Forty per cent of this came from the accounts of the Kara Corporation, which were still open. Since August 1931, this money had been accumulating in these accounts as a result of the German Credit Agreement and the ensuing exchange control.[138] The American Warburgs had reduced their demands to 1.7 million Reichsmarks. Instead of casting the money into the greedy maw of the National Socialists, it was now used to pay for sworn affidavits, passports, residence visas, and boat tickets for Jewish refugees. In consultation with his cousin Bettina, a trained psychologist and member of the American Psychoanalytic Association, Erich advanced money from the Kara fund to impecunious Jewish psychologists and psychiatrists. This enabled a total of 154 people to escape from Germany.[139]

*

93

In June 1936 John McCloy, Frederick Warburg's tennis partner and company lawyer, arrived in Germany. He was representing the Bethlehem Steel Company, a Cravath client, which in 1916 had lost munitions to the value of some 3 million dollars in a huge explosion at a railroad freight yard in the New York harbour basin, the so-called Black Tom Depot. Because this occurred as the result of German sabotage, Bethlehem Steel and 153 other plaintiffs were claiming compensation before the international German–American court of arbitration. The German Empire had to defend itself against the accusation that it had been responsible for carrying out at least two major attacks with explosives on American soil during the First World War, even at a time when the two countries still maintained diplomatic relations. Unlike the torpedoing of the transatlantic liner RMS *Lusitania*, it had never accepted responsibility for the bombings. In an initial judgment in 1930 the Mixed Claims Commission had found in favour of Germany, whereupon the plaintiffs' lawyers demanded that the judgment be set aside and ultimately succeeded in securing a retrial. By the time the NSDAP suggested to the legal representatives from the USA in May 1936 that these so-called 'sabotage claims' be dropped in favour of a settlement, the action was already entering its ninth year. At the end of June 1936, the American delegation arrived in Munich. Hermann Goering had delegated Franz Pfeffer von Salomon to head up the German negotiating team. In the 1920s, Pfeffer had been instrumental in developing the SA into Hitler's personal instrument of power within the party. After standing down from the senior leadership ranks of the SA, Pfeffer joined the staff of Rudolf Hess on the party's governing body and carved out a niche for himself as a 'gun for hire'.[140] It was in this role that Goering deployed him in the negotiations with the Americans.[141] The sabotage claims had long been a thorn in the side of the National Socialists. While the international arbitration commission was still investigating the role of German agents in the First World War, the Nazis were already busy building up their intelligence services for the next war.[142] The Olympic Games, which were due to take place in Germany in August 1936, opened up a favourable window of opportunity for the negotiations. Moreover, Pfeffer proved himself to be a skilful negotiator, and reached an agreement with the Americans after just a few days. Those who were astonished by this outcome found out the truth at the end of proceedings, when Pfeffer played the American delegation recordings of their telephone conversations.[143] The National Socialist negotiator had listened in on the conversations between the American attorneys and their clients back in the USA and used the information he gleaned to his tactical advantage. Pfeffer, who had been a member of the right-wing Freikorps militia back in the early 1920s and taken part in the armed resistance to the French military occupation of the Ruhr in 1923, had during his time there got to know Kurt Jahnke, the leading figure in the German spy ring that had been active on the Eastern seaboard of the United States until April 1917. On Rudolf Hess' staff in 1935, Pfeffer developed a foreign intelligence service based on Jahnke's model.[144] Goering had carefully weighed up whom he should appoint to lead negotiations and quite deliberately put in place an expert in clandestine activities. Yet ultimately, Pfeffer was cheated of success. For after the American government had made it clear right at the outset that the delegation in Munich was not authorised to make any trade concessions, Goering and Hitler quickly lost interest in an out-of-court settlement. When the German Foreign Office refused to ratify the agreement because it had been misled by Pfeffer during the talks, there were no further repercussions. Instead Hitler gave instructions for the entire case to be shelved.[145]

*

No sooner were the Olympic Games over than the regime intensified its Aryanisation programme. Now even those Jewish firms were affected that had previously been spared because of their importance to the German economy. Friedrich Flick, who for a long time had been putting pressure on Jewish shareholders in the Lübeck blast furnace works, aggressively forced them out at the end of 1937. To start with, he browbeat the Eisner family into selling him their firm Rawack & Grünfeld. To achieve this he made use of the Office of the Chief Representative of Iron and Steel Management, a body newly formed by Hermann Goering, which threatened R & G with having its import licence revoked. The Eisner family capitulated. Through his takeover of R & G, Flick became a shareholder in the Lübeck blast furnace works. Now Flick exerted pressure on the Hahn family too, telling them it would be better for them to sell their shares in the Lübeck steelworks, since the powers that be were already planning for 'Aryan' proprietors to take charge of the enterprise.[146] Anticipating harassment by the state, the Hahns gave in to Flick's cajoling. They attempted to gain an assurance on the government's part that they would not be forced out of their original works in Duisburg-Großenbaum, and initially the chief representative of Iron and Steel Management magnanimously conceded this. Well aware that such assurances had no binding legal force in any case, he informed them that he had no intention 'in any shape or form of putting pressure on the Hahn and Eisner families to renounce their ownership of Großenbaum too.'[147] Soon after, Wilhelm Zangen, director of Mannesmann Pipeworks AG, submitted a claim to acquire the Duisburg works.[148] Attempts by the family to have some influence over the sale of their original plant were stymied by the Reich Industry of Economic Affairs, which summarily cut the supply of raw materials to their works.[149] The Hahns had no choice but to sell their works to Mannesmann for 15.3 million Reichsmarks.[150] After this massive intervention by the Ministry of Economics, the Warburgs also signed over their blocks of shares in both the Berlin iron-ore plant of R & G and the Lübeck blast furnace to Flick. Erich Warburg, Rudolf Hahn, and his cousin Peter – a son of Georg Hahn, who had carried on the business after the death of his brother Oskar in 1907 – considered how they might manage to transfer at least a portion of the proceeds from the sale of their shares overseas. Alongside the Paltreu, in 1934 Max Warburg had also, in the 'Society for the Promotion of Business Interests of Jews Currently or Formerly Resident in Germany', created another instrument for the transferring of Jewish capital abroad.[151] This involved transactions with Germans living overseas who intended to return to Germany. Doing business with them attracted neither the Reich Flight Tax nor any duties, because the capital transfer entailed no exchange of foreign currency. The property that changed ownership was in a foreign country, while the business transaction was conducted wholly within Germany. The Warburgs knew of a family from the Ruhr who owned a steelworks and rolling mill in the south-west of Finland. This plant, which had been acquired during the French occupation of the Ruhr in order to circumvent the ban on arms production in this German industrial heartland, was now to be sold, because all the pointers in the German Empire

were to growing armaments production and the steel producers who had temporarily moved their operations to Finland
wanted to secure a share of the arms contracts – for which they
would have to invest in their outdated plants in the Ruhr.[152]
As a result, the Aktiebolaget Dalsbruk was now up for sale.
Peter, Rudolf, and Erich travelled together to Finland to close
the deal. The purchase was handled by the Finnish State Bank,
with whose director general Risto Ryti M. M. Warburg had
already worked back in the 1920s. Yet because Erich Warburg
and the Hahns on no account wished to acquire more than a
49 per cent stake in the works, the remaining 51 per cent were
taken on by Gustav Wrede, the Dalsbruk works manager. This
meant that the firm remained preponderantly in non-Jewish
ownership and so could not at some later date be transferred
'into German hands' by the National Socialist government
as a 'Jewish' enterprise. The plant was handed over to them
in Finland; meanwhile the purchase sum was paid into an
account in Germany. Subsequently the Hahn family left
Germany. Georg Hahn and his son Peter emigrated to Brazil.
Rudolf and Lola Hahn moved with their two children to
Great Britain and became neighbours of Kurt Hahn, who in
1934 had opened another boarding school at Gordonstoun in
the north of Scotland. The greater part of the sales proceeds
from their German steelworks went to the foreign exchange
bureau of the Reichsbank. And the funds they might have
been able to draw upon abroad were now tied up in a Finnish
steelworks.

*

As late as May 1936 none of the employees of the Warburg
Library had any idea how things would proceed once the

three-year arrangement had come to an end.[153] After the period agreed with Kleinschmit had elapsed, the foreign currency export department of the Reichsbank promptly enquired when the return of the books might be expected.[154] But just as in ancient Roman dramas, where a *deus ex machina* intervenes in a completely muddled situation and resolves it, so too in the case of the Warburg Library. At literally the eleventh hour a surprise brought about an unexpected turn of events: the Courtauld Institute found itself under threat of having its academic accreditation to confer degrees withdrawn, because the quality of its teaching did not meet the required academic standard.[155] In this situation the Warburg Library turned out to be a knight in shining armour. It immediately placed its own academic expertise at the disposal of the beleaguered Institute and so made itself indispensable. As a consequence, in July 1936 the Courtauld Institute extended its collaboration with the Warburg for a further seven years. The annual subvention was raised to £5,500 and the University of London held out the prospect of the library moving into rooms in one of its buildings in West Kensington.

*

Erich Warburg informed Kleinschmit that they had taken up the British offer of bringing the library into closer partnership with the University of London.[156] If the situation in Germany did not change for their colleagues over the next seven years, then they would consider the loan to the University of London a permanent arrangement. Kleinschmit took note of this information but gave no further response. Erich Warburg told the library employees in London that 'the people over there' had accepted the inevitable.[157] He asked his father to refrain from mentioning the idea of a dual-site institution ever again.[158] Such an arrangement would, he surmised, still fail to satisfy 'Uncle Felix'. And the British, who 'place so much hope in the personal involvement of our people at the Courtauld Institute and indeed are only entering into the arrangement for that reason' would have no use for a dual-site institution at this time.[159] But to his great surprise New York University now expressed an interest after all in collaborating with the Warburg Library in London. The founding director of the Institute of Fine Arts (IFA), Walter W. S. Cook, wanted to use at least 20,000 volumes from the holdings of the Warburg Library to establish an art history library in New York. The IFA was willing to pay the original list price for the books, so that the library in London could immediately replace them. Felix Warburg was also back in the game. He offered to make US$50,000 dollars available for the purchase of books, so long as a third party put up the same sum. He would have had sufficient means to fund the development of the library in New York entirely from his own pocket, but this would have meant the American KBW remaining merely a private Jewish library with only a loose connection to the university. Only as a university institution could it free itself from an existence that was dependent upon the interests and prospects of individual family members and establish itself as a channel for academic cooperation that would be used equally by Jewish and non-Jewish scholars. The London library was already well on the way to being just that. Hence the revival of his interest.

*

However, all the discussions about the library's location came to an abrupt end when Felix Warburg unexpectedly died of a heart attack on 20 September 1937, aged sixty-six. The cause of Felix's death was linked to an argument that erupted between him and Chaim Weizmann over the report by the British Peel Commission. This report, which was published in July 1937, envisaged the partition of Palestine into a Jewish state and an Arab state. Felix Warburg regarded Chaim Weizmann's approval of this plan as a betrayal, since he had always supported the work of the Jewish Agency in the belief that religious and nationalistic tensions could be overcome and a partition of Palestine avoided by an improvement in economic conditions and the standard of living across the board.[160] With the death of its most important backer, development of a second library in New York ground to a halt. And although New York University acquired Paul Warburg's former house at 17 East 80th Street for the graduate programme of the Institute of Fine Arts, the plan to cooperate with the Warburg Library in London never came to fruition.

*

In June 1938 the Foreign Exchange Board of the Reichsbank blocked the library's account without citing a reason.[161] In order to get this revoked, the Warburgs planned to donate the books belonging to Aby's war library, which had been left behind in Hamburg, to the city's State and University Library.[162] Until very recently, within certain parameters this kind of *quid pro quo* would have achieved its aim. Now, however, the State and University Library no longer attached any value to this book bequest.[163] The policy of *Gleichschaltung* had taken hold of all authorities. In October 1936 the Bureau for National Tradition, Church, and Art, which had authorised the export of the books to London, was dissolved. In

1938 Kleinschmit was dismissed from the civil service and the education authorities now assumed responsibility for all cultural administration.[164] As if by some miracle, no objection had thus far been raised to the concept of the fixed-term book loan. Yet the Warburgs could still not afford to make any mistakes. After Felix's death Max and Fritz had transferred their shares in the property at Heilwigstraße to Aby's children. When, in August 1938, they suggested demolishing the building in order to rid themselves of the burden of the ongoing maintenance costs, Erich vehemently opposed it.[165] After all, he objected, tearing down the ancestral home might well lead people to read this as a signal that the library was staying in London in perpetuity. And then each and every one of them would be required to pay 90 per cent of its value to the National Socialist exchequer (in the meantime the Reich Flight Tax had been increased to this level).[166] Ultimately, it was the unrestrained looting of Jewish assets after 1933 that had prompted them to carry out the library transfer in the form of a loan arrangement in the first place. In August 1938, books from the London Warburg Library were still being lent to Germany through the Prussian State Library. Erich and his father ensured that the library's activities remained below the public radar. When the librarian Hans Meier was drawing up the annual report, Erich asked him mildly sarcastically to 'make sure you don't mention the State Library while you're about it, because I don't imagine that you'd be doing the State Library any favours by mentioning their name. You understand?'[167] And in January 1938, when the Jewish *Central-Verein-Zeitung* (the journal of the Central Association of German Citizens of Jewish Faith) reported on new publications from the Warburg Institute, Max Warburg wrote to the newspaper's editor-in-chief Alfred Hirschberg: 'I would be greatly obliged to you if you would report nothing about the Library in future.'[168] In no further publications was the aggressiveness identified so plainly as it had been in the 1934 *A Bibliography on the Survival of the Classics*, with which phenomena that they studied academically as cultural, historical, and religious symbols all of a sudden irrupted very tangibly and menacingly into their lives under National Socialism.[169] The only good news during this period came from London. The University of London made rooms in its own Imperial Institute Building available to the Warburg Library rent-free. Since its completion in 1893, this building in West Kensington had been used to host overseas exhibitions and trade fairs. The university's own administrative department had also been housed there since 1899, and it was now relocated to Bloomsbury. Thus, the former administrative wing of the building was now free for the Library to take occupancy.

*

If in the first years of National Socialist rule Max Warburg had still believed that their business associates, many of whom were also personal friends, would be courageous enough to resist the pressure to conform, in the interim he had been forced to admit that he was fooling himself. 'It was only a matter of time, and sooner or later they all caved in. The propaganda that appealed to people's basest instincts, combined with terror, was incredibly successful.'[170] Since 1936, economic 'enforced uniformity' had put a stop to all their remaining business contacts. Between 1936 and 1938 the bank had been removed from eighty posts on boards of directors. Things went quiet at the banking house. In May 1938 the National Socialist policy of Aryanisation also reached M. M.

Warburg in Ferdinandstraße. So as to continue to profit from its international reputation, at the Aryanisation negotiations the authorities refrained from changing the bank's name.[171] As late as 1941 the bank was still trading under the name of M. M. Warburg. It became a limited partnership, headed by its former chief representative Rudolf Brinckmann. His right-hand man, Paul Wirtz, was a business friend of the Warburgs. The former shareholders received 11.6 million Reichsmarks.[172] As a result of the remaining shares in land and real estate, as well as the Amsterdam subsidiary, none of which formed part of the limited-partnership agreement, the credit balance was reduced to 6.4 million Reichsmarks.[173] Minus the sum of 3 million Reichsmarks, which Max and Fritz Warburg had made available to the limited partnership as sleeping partners, the final proceeds from the compulsory sale amounted to 3.4 million Reichsmarks. From this sum a further 850,000 RM in 'Reich Flight Tax' were deducted, along with an 'authorisation fee' for the Aryanisation that came to 1 million Reichsmarks. In the end, all that remained of the assets of the bank, which had been in the hands of the Warburg family for 140 years, was a mere 155,000 Reichsmarks, to be split between the four shareholders and converted into foreign currency.[174]

*

In the years since 1933, when they had clung on in Germany, Erich had seen his most important role as supporting his father. Ever since the Nazis had come to power, he had stayed by his side. He had accompanied him to conferences, defended his various plans concerning how to organise a mass emigration of German Jews, and taken the part of his father's emissary in the matter of the library. In doing so, as he later described it, he had 'always had one foot in a concentration camp, so to speak.'[175] Ever since his first visit to the United States, when the immigration official on Ellis Island had, unbidden, included him in the immigration quota, every year Erich Warburg had renewed his 'permanency of residence'. After 1933 Woodlands, the family seat of the American Warburgs, became an unreal antithesis to the reality of Jewish life in Hitler's Germany. And yet every time Erich Warburg had returned to Germany from his visits to the USA.[176] It was his loyalty to his father which made him put up with the Nazis for so long, even though he could have escaped their clutches far earlier by becoming a naturalised US citizen. 'As his only son, I could not bear the thought of him in a concentration camp while I was living on Park Avenue in New York'.[177] Since the Aryanisation of their bank, however, father and son found themselves fighting a losing battle in Germany. But Max Warburg was loath to admit it; what kept him going was the sense that he should not give in unless he was absolutely compelled to do so.[178] Together with his office, he moved across the street from the banking house and resumed his work helping refugees. As the scope for action grew ever more limited, his office became increasingly important to the work of the Jewish aid organisation.[179] Erich's sisters were also engaged in the refugee aid programme. As early as January 1933, an Aid Committee had been established in Berlin to help young Jewish people who had lost their parents emigrate to Palestine. With the support of Lola Warburg, this evolved in May of that same year into the Youth Aliyah organisation.[180] And from 1935 on, her sister Gisela headed the department responsible for child emigration at the Reich Deputation of German Jews. In Office II-112 of the secret service of the SS, where Adolf Eichmann worked from 1935 on, and which was responsible for 'Jewish affairs', it had long been assumed that the Foreign Exchange Board was profiting from the millions in aid that Jewish organisations were collecting for German Jews. When Eichmann found out in 1938 that the clearing system developed for emigration was managing without foreign exchange transfer, the security service took control of Jewish emigration. In August 1938 Eichmann set up the Central Office for Jewish Emigration in Vienna.[181]

*

In 1926, after returning from the USA, Erich Warburg had bought an old customs cutter and restored it with the help of Wolfgang Rittmeister, his friend since childhood who worked at the Hapag shipping company. They christened the boat *Kong Bele* and sailed around the Baltic every year. Erich was very attached to the vessel and submitted an export application, which he was granted. With the plan of berthing her at a mooring in a Swedish harbour, in the summer of 1938 he once again sailed up into Scandinavian coastal waters. He put in at the Finnish Åland Islands. In the small cinema in Marienhamn, the capital of the Ålands, a film was playing about the final voyage of *L'Avenir*, a barque belonging to Gustav Erikson, the last Finnish ship owner to maintain a fleet of tall ships.[182] In 1937, Erikson had finally parted with *L'Avenir* and sold the vessel to the Hamburg Hapag shipping company. But in March of that year, on her maiden voyage under the Hapag flag, she had foundered off Cape Horn. Erich felt a great sense of melancholy at the sight of the proud tall ship on the screen. *L'Avenir* is the French word for 'future'. But in the summer of 1938, as the fate of the *L'Avenir* demonstrated, tall ships had no future. All that awaited them, at best, was life as a museum exhibit. Ship owners like Gustav Erikson were dealers and businessmen. Their epic voyages around the world demanded a willingness to take risks.[183] The flip side of trade was the struggle for mastery of the world. In this moment, Erich Warburg did not dare to imagine what the Germany of the future might look like if, against all expectations, war did not break out again.[184]

*

When, on 23 August 1938, he set off from the Kösterberg on his next passage to New York, he travelled without a return ticket. Not long after, his parents followed in his wake.

4

The Finland Connection

By the time Erich arrived in New York in September 1938, CBS had for several days been broadcasting a special programme on the escalating crisis in the Sudetenland. After every new ticker-tape message, H. V. Kaltenborn, a popular radio journalist, commented on how events in Europe were unfolding, almost on a minute-by-minute basis. His voice could be heard everywhere, be it in the drugstore, the supermarket, or taxis – the whole of New York listened, spellbound, to the radio when the running news broadcasts were interrupted and H. V. Kaltenborn's voice broke in.[1] The transmissions began on 12 September, with Hitler's closing speech at that year's Nuremberg Rally, and ended with the signing of the Munich Agreement on the night of 29–30 September. On that same day, Erich Warburg was formally granted US citizenship. When applying for his new papers, he opted for the Anglo-Saxon spelling of his Christian name: he was now called Eric M. Warburg.

*

Max and Alice Warburg, who came to the USA shortly after their son on a visitors' visa, were now the parents of a US citizen, and as such were entitled to remain in the United

States indefinitely. Yet Max Warburg had already booked a return passage to Germany for himself and his wife on 2 December.[2] In spite of being seventy-one, the banker was resolved to once more brave all the anti-Semitic harassment he would encounter in Germany. Alice Warburg, who would never have dreamt of letting her husband travel alone, was determined to accompany him on his return journey come what may. Their trip to the United States was for the sole purpose of collecting money from Jewish aid organisations there for the Benevolent Society for German Jews (*Hilfsverein der Deutschen Juden*), which was threatened with bankruptcy. They were accompanied on this begging expedition by their daughter Gisela, since her department for child emigration at the Reich Deputation of German Jews – which the authorities had legally downgraded – was also facing the same problem. Gisela too wanted to be back in Berlin in a few weeks' time. But then, on 10 November, reports came in from Germany on serious disturbances that had broken out the previous night: synagogues had been set on fire, Jewish businesses and organisations systematically vandalised, Jewish children's and old people's homes attacked, and thousands of Jewish citizens rounded up and imprisoned. Kurt Sieveking sent Max Warburg a telegram, warning him that if he came back to Germany he would be arrested the minute he stepped off the boat. His brother Fritz, who on the night of the pogrom in Hamburg rushed to the Israelite Hospital, had been seized and promptly carted off to the concentration camp attached to the city's Fuhlsbüttel Prison. It was only at the instigation of a banker who was a friend of the family, Cornelius von Berenberg-Gossler, who interceded with Heinrich Himmler's adjutant Karl Wolff, that Fritz Warburg was finally released at the end of January 1939, with the proviso that he leave

Germany immediately.[3] However, for this he needed a passport with valid emigration papers, which he was refused, thereby making his continued stay in Germany tantamount to house arrest. Berenberg-Gossler duly paid the Gestapo a second visit, having got the impression that they wanted to hold a prominent Jew as a hostage. All the same, an exit permit was now linked to the condition that Fritz Warburg and his wife would have to organise the emigration of a hundred Jewish children at their own expense.[4] But what the German authorities had devised as a coercive measure was eagerly embraced by the Warburgs. At this stage, the *Kindertransport* rescue mission was already underway. Eva, the Warburgs' middle daughter, who like her mother was a nursery-school teacher, had set up a refuge on the Hochallee in Hamburg in 1933 and used the family's summer house on the Kösterberg as a summer refuge for the children. Up to thirty children would stay over the summer months at the white villa, eating a midday meal there, spending time in the garden, and doing their homework in a calm atmosphere.[5] And now it was Eva who organised foster families in Sweden for the hundred children who emigrated with Fritz and Anna Warburg in May 1939. The head of the Youth Aliyah in London then asked her to continue her work in Stockholm and to do everything she could in the context of the *Kindertransports* to ensure that even more Jewish children gained asylum in Sweden. Eva Warburg succeeded in getting the Swedish asylum quota for refugees under the age of seventeen raised from 60 to 500.[6] However, their residence permits were limited to two years, after which the young people had to emigrate to Palestine. But because the quota in Palestine set by the Jewish Agency for young emigrants was pegged at an extremely paltry ninety-five, Eva used the family's network to pull strings. With help from her cousin Gisela, who meanwhile was carrying on her work for the Youth Aliyah from the United States, some of the young people registered for the Aliyah were able to emigrate to the USA. In the case of the *Kindertransports* too, which after the November pogroms saw 10,000 Jewish children between the ages of two and seventeen, not only from Germany and Austria but also from Poland and Czechoslovakia, find asylum in Great Britain, the organisation profited from the ongoing involvement of those who had long been engaged in the field of child emigration. Lola Warburg-Hahn, who had been living in England since 1938 with her husband Rudolf Hahn and their two children, was one of the main organisers there of the *Kindertransports*. One of those supporting her in her efforts was her sister Anita, who was also resident in England. The last train, with 251 children on board, was due to leave German-occupied Prague on 1 September 1939. But on that same day, Germany invaded Poland and closed the borders throughout its area of control.

*

After the Munich Agreement of September 1938, H. V. Kaltenborn's US listeners were convinced that it had been the pressure of world public opinion, generated by the radio, which had ensured that politicians had been forced to bow to a universal wish for peace.[7] After enduring more than five years of Nazi harassment and their steadily intensifying anti-Semitic measures against the Jews, Eric Warburg was one of those who took the view that the policy of appeasement would only enable Hitler to transgress all boundaries. For if he was allowed to occupy the Czech lands and annex the Sudetenland with impunity, then he could also continue to terrorise a section of his own populace without having to fear any serious consequences. 'I was sure that only a military victory over Hitler would bring about change.'[8] But such a victory could not be achieved without the involvement of the United States. And over the preceding years US policy had made legislative provisions to ensure that America would never again – as in had been in 1917 – be drawn into a war in Europe. Between 1935 and 1937 laws came into force committing the USA to military neutrality and coupling this commitment with an arms embargo. So as not to harm the whole of the American export market, civilian goods were exempted from this ruling, so long as these shipments were paid for in cash and not carried on American vessels. In addition, a Senate investigative commission examined the question of whether American arms manufacturers had worked towards getting the USA involved in the First World War in 1917. Because around a quarter of all the materiel that was deployed during the conflict was made in the USA, the Republican senator Gerald P. Nye spoke of a conspiracy between arms manufacturers and bankers operating at an international level, and identified this as the reason why the United States entered the war.[9]

*

As a result of his numerous stays in the USA and his family background, Eric Warburg did not find the transition to his new life at all difficult. To begin with he lived with his family, before moving into a small apartment on 52nd Street, where an ever-increasing stream of employees of their former Hamburg banking house, who had managed to flee to New York via Cuba, pitched up outside his door looking for work. Before Eric Warburg had time to decide whether he even wanted to be the proprietor of a bank henceforth, he found himself in the process of establishing a new one. It traded under the name of E. M. Warburg & Co. – his own initials, since at this stage the expropriated bank in Hamburg still carried the name M. M. Warburg. E. M. Warburg occupied premises in the Kuhn–Loeb Building at 52 William Street in Lower Manhattan. Since Felix Warburg's death, Kuhn, Loeb & Co. had been headed by Frederick. Frederick Warburg wasn't facing competition from the bank founded by his cousin, for while the American bank's clients were large American firms, E. M. Warburg was a bank founded by emigrants and for emigrants. Its employees had all once worked at M. M. Warburg in Hamburg, and its customers belonged to that tiny minority among emigrants who still had savings. Max Warburg moved into a small office in his son's bank and incidentally acted in a supervisory role, while continuing to take on responsibility for the fate of German Jews.[10] He remained involved in the European refugee aid programme, founded organisations in America that offered help to new Jewish arrivals, and lobbied for the Rublee–Wohlthat Plan, which he saw as the last opportunity for an organised emigration scheme.[11] The American diplomat George Rublee was executive director of the Intergovernmental Committee on Refugees, a body formed at the Évian Conference in July 1938, which was intended to address the financing and planning of Jewish emigration at a government level in the wake of the failed conference. In December Rublee and Hjalmar Schacht held secret talks in London about a programme that planned for the emigration of all employable German Jews within the next five years. The Rublee–Wohlthat Plan had some similarities with Max Warburg's schemes based on the transfer of Jewish assets, but with the difference that Max was trying to save Jewish capital, whereas the plan devised by Schacht robbed Jewish emigrants of their final savings. After Schacht was dismissed as president of the Reichsbank in January 1939 Rublee continued discussions with the civil servant Helmut Wohlthat, who was responsible for managing the foreign exchange control system. But after Rublee too was relieved of his post in February 1939, there was no one left to promote the plan. And so the last attempt to reach a negotiated emigration settlement ran into the sand.

*

In the summer of 1939 Eric once more travelled to Finland, in the company of Rudolf Hahn, who had joined him from England. The reason for their trip was that there was a buyer interested in the Finnish steelworks and rolling mill, in which the Hahns and the Warburgs still jointly had a 49 per cent stakeholding. Wilhelm Wahlforss, owner of the largest Finnish conglomerate Wärtsilä, wanted to purchase their shares in the Dalsbruk Works.[12] It was no coincidence that Wahlforss was interested in the plant. For some months, the USSR had been pressing Finland to form a military alliance. A Non-Aggression Pact had been in place between the two countries since 1932, but now Russia demanded that Finland give up some militarily important strategic territories. For its part Finland had always been careful to maintain a politically neutral relationship with its communist neighbour and was prepared to make some minor symbolic concessions regarding the demands for territory. But the USSR had intensified its pressure and now the Finnish military was urging the political leadership to provide them with better armaments. Wahlforss' bid for the Dalsbruk Works took place against this backdrop. As purchase agreements were being drawn up in Helsinki, on 23 August 1939 foreign ministers Molotov and Ribbentrop signed the German–Soviet Non-Aggression Pact.

*

When Hitler came to power, Eric Warburg would never have thought it possible that Britain and France would maintain their stance of appeasement for so long. Their conciliatory policies had smoothed the path for German rearmament, the occupation of the Rhineland by German troops, the Nazi takeover of Austria, the incapacitation of Czechoslovakia, and the annexation of the Klaipėda Territory (or 'Memel region') of Lithuania on 23 March 1939. And finally, just a week after concluding the Non-Aggression Pact with the Soviets, Hitler felt emboldened to attack Poland on 1 September 1939.[13] 'Someone must to do something to stop this regime!' Eric cried in desperation when, not long after his return from Finland, Adam von Trott zu Solz paid him a flying visit in his office. 'You organise something here, Herr Warburg, and I'll do something in Germany,' his visitor replied.[14] Adam von Trott was a good friend of his cousin Ingrid, Fritz Warburg's eldest daughter. The two knew one another from their time as students at Oxford. An invitation by the Institute of Pacific Relations had furnished the China expert Trott with a pretext to travel to the USA. In actual fact, he was here to make contact with representatives of the US government and brief them about German resistance to Hitler. In the course of her work for German–Jewish children's aid, Ingrid Warburg had got to know Eleanor Roosevelt. She managed to secure Adam von Trott an invitation to tea at the White House, although in the event he did not get to meet a single representative of the administration.[15] On his return from New York, Adam von

Trott joined the inner circle of conspirators who would later attempt to assassinate Hitler on 20 July 1944.[16]

*

Eric Warburg was itching to play an active role. He could not imagine spending his days working quietly at the bank while Hitler and Stalin carved up Europe. He had long been convinced that US entry into the war was the only means of stopping Hitler. And at Kuhn, Loeb & Co. he found like-minded individuals such as the now seventy-seven-year-old commercial lawyer Paul Cravath, who believed that the security of Western democracies in the coming century depended upon a strong Anglo-American alliance. Even before the Sudetenland crisis, Paul Cravath had declared that, in view of Hitler's aggressive and determined pursuit of German rearmament, Great Britain and France would sooner or later go to war with Germany.[17]

His fear at that time, that they would in this event surely have to do without military support from the United States, at least initially, was indeed realised. Hitler's invasion of Poland, followed two days later by France and Britain's declaration of war on Germany, did not bring about any change of heart in the USA. The American public's opposition to a military intervention remained just as strong as ever. The fact that Paul Cravath nonetheless held fast to the idea that Great Britain and France could still win the war against Germany even without the USA was at that stage based solely on the belief that certain things simply should not be allowed to happen and therefore would not happen.[18] On 5 September the US Congress extended the 'cash and carry' provision to the supply of war materiel, which amounted to a de facto overturning of the arms embargo. In addition, Soviet aggression toward Finland had starkly revealed the shortcomings of US neutrality legislation.

*

When, on 17 September, in the wake of Hitler's attack on Poland, Soviet troops also marched into Eastern Poland, despite the Soviet Union and Poland having signed a non-aggression pact in 1932, the Finns sensed that the Russians would no longer abide by existing treaties where they were concerned either. On 30 November 1939 the Soviet Union duly launched its expected invasion. The fact that Germany did not intervene, as it had done in 1918 when the German Baltic Division had supported conservative forces against the Red Guards, was down to a secret additional clause in the German–Soviet Non-Aggression Pact, which planned for the geostrategic division of Europe between the two countries. The USA kept its distance from events in Europe. And yet since Herbert Hoover's active support for Finnish independence, Finland was precisely the European country that was somewhat closer to Americans than the rest of the continent. Until 1917 Finland had been a Grand Duchy of Russia, but broke away from it during the October Revolution and underwent a process of nation-building that began with a civil war between 'white' and 'red' factions. After the civil war came to an end with the defeat and execution of all the red guards, Finland flirted with the idea of a monarchy and had its fledgling army trained by generals of the German Kaiser. For this reason, the United States initially refused to recognise Finland's independence. But when the Finns clearly demonstrated their republican disposition in the first parliamentary elections in March 1919 and the USA still made no attempt to formally recognise the country, the Finnish diplomat Rudolf Holsti solicited the support of Herbert Hoover at the Paris Peace Conference. At that time, the future US president was head of the American Relief Administration, which organised food supplies to war-ravaged Europe. Hoover's private secretary was Lewis L. Strauss, who after the Second World War, under the presidency of Dwight Eisenhower, would become chairman of the US Atomic Energy Commission. But at the time of the Armistice in 1918, he was just one of 700 volunteers who had reported for duty in the USA for this humanitarian aid mission. In April 1919, Holsti had taken the opportunity to brief Hoover's private secretary on the disastrous situation in Finland. On learning of this, Strauss drafted a letter, signed by Hoover, to Woodrow Wilson, in which he explained to the President why Finland's struggle to establish itself as a liberal democracy deserved to be recognised by the USA.[19] When all was said and done, he stated, the Finnish people had thwarted a communist coup in their own country. But if Finland now failed to gain formal recognition, it would be easy prey for the Soviet Union. Thereafter, it took barely a fortnight for the USA to recognise Finland as a sovereign nation, and also over time to provide it with millions of dollars of trade credit alongside food aid.[20] On the occasion of the twentieth anniversary of Finnish independence in 1938, Herbert Hoover had visited Helsinki and pledged never to forget the Finnish people's friendly attitude.[21] Over the preceding twenty years this had manifested itself above all in the Finns' good payment practice. Even during the global financial and banking crisis, Finland had been the only debtor country to fully reimburse the USA for the credit and aid it had received after the First World War.[22]

*

When, one year after Hoover's visit to Helsinki, Soviet pressure on Finland began to increase, the Finnish ambassador in Washington, Hjalmar Procopé, hurried to the office of US secretary of state Cordell Hull and asked him for a 60-million-dollar loan. In return, he was treated to more fine words about the friendly Finnish nation, though Hull failed completely to address the request for credit.[23] President Roosevelt was keen to avoid a split with the Soviet Union because he was counting on the Hitler–Stalin Pact being of only very transient benefit to both sides. As a result, everything that might have strengthened the Nazi–Soviet alliance was to be avoided.[24] The Finns were free to stock up on weapons from the open market, but unlike the great nations of Great Britain and France, little Finland had neither sufficient cash reserves nor merchant ships to be able to take advantage of the 'cash and carry' provision. When, on 30 November 1939, the country found itself facing an overwhelming force of some 180,000 Red Army soldiers, who advanced into Finnish territory backed by huge numbers of tanks and warplanes, the Finnish Army could only muster 9 poorly equipped divisions, 60 obsolete tanks, and 150 aircraft.[25]

*

In desperation, Hjalmar Procopé turned to Hoover's private secretary Lewis L. Strauss, just as his colleague Rudolf Holsti had done twenty years before. 'I am at the end of my rope and Finland is near the end of hers,' a distraught Procopé began. 'Everywhere I go in Washington – to the State Department, to the Treasury, to the White House, even to the Red Cross – I get sympathy but nothing more. We can't defend ourselves with sympathy.'[26] Hoover's old team, which had coordinated the fundraising campaigns in 1915 and 1916 for the Commission for Relief in Belgium, was already engaged in getting an aid programme for Poland off the ground. Procopé asked Strauss whether something of the kind could also be organised for Finland.[27] Within a few days, Hoover's mighty PR machinery was set in motion.[28] Once again, the legendary fundraiser acted as the chief crowd-puller: Hoover presided over benefit events and went on the radio to ask people to organise fundraising activities. American towns and cities held 'Finland Days'. Greta Garbo donated $5,000, the Danish physicist Niels Bohr gave his Nobel Prize medal, while in the US state of Washington all the box-office takings for the première of the movie *Gone With the Wind* were sent to the Finland Relief Fund. Hoover placed advertisements in no fewer than 1,400 newspapers. The impetus that the Finland campaign generated was evident from the figures. Within the space of just three months, $3.5 million in donations flowed into the Finland Relief Fund. This was fully fifteen times the amount that was raised by the Finland fundraising campaign of the American Red Cross.[29]

*

The high regard in which Hoover and Strauss held one another went back to the beginning of their work together during the First World War, when the aid programme for Poland threatened to founder on the widespread public protests in the USA against the anti-Semitic abuse that was taking place in Polish cities.[30] At Strauss' suggestion Hoover put it to President Wilson that the events in Poland should be investigated by an official commission that included at least one Jew.[31] The Jewish member of the commission was ambassador Henry Morgenthau Sr., not to be confused with his son Henry Morgenthau Jr., who became secretary of the treasury in the administration of Franklin D. Roosevelt. In his report Morgenthau Sr. cited the nationalistically charged atmosphere that accompanied the nation-building process in former multiethnic monarchies as the cause of the eruption of anti-Semitic hate on the streets. However his two non-Jewish colleagues thought that his description of the events occurring on the streets of Poland as a pogrom was wildly exaggerated. In their opinion, the fault for the violence that was being directed at the Jewish population lay squarely with the Jews of Poland themselves, who in their view had not distanced themselves sufficiently from Bolshevism. Besides, they further maintained, there was plenty of evidence that ever since the Middle Ages Jews had tended to segregate themselves from the Gentile majority society.[32] The majority finding of the Commission was that the anti-Polish sentiment in the USA was not fact-based but was the result of Jewish propaganda. After publication of the Morgenthau Report the US ambassador in Warsaw, Hugh S. Gibson, advised the US government that it should in future focus solely on American Jews and intervene in matters concerning Jewish populations in other countries only in the case of extreme atrocities and injustices.[33] The unequivocal message sent by the report was that in an emergency European Jews could only count on the help of Jewish organisations. Around this time Lewis L. Strauss took the decision to join the committee of the Jewish Joint. At the same time he made it a firm rule that when working with Hoover he should create channels of communication on his own account that also benefitted the non-Jewish side.[34] It was on this basis that a stable, friendly relationship between the two men had evolved over the preceding twenty years.

*

The drive to aid Finland pursued a dual strategy. The Hoover campaign was the public face, while the Finnish–American Trading Corporation, on the other hand, was the vehicle for all transactions involving arms purchases and loan agreements. The lawyers from the Cravath chambers took only a few days to draw up the regulatory underpinnings for a Finnish–American trading company which, despite having its registered office in New York, would be one-hundred per cent Finnish-owned.[35] The Finnish–American Trading Corporation was given its own office in the Kuhn–Loeb Building. As its director, the foreign trade expert Julius Klein was appointed, who had been deputy trade minister in the Hoover administration from 1929 to 1933. Eric Warburg, meanwhile, was named managing director on the basis of his contacts in Finland and his knowledge of the country.[36] In this role he worked *pro bono*, acting in solidarity with a country that was beset by totalitarian regimes. He left the business of running his own bank to his colleagues; he himself was henceforth busy round the clock working on behalf of the Finns in a race against time. Thus far, Finland's greatest ally had proved to be the winter. Dressed in white camouflage gear and operating on skis, Finnish forces attacked the foreign troops from all sides, almost invisibly and silently. While these guerrilla tactics did not secure an outright victory, they did buy the Finns time. They hoped to hold out until one of the countries with which they shared democratic and liberal values came to their aid.[37] As early as 1931, in the Hamburg municipal elections, Eric Warburg and his friends had already warned about the situation that was now unfolding: 'If Hitler comes to power, and if the world ostracises Germany or Hitler shuts Germany off from the rest of the world, then of necessity the final consequence will be an alliance with the Soviet Union.'[38] Back then they had come up with the slogan 'Keep the gate open' and urged the people of Hamburg not to vote for any radical parties.[39] They produced a small leaflet, whose cover image showed a sailor fending off attempts from both left and right to close the gate that appears on the coat of arms of the city of Hamburg. The group that formed the Finnish–American Trading Corporation shared the liberal worldview and a strong economic orientation towards foreign trade, as symbolised by the gate on the Hamburg city crest. Eric Warburg experienced a feeling of liberation that he had finally been able to take the initiative amid the debilitating atmosphere of political inactivity. He knew the ruling Finnish prime minister Risto Ryti from the days when Ryti had still been president of the State Bank of Finland. One of the members of the handpicked Finnish Purchasing Commission that Ryti sent to the USA to buy armaments was Wilhelm Wahlforss, the head of Wärtsilä, who had bought Eric Warburg's shares in the steelworks and rolling mill.[40] Secretly, the Finns were counting on the credit that they had asked for being approved by the US Senate after all. But when, instead of the 60 million they had requested, they found that only 10 million was to be made available, and in addition that they would only be allowed to use this money for non-military purposes, Hjalmar Procopé declared testily that this was of no use to Finland. 'We need much more money … we need guns and planes and ammunition.'[41] And when Cordell Hull once again referred them to the private munitions market that was open to Finland an all other combatant nations,[42] Wahlforss' patience finally snapped. He found it a total waste of time to keep going begging door-to-door around Washington while

Finland was bleeding to death. Yet even in Congress now, a few lone voices made themselves heard, calling for a more robust stance towards the Soviet Union: 'The Finns ask for bullets, and we give them beans; they ask for powder, and we give them peas; they seek cannon, and they get broomsticks; they covet planes, and we send them pancakes. We must aid Finland, and we must render that aid quickly,' the Democratic congressman Emanuel Celler told the House of Representatives on 27 February 1940.[43] The anti-Soviet voices grew louder. 'I see no violation of neutrality when the issue is one against Communism.'[44] The Republican representative William A. Pittenger was not alone in this assessment.

*

While the political wrangling continued in Washington over what form the support should take and its scope, the Cravath lawyers drew up contracts with arms firms from which the Finns were ordering weapons and munitions. They had at their disposal US$7,188,000 from Finnish cash reserves. Alongside several hundred thousand rounds of ammunitions, warplanes, heavy artillery pieces, lorries, and tractors were on the shopping list, plus 1,000 gas masks for horses and 4,000 boots for horses.[45] However, the delivery time for orders on the private market was several weeks, since in addition to Great Britain and France, smaller countries too were increasingly equipping themselves with weapons from the United States' 'arsenal of democracy'. Eric Warburg chartered ships and dealt with so-called 'Navy Certs'. Without these permits issued by the navies of combatant nations, cargo ships laden with military equipment, vehicles, goods, war materiel, and medicines would run the risk of being fired upon in those stretches of water in the Atlantic, the North Sea, and the Baltic that had become war zones. Up to seventy people were involved in the work of the Finnish–American Trading Corporation.[46] While Eric Warburg prepared the shipment of goods from New York, his Finnish counterpart was Robert Jansson from the Bensson banking house in Helsinki.[47]

*

'Too much time had been lost,' was Lewis Strauss' verdict.[48] After weeks of debate, the US Congress finally agreed to provide a second tranche of credit to Finland on 18 February 1940. The country was to receive another US$20 million from the state Export–Import Bank. Yet by this time the Finnish army had already lost a fifth of its strength, with 25,000 men killed and another 44,000 wounded.[49] On 12 March 1940, Finland offered the Soviet Union a ceasefire, which Stalin accepted, even though he could have annexed the whole of Finland within a few weeks. But Great Britain was planning to send troops and equipment to Finland and Stalin fought shy of getting involved on the side of the Third Reich in a war against the West.[50] So he settled on control over those areas to which the Soviet Union had laid claim even before the war.[51] Finland ceded 12 per cent of its sovereign territory to the USSR. In Karelia, the Finnish border shifted 130 kilometres to the West.[52] After 107 days, on 13 March, the Finnish–Soviet Winter War was at an end.

*

Nonetheless, the Finnish–American Trading Corporation carried on regardless with its work. Despite being in possession of Navy Certs, four of the sixteen ships chartered by Eric Warburg were torpedoed by German U-boats. A further complication came with the German army's occupation of Denmark and Norway in April 1940. The charter vessels of the trading company were now forced to make a detour with their cargoes via the Arctic Ocean route. The town of Petsamo in the far north, which still belonged to Finland at that time, was the port of discharge. The newly arrived lorries were immediately pressed into service to ferry the goods south, shuttling between Petsamo and Rovaniemi, the country's northernmost railhead.[53] Finland had lost important industrial and agricultural areas with the territory that it had ceded to the Soviet Union; some 400,000 Finns who suddenly found themselves on the Russian side of the border fled to Finnish territory and required accommodation. The late US$20 million provided by the Americans was channelled into reconstruction work.

*

In May 1940, just a few weeks before his death, Paul Cravath, who in 1914 had supported the Allies and spoken out in favour of the United States becoming involved in the war on the side of Great Britain, saw the first indications of a rethink in US policy after the German occupation of the Netherlands, Belgium, and Luxembourg: 'I begin to see signs that, determined as American public opinion is against our entering the war, it might change very quickly if it seemed probable that without our help Great Britain and France would lose the war.'[54] After the defeat of France in June 1940 the change in political course that Cravath had anticipated duly came about in Washington. President Roosevelt replaced the Secretary of War Harry Woodring, a firm advocate of isolationism, with

Henry L. Stimson, a seasoned Republican politician and advocate of intervention. Stimson was tasked with stepping up arms production for a foreseeable war without thereby jeopardising Roosevelt's re-election in November 1940 – for the opponents of intervention were still in the majority in Congress. And so Stimson outsourced the preparation of legislation on compulsory military service to the Council on Foreign Relations. The legal team responsible for drafting this bill was a group of lawyers from the Cravath firm, among them John McCloy.[55] The action regarding the 'sabotage claims', which had dragged on into 1939 after the failed attempt to reach a settlement in Munich, made McCloy's name known beyond New York legal circles. In his role assembling all the evidence that eventually saw Germany convicted on sabotage in the 'Black Tom' case, he drew the attention of Washington. Stimson engaged McCloy in September 1940, initially as an external advisor. He needed an expert in the Department of Defense who knew how armaments factories could be protected in time of war. After Roosevelt was re-elected in November, McCloy was made special assistant to the Secretary of War, since Stimson now required a trouble-shooter to steer through Congress the unpopular Lend-Lease Act. This act would circumvent the neutrality laws and lay the legal groundwork for supplying the British, who were in desperate straits following the fall of France, with vital war materiel. McCloy took care not to speak about 'essential war preparations' when taking to members of Congress. Instead he extolled the Lend-Lease Act to sceptics as a way in which America might prevent itself from becoming drawn into the war, namely by shoring up combatant nations whose military strength would serve to bolster the United States' own security. When the Bill passed in Congress in February 1941 with a slim majority, Stimson enthusiastically hailed his new colleague as a 'great find.'[56]

*

Just once more in the course of the forthcoming Lend-Lease arrangement, in March 1941, the American Import–Export Bank approved a loan to the tune of $5 million for aid consignments to Finland,[57] which moved into Hitler's sphere of control following the breakdown of the pact between Germany and the USSR in June 1941. For Operation Barbarossa, the long-planned invasion of the Soviet Union, the German army exploited the strategic advantages offered by Finland. Troops of the Wehrmacht began to assemble on Finnish territory in the days running up to 22 June. Great Britain refused to grant any further Navy Certs to ships of the Finnish–American Trading Corporation, and with the start of the German campaign against Russia extended its blockade of all Finnish overseas shipping. At the same time it promised the USSR support.[58] Now, as an ally of Britain, the Soviet Union profited from the American Lend-Lease policy, whereas Finland suddenly found itself once more in the enemy camp. Even so, diplomatic ties with the USA were not severed entirely,[59] since as the only functioning democracy within Hitler's sphere of influence Finland did not want to lose its independence. Germany was a war partner, not an ally, Ryti assured the United States.[60] His country, he went on, was waging its own war, which would end when the original border between Finland and the Soviet Union was restored. Finland had no intention of making any further advances into Russian territory.[61] Finland also demonstrated its independence through its refusal to hand over Jewish soldiers to the Germans; the Finnish prime minister

Johan Wilhelm Rangell observed that there was no 'Jewish question' in his country, and that Finland's Jews were totally normal citizens.[62] Practically all Jewish men of 'call-up' age were fighting at the front. They were joined by Jewish volunteers from Sweden, Norway, and Denmark.[63] The situation was a truly bizarre one: in the Finnish army several hundred Jews were fighting on the side of the Germans, while at the same time in Poland and in the Balkans campaign, thousands upon thousands of Jews were being murdered by special units of the SS.[64]

*

After Britain issued the Finns an ultimatum, Finland declared the restoration of the original Finnish–Soviet boundary line as finalised on 6 December 1941. It is idle to speculate whether Eric Warburg would have continued his involvement with the Finnish–American Trading Corporation after the lifting of the naval blockade by Great Britain. For just one day after the end of hostilities on the Finnish–Russian Front, aircraft of the Japanese Imperial Navy attacked the US Pacific Fleet's base at Pearl Harbor on Hawaii, turning the United States overnight into an active theatre of war.[65] The Finnish–Soviet Winter War was now history. For his efforts, Eric Warburg was awarded the Order of the White Rose, the greatest honour that the Republic of Finland could confer.[66]

5

Lieutenant Colonel Eric M. Warburg, USAAF

Japan's aggressive pursuit of expansion throughout the Asia–Pacific region (the so-called 'Greater East Asia Co-Prosperity Sphere') had already prompted a condemnation of the Japanese occupation of Manchuria in north-eastern China by the administration of Herbert Hoover in 1932. The US secretary of war during the Second World War, Henry L. Stimson, was secretary of state under Hoover and had publicly declared that the USA was not prepared to recognise any expansion that had been achieved through the use of military force. In 1940, Japan broadened its territorial claims to take in the whole of the South East Asian–Pacific region. Because the United States saw its own interests, in the shape of the Philippines, threatened by this move, a confrontation with Japan seemed ever more likely. Cryptologists in the USA[1] had succeeded in cracking the encoding device used by the Japanese. One of those who was authorised to read Tokyo's directives to its embassies as they were decrypted every day at the US Department of Defense was John McCloy.[2] Warnings of a Japanese attack had been growing for some weeks – the only question was where they would strike. McCloy's best guess was Singapore; as someone who had formerly specialised in rooting out German saboteurs, he believed that the greatest danger to the United States came from the subversive activities of espionage cells controlled by the Japanese secret services along the Pacific seaboard.[3] On 7 December 1941, 180 dive- and torpedo bombers of the Japanese Imperial Navy appeared in the skies over the island of Oahu in Hawaii and launched an attack on the main naval base of the US Pacific Fleet at Pearl Harbor, in the first of two waves. Five American battleships were sunk among a total of eleven warships destroyed or damaged beyond repair, and 188 fighters and other aircraft destroyed on the ground. The number of US service personnel killed in the raid was 2,403. On 8 December, the USA declared war on Japan. Three days later Italy and Germany threw in their lot with their alliance partner Japan by declaring war on the United States. In one fell swoop, America found itself embroiled in a global conflict in two different theatres of war simultaneously.

*

On the eve of the Second World War, many friends and acquaintances of Eric Warburg switched from leading positions in New York banking houses and law firms to go and work for government agencies in Washington, DC. Together with John McCloy, Allen Welsh Dulles also gave up his job as an attorney at this time and took up a post at the newly created Office of the Coordinator of Information, a US government intelligence agency. Aside from the decoding of the Japanese 'Purple' encryption device in August 1940, the US security services sector had had little to celebrate thus far in the way of successes.[4] As recently as 1936 the Democrat Senator Kenneth McKellar had openly questioned the need for secret services departments in democratic societies like that of the United States.[5] There was a widespread conviction that America was safe enough as a result of the continent's geostrategic location. President Roosevelt received secret intelligence briefings from abroad through a group of friends who in their roles as international bankers and businessmen were able to glean sensitive information to which even politicians were generally not party. Among this group of around three dozen individuals who met regularly was William Donovan, a Wall Street lawyer – though his fellow Americans knew him best as the most highly decorated US soldier of the First World War. And since the renewed outbreak of hostilities in Europe, Allen Welsh Dulles also took part in these clandestine private gatherings. It was clear to everyone in the group that the United States would sooner or later become involved in a global conflict while lacking any properly functioning government security services.[6] To be sure, there was a whole series of intelligence-gathering government agencies, none of which was aware what the others were doing. Even the intelligence arms of the Navy, Army, and the State Department were in competition with one another. The situation was further complicated by the fact that, during the First World War, the realm of counterintelligence had been transferred to the Federal Bureau of Investigation. In January 1941, after his re-election, Roosevelt met the head of British naval intelligence, John Godfrey, who had come to Washington with his adjutant Ian Fleming (later creator of the fictional spy James Bond) and a message from British Prime Minister Winston Churchill, urging the USA to begin creating a modern secret service with all haste.[7] Six months later – too late to stop the Japanese attack – Roosevelt tasked Donovan with establishing a central coordinating hub for the state security services, in the shape of the Office of the Coordinator of Information (COI). As the Japanese planes were massing over Hawaii,

Allen Welsh Dulles was just starting his new job as head of the New York COI bureau. Before long, 600 men and women were reporting to him.

*

After the attack on Pearl Harbor Americans enlisted in droves, and Eric Warburg was no exception. Thus far, he had not started a family and had no ties, and so did everything in his power to try and get accepted into the American military. He wanted to get involved in the war in Europe and no longer stand by and watch Hitler conquer the world. On account of his age – he would soon turn forty-two – he stood little chance of being enlisted as a front-line soldier, but he pulled all the strings he could in Washington and New York and duly received his call-up papers in the spring of 1942. He was drafted into the US Army Air Forces and initially underwent a two-month training programme in Palm Beach to become an officer cadet; at the end of this training period he was posted to Harrisburg, Pennsylvania, where the first US airforce intelligence academy was just commencing operations. At this stage, though, virtually none of the lecturers had any practical intelligence experience in the field. Even in 1941, the entire intelligence division of the USAAF consisted of no more than a couple of dozen officers.[8] Courses on aerial photography dominated the curriculum. But before they could even explain to their students how to interpret reconnaissance photographs, the course leaders had to furnish themselves with the necessary knowledge from their British colleagues.[9] The Harrisburg Academy was under the command of Egmont König, the only regular army officer on the base. Taking his cue from the Royal Air Force, his preference was to train more mature people to lead operational activities. Ideally they should already have had a proven track record of success in their careers, possess a good general education, and above all bring with them an interest in business and politics. Eric Warburg fitted this template of a gentleman secret service agent.[10]

*

In June 1942, barely a year after it was founded, the COI became the Office of Strategic Services – or OSS for short, and Donovan opened a liaison bureau in London.[11] This predecessor organisation to the CIA was designed, along the lines of the British foreign intelligence service MI6, to coordinate secret service operations behind enemy lines. The line of reporting was no longer with the US president directly but with the Joint, a military committee which together with its British counterpart comprised the Combined Chiefs of Staff; this was the body that assumed responsibility for directing military operations in Europe and North Africa. Around the same time that the OSS and MI6 began working together, in Suite 3603 of the Rockefeller Center – the headquarters of MI6 in the United States, officially known as the British Security Coordination – a meeting took place between the head of MI6 Thomas Kendrick and US Army intelligence officers. An agreement was reached on close British and American cooperation in the realm of military intelligence gathering. Hitherto, cooperation had been confined to the codebreaking station at Bletchley Park 50 miles north-west of London, where German encryption systems were decoded. Henceforth, the plan was for MI6 to train up in Britain both OSS operatives and officers of the United States Army

Air Forces to be interrogation specialists, on courses lasting between two weeks and two months.[12] In the same month – June 1942 – Lieutenant Colonel W. Stull Holt of the USAAF was appointed commander of the American intelligence officers who were being trained by sections MI9 and MI19 of the British security service.[13] Section 9 directed agents in the field and organised the repatriation of Allied servicemen trapped behind enemy lines; section 19, meanwhile, was responsible for gathering intelligence from the interrogation of prisoners of war (POWs) in specially equipped Combined Services Detailed Interrogation Centres (CSDICs). The headquarters of these CSDIC interrogation facilities was at Latimer House in Buckinghamshire, north-west of London.[14] Eric Warburg arrived there in October 1942 as one of the participants on a course for training liaison officers.

*

The plane on which Eric was travelling landed at Prestwick aerodrome in Scotland, 32 miles south-west of Glasgow and the only airfield that was both safe from attacks by the German Luftwaffe and suitable for transatlantic flights. There he boarded a two-engine Douglas Dakota for the onward journey to London. He travelled the final 40 miles to Latimer House in the back of a staff car belonging to the USAAF.[15] At the wheel was Lt. Col. Holt, who stopped the car mid-journey to issue Eric Warburg some final instructions: not even his closest relatives could know his whereabouts over the coming weeks, he was told.[16] The success of their operation depended at this moment on the British, specifically on their willingness to cooperate and to share their intelligence experience with the Americans. Nothing, Hull said, should be done to antagonise the British. 'Whatever happens, don't step out of line, like Americans are prone to. If the British smile, you smile along with them. If they say yes, you say yes too, and if they say no, so do you. This is supposed to be a joint British–American operation, and whether the British play along ultimately depends on how you conduct yourself.'[17]

*

In addition to Latimer House, there were also two other CSDIC facilities: Wilton Park near Beaconsfield and Trent Park in the vicinity of Cockfosters in North London.[18] At each of these centres, German POWs were interrogated. Latimer House and Wilton Park specialised in questioning U-boat crews and pilots of the Luftwaffe. High-ranking German officers were housed at Trent Park, where their stay was made as pleasant as possible. They were allowed to stroll in the extensive grounds of the house and given wine with their evening meals, while in the fireside lounge there was a billiard table at their disposal. The idea was to make them forget that they were being held captive, and to induce them to start talking. For all these facilities had one thing in common: secret service agents were able to eavesdrop on the officers' conversations via electronic bugs concealed in the rooms and in buildings in the park. Even the trees had microphones hidden in their branches. The 'M Room', the listening station, was staffed by native German speakers, many of them German–Jewish emigrés, who could also cope with dialects that were hard to understand. They had all signed the Official Secrets Act, which obligated them to say nothing about what they did in the M Room. But alongside the M Room there were also other rooms that were fitted with listening devices. Finally, agents also listened in on official interrogations. This was where a large part of Eric Warburg's training took place. He listened in when German POWs were being questioned, and before long he was also conducting interrogations himself. Each interview was assessed by his instructors. Later, when he was deployed at the front, he would need to be able to extract all the necessary information from Luftwaffe pilots who had been shot down and survived, while they were still in a state of shock.[19] A large part of his work consisted of writing reports on interrogations; over the course of the war, more than 60,000 such records were filed in the Document Centre.

*

Eric's training ended in November 1942, the date when Operation Torch began, the landing of British and Americans forces in North Africa. Eric Warburg was sent to Birkhadem, 7 miles outside Algiers, which was the headquarters of the Allied intelligence division. In this French-governed part of North Africa, the two-nation operation turned into a tripartite enterprise. Following a long period of rain, the corrugated-iron Nissen hut in a remote corner of the base that was assigned to the Air Section had become a breeding ground for swarms of flies that buzzed around the heads of the officers as they assembled standing working parties from the British, American, and French men under their command.[20] The Americans had no desire to work with the British or French, and vice versa.[21] The commanding officer of the Air Section, George McDonald, an American of Irish extraction, even withheld information from British members of his own section.[22] When Eric Warburg disobeyed his orders and passed internal documents on to a British colleague, McDonald disciplined him and his interrogation unit by sending them to Tebessa in Algeria. Eric Warburg was quite at ease with the new situation, because in Tebessa he was responsible for the entire southern section of the front and no longer answerable to anyone.[23] There, at the Kasserine Pass in February 1943, he saw how the inexperienced American units were pushed back almost 40 miles by Rommel's latest offensive. General Eisenhower visited Algeria twice to try and shore up his troops' morale.[24] In March, the tables began to turn: now the Allied forces sent the German and Italian armies into retreat, driving them onto the peninsula of Cap Bon in Tunisia, where they were forced to surrender. By this stage Eric Warburg and his men had interrogated over a thousand pilots. The details of how and where they had been shot down were painstakingly recorded in the 'crash book' that each man in the unit had to carry around with him. Among the most highly prized information were details about the airstrips that the planes had taken off from and about the scope of their sorties, as well as special technical features such as new cockpit instrumentation. Other vital data from the interrogated pilots included lists of the personnel, the losses suffered by various units, and details about future sorties.[25]

*

As a field test, North Africa yielded somewhat unsatisfactory results for Eric Warburg. The lack of willingness to cooperate among the Americans, British, and French jeopardised the whole operation. When the Allies had to hastily retreat in the face of Rommel's advance at the Kasserine Pass, they lost a lot of equipment just because it could not be evacuated quickly enough. As a result, that very same night Eric Warburg was

139

tasked by the American major who was responsible for resupply with organising dozens of lorries to clear out the nearby munitions depots and arms dumps. Of course, in the wasteland of the Tebessa Mountains, it was impossible to get hold of lorries in the numbers that were required. However, not far off there was a railway line that was administered by the British, and on which the supplies could be transported the next day. Eric Warburg got in touch with the major in question that same evening. The fact that the American major who was responsible for resupply did not even know who he was was further proof to Eric Warburg of the 'pettifogging' level of cooperation between the Americans and the British.[26] Furthermore, the intelligence section, which was still in its infancy, lacked organisational experience where administration was concerned. No one had any idea about the importance of matters of logistics. Prisoners, documents, or personnel were constantly having to be transported long distances from the front to the interrogation centres. Prisoners who it was hoped might divulge important information were often taken straight to the ports of Oran and Casablanca and shipped off from there to the United States. Because the interrogation centres were frequently located far behind the front line, it wasn't always easy to retain an overview of what was going on.[27] Even after German and Italian forces surrendered, the greatest challenge was still of a logistical nature.[28] Some 25,000 Axis POWs were being held on a barren tract of land near Algiers, which in peacetime had been used as a horseracing track. Many men were suffering from dysentery. Eric Warburg discovered that there were certain situations where both friend and foe had an equal interest in a problem being solved, and so persuaded a German POW to show him one of their abandoned camps where rations and tents were still to be found. He also managed to get hold of the most important medicines for treating the sick from a German field hospital in Carthage.[29]

*

The invasion of Sicily began on 10 July 1943, with British troops landing in the south-east of the island and the Americans on the southern coast. Eric Warburg asked himself why intelligence units and interrogation specialists needed to be in the first wave of the landings at Gela.[30] The spaces in the landing craft were required for the assault troops, and the presence of intelligence personnel only served to unsettle the other men, and besides intelligence officers were not easy to replace. In his view, the scraps of information that they would be able to gather during the confusion of the initial fighting would not outweigh the risk of losing valuable trained specialists.[31] Yet the situation looked very different once troops under General George Patton had captured the German Luftwaffe headquarters at Comiso. Now it was good that they were first on the scene, rounding up prisoners and collecting documents. Meantime, the interrogation units in the British sector, which included Palermo, were in difficulty, since it transpired that they had landed with the troops on the island without any clear orders. It was frustrating that their CSDIC unit was always thought of as a last resort because no one felt responsible for them. After the capture of Naples, Air Intelligence set up an interrogation centre in Bari, which after a few months became a reception centre for refugees. But when Eric Warburg also succumbed to dysentery and wasted away until he was nothing but skin and bones, he was put on board one of the flights transferring POWs to England, so that he could be treated by a doctor who worked with German emigrants. After a week, he had rallied to such an extent that he could be considered fit for active service once more. But now he was no longer needed in North Africa – instead, in November 1943, he was posted to the Pentagon in Washington. A liaison officer with the Royal Air Force was required in light of the planning that had already begun to launch an invasion of mainland Europe.

*

After the months he had spent in Tebessa, left to his own devices and responsible for a long section of the front, Warburg did not find it at all easy getting used to the bureaucracy of the Pentagon. Whereas in Tebessa decisions were immediately followed by action, here he was at a loss to see how anything he was now doing had any effect whatsoever. But at least he encountered some old friends again: John McCloy had in the meantime become a very skilled operator in the corridors of power at the Washington nerve centre of US defence policy. To outsiders it even appeared that he was the one who called the shots in the ministry. Even Secretary of War Stimson wondered ironically whether there was anyone at all left in the administration who didn't first consult with McCloy before coming to a decision.[32] McCloy was well aware of the influence he wielded: as he said of himself, 'I get things done.'[33] Eric Warburg knew this too. His own influence within the bureaucratic apparatus of the Pentagon was noticeably less significant. He had neither his own area of responsibility nor a high military rank. However, neither of these disadvantages prevented him from intervening when he learned that there were plans afoot in the Royal Air Force to launch another bombing raid on the city of Lübeck after the devastating attack on 29 March 1942. In 1943 the British Ministry of Economic Warfare (MEW) had published a review of suitable targets in Germany under the title *The Bomber's Baedeker: Guide to the Economic Importance of German Towns and Cities*, which listed all the cities with more than 15,000 inhabitants hosting industries that were important to the war effort. Lübeck now appeared again in this publication as a potential target, despite the fact that, even according to the MEW's own assessment, it did not contain a single 'Category 1+' industrial facility, the ministry's designation for prime military strategic targets.[34] Accordingly, an attack on the city would have been of questionable value from a military point of view. In his capacity as a liaison officer, Eric Warburg initially attempted to make contact with Arthur Harris, the chief of RAF Bomber Command. But after getting nowhere using official channels, he switched strategy and instead approached the Swiss diplomat Carl Jacob Burckhardt, who since 1941 had headed the Joint Commission of the International Committee of the Red Cross (ICRC) and the League of Red Cross Societies. In this role Burckhardt had held talks in London in December 1941 with the MEW about lifting the naval blockade to allow the passage of ships bringing relief to the victims of war and the civilian population. After this meeting the MEW allowed the Joint Commission to use the sea route to send relief packages to POWs. This applied equally to German POWs in England and the USA and to Allied prisoners in Germany. Because Burckhardt was a great-nephew of the nineteenth-century art historian Jacob Burckhardt – who in turn had been one of Aby Warburg's great spiritual mentors – there was a personal connection between the two men, which Eric Warburg now used to try and avert another bombing raid on Lübeck with Burckhardt's support. Without further ado, Burckhardt made Lübeck the port of destination for ships of the Swedish Red Cross delivering relief packages to British and American POWs. As a result, Lübeck was spared from any more raids.[35] Thereafter, word got around that there was a clever and practically minded individual working in a department of the Pentagon with a quick eye for seeing connections which others – especially those who had been engaged for a long period on special projects – had failed to spot. During his officer training in Florida in 1942, Eric Warburg had struck up a friendship with a young lieutenant by the name of Warner Marshall, a nephew of General George Marshall, who as chief of staff of the US Army during the war coordinated Allied operations in Europe and the Pacific, and who was appointed secretary of state under President Truman after the war. Warner Marshall was a member of the planning staff of the Air Force for the Allied strategy conference that was to be held in Tehran in November 1943, where Roosevelt and Churchill were to meet with Stalin for the first time. One day, Marshall knocked on Eric Warburg's office door and asked for his opinion on a particular matter. He led Warburg to a room to which only officers of the planning staff normally had access. As part of the preparations for the Tehran Conference, potential different scenarios for how Europe might be carved up after the war had apparently been rehearsed. The room contained a map that showed a future border between East and West Germany running along the course of the River Elbe. Eric Warburg could barely conceal his horror. He was clearly the only person in the room who had any idea of the implications of this boundary line. It would mean not only Schleswig-Holstein and his home city of Hamburg, home to the most important port in Germany, falling into Russian hands, but also the Kiel Canal.[36] Asked to give his opinion, he argued that the Western Allies would lose access to the northern Baltic region if the border between East and West ran along the Elbe. In the event, however, he would never discover whether his objection had been the decisive factor in getting this plan rejected: his friend Warner Marshall was killed when the transport aircraft carrying him from the Tehran Conference to the China–Burma–India theatre of operations crashed over East India on 12 December 1943.[37]

*

At the meeting between the 'Big Three' in the Soviet Embassy in Tehran, a far more momentous episode involving a map had taken place. In discussions with Churchill, Stalin had produced a world map and sketched in his idea of where the western border of the Soviet Union should run in a future post-war Europe. According to this, he would continue to lay claim to those regions that had been ceded to the Soviet Union in the secret ancillary agreement attached to the Hitler–Stalin Pact of 1939: Eastern Poland, Bessarabia, Northern Bukovina and the Baltic states.[38] This meant that the Hitler–Stalin Pact had effectively predetermined the post-war order in Europe. Admittedly, Stalin displayed some willingness to compromise when, in September 1941, he accepted the terms of Atlantic Charter agreed between Churchill and Roosevelt, which promoted people's right to self-determination. And in 1943 he once again accommodated the West by disbanding the Communist International. But the territorial claims which Stalin announced at the Tehran Conference unmasked his commitment to the self-determination of peoples as mere strategic lip service and revealed that Russia was no ally in the fight for democracy. For Eric Warburg, the concessions made to Russia raised the question of what grave consequences the West's cooperation with Russia would have for the post-war order in Europe if the right to self-determination for people in Eastern Europe was sacrificed to the Russian ambition to become a superpower.

*

When plans were made to assemble an interrogation unit that would land in Normandy alongside the invasion troops in June 1944, Eric seized the opportunity and got himself posted back to England. The training units were within the Air Intelligence sector of the Combined Services Intelligence Centre. Eric Warburg felt more useful here than in the bureaucratic apparatus in Washington, where he witnessed many things with which he disagreed without being able to exert any influence on decision-making. This also related to how politicians handled the news of the mass murder that the Germans were planning to perpetrate against the Jews of Europe, which the American public had learned about from the chairman of the World Jewish Congress, Stephen S. Wise, as early as November 1942. Why, Eric wondered, couldn't the government incorporate rescue missions into the US war strategy? The State Department still echoed to the infamous words spoken by the American ambassador Hugh S. Gibson, who had reacted to reports of pogroms against Polish Jews after the First World War by recommending that the USA should only concern itself with the fate of American Jews, and had urged the country to exercise caution regarding news of violent excesses lest this simply be Jewish propaganda.[39] Reports from Jewish organisations about the extermination camps were treated with mistrust. Instead, the US State Department favoured a restrictive immigration policy. At a time when Jews were trying to escape extermination in Europe, the ministry did not even meet the regular quotas.[40] The visa section of the State Department was far less troubled by the fate of those being persecuted than it was by the idea that there might be a growing clamour to allow more refugees to enter the country. News about the Holocaust was systematically suppressed and the figures showing the number of visas issued carefully massaged. Eric Warburg was of course well aware of the appeals that the World Jewish Congress was making to President Roosevelt, though he had never expressed his views on this. He did not voice any criticism regarding the policies of the country that was helping them defeat Hitler. In this, Eric stood in a line of tradition with generations of German immigrants to the United States who felt immense gratitude towards their new homeland and would never have taken the liberty of denouncing US government policy. But even his new homeland was not immune to anti-Semitism. The government bent over backwards to avoid raising the spectre of the sons of American families losing their lives in Europe in order to save European Jews. In the Department of Defense there was even concern that such an idea might undermine the combat morale of US troops. It was only in January 1944, at the urging of the treasury minister Henry Morgenthau Jr., that the War Refugee Board (WRB) began its work. The WRB was an inter-ministerial body that Roosevelt positioned at the interface between the remits of the Treasury, the State Department, and the Department of Defense. And since the Department of Defense in its turn had a Civil Affairs Division, headed by John McCloy, which sat at the interface between the military and civilian domains, Stimson's assistant secretary also became the contact person for matters relating to the WRB. The WRB asked McCloy to encourage relief or rescue operations at commanding officer level whenever they could be squared with the department's military agenda. McCloy, who prided himself on getting things done, only acceded to the WRB's request reluctantly: 'I am not at all keen on involving our forces in this while the war is still going on.'[41] The armed forces general staff responded promptly by issuing a rejection that was couched in terms of a point of principle: the most effective assistance for the victims of enemy persecution would be the swiftest possible victory over Germany and its allies, an enterprise in whose service all available means should be deployed.[42] At this time, some eyewitness accounts from the extermination camps were already becoming known. The mass murder of Jews that the Germans were carrying out in camps in Eastern Europe far exceeded any previously conceived category of 'great cruelty and injustice' that Gibson had presented to the State Department as a guideline for action on the major human catastrophes of the twentieth century. When the deportation of Hungarian Jews to Auschwitz began in the spring of 1944, Jewish groups appealed to the US administration to bomb railway lines and gas chambers. The idea that it might thereby be possible to halt the machinery of extermination for a while, or at least slow it down, came about because, from May 1944 onwards, the USAAF's Fifteenth Air Force started flying bombing missions from its base at Foggia in southern Italy against the Buna industrial complex of IG Farben, which was located just 4 miles east of Auschwitz.[43] In his correspondence with the WRB, John McCloy, who saw his primary task as smoothing the armed forces' path to achieving victory at all costs, cited questions of military and organisational practicability as reasons for turning down its pleas to bomb the camp.[44] He took the view that such requests were not something that the US military ought to be worrying about at this juncture.[45] McCloy even instructed his secretary to 'stall for time' on this matter.[46] For at the same time as Hungarian Jews were being transported by train to Auschwitz and ever more urgent requests from the WRB were landing on the desk of the Civil Affairs Division, Operation Overlord was getting underway in Normandy – the largest landing operation in history. Eric Warburg, who in the meantime had been promoted to lieutenant colonel, directed a group of ten interrogation units[47] who landed with the US Ninth Air Force at Omaha Beach on 7 June 1944 (D-Day+1).

*

The interrogation units of the individual sections proceeded to land at Omaha Beach over the following four weeks, moving forward in a south-easterly direction with the Allied advance and taking up various positions along the front. The Air Section was based at the Ninth Air Force's headquarters in Grandcamp-les-Bains.[48] Although they were directly behind the front, in the first few weeks of the invasion Allied troops shot down only a handful of enemy aircraft behind the lines, with the result that there were very few captured Luftwaffe pilots to interrogate. When they did manage to do so, they gathered a wealth of useful information from them. One of those interrogated belonged to the German radio monitoring service and revealed where their transmission intercept stations were located.[49] In the logbook of another man they found a map containing information on Axis airfields that they had not known about.[50] On the other hand, Allied ground troops contrived to make their lives more difficult. It was hard to impress upon them that items belonging to aircrew which they found strewn about at crash sites were not trophies or souvenirs but had intelligence value that might potentially even be decisive to the outcome of the war. Eric Warburg's units marched into Cherbourg, Rennes, and Angers with the Allied forces and immediately set about looking for Luftwaffe headquarters, airfields, radio signals, and V-weapons bases. On the day that Paris was liberated, 25 August 1944, Eric was with the baggage train of General Philippe Leclerq of the Free French Army and his Second Tank Division. His units took control of several dozen buildings that had been used by the city's Nazi administration. Among these were the headquarters of the Gestapo and a number of factories in the Greater Paris area. In the process, they got their hands on complete sets of documentation detailing the development of the Messerschmitt Bf 109 and the Focke-Wulf Fw 190.[51] The first of these was the most widely produced fighter of the Second World War, while the latter was reputedly the best such aircraft. As the front advanced, the Air Section's headquarters, which was initially based at Grandcamp-les-Bains, had moved forward step by step to Saint Saveur, Lendelin, and then Saval, and now found itself in Versailles. Warburg's unit was stationed there for a fortnight before moving on with the advancing front to Verdun, Luxembourg, and Namur, a small Belgian town on the River Meuse with a citadel, where the first high-ranking Luftwaffe officers to be taken prisoner since the invasion began were interrogated. When Eric entered Aachen, it was the first time he had set foot on the territory of the German Empire since 1938. The advance of American troops towards the city on 11 September had prompted a hasty retreat by Nazi functionaries, policemen, and local officials. When unrest broke out among the city's inhabitants as a result, Hitler ordered that its civilian populace should also be evacuated. Anyone refusing to leave the city was considered a traitor.[52] Even so, a quarter of Aachen's 160,000 civilian population stayed put and witnessed the battle for the city. Eric Warburg wrote a letter to his parents with his first impressions. He told them how the Nazi officials had been the first to disappear, leaving the ordinary people behind. He described how people held out in foxholes, cellars, bunkers, and sheds, hoping that the juggernaut of war would roll on past them and leave them unscathed. 'As always, the little people are paying the highest price,' he wrote. 'They probably *Heiled* when things went their way and they kept silent when they should have rebelled at a time when they still could have.'[53] And yet he still did not see ordinary people and Nazis as one and the same thing. In spite of the crimes of the National Socialists that were coming to light, he drew a distinction between between perpetrators and fellow-travellers. To be sure, the latter also bore some responsibility, but in his eyes they weren't National Socialist political criminals.

*

In the spring of 1944 the prevailing view in the US Department of Defense was still that the war would be over by the autumn of that year. For the moment when Allied forces entered Germany and the period immediately before the final surrender, the ministry had prepared Directive CCS 551 and circulated it among staff officers. It was admittedly based on the assumption that the invading troops would encounter infrastructure in Germany that was still at least partially intact.[54] Under such conditions, National Socialist organisations were to be disbanded forthwith, Nazi laws repealed, Hitler and leading party members arrested, Nazis dismissed from positions of leadership, and economic normality restored so that Germany could as soon as possible be placed in a position where it could cater to the needs of its own population. The top priority was to avoid an economic collapse. But by the early summer of 1944, the Allied Supreme Command was working from a totally different set of circumstances in a defeated Germany. It was now certain that the German leadership would not surrender but would continue to fight on even within the country's borders. As a result, the Supreme Allied Commander General Eisenhower spoke in terms of a prolonged interim phase in which government would have to be conducted by decree. Accordingly, in the Department of Defense John McCloy drew up Directive JCS 1067, which was better suited to the real conditions on the ground than CCS 551. Where dealing with Germany was concerned, an immeasurably harsher tone was now adopted. For in the interim the treasury minister Henry Morgenthau had protested to the President about the kid-glove treatment that the Allied forces wanted to apply to the Germans. During a tour of inspection that he took in Germany at the beginning of September 1944, he had got hold of a copy of the new occupation handbook, which was based on Directive CCS 551. In it there was talk of working together with German administrative agencies and of economic normalisation ensuing as quickly as possible. And the recommended treatment of the German population sounded positively solicitous. By contrast, the military handbook had nothing to say on the question of how to deal with Nazi mass murderers and war criminals. Nowhere was there even the slightest mention of the fact that Germany had been guilty, and was still guilty, of crimes against humanity on a hitherto unimaginable scale.[55]

Such an approach would mean that, after the war, a pall of silence would soon shroud these crimes in oblivion – as had happened with every previous conflict. Roosevelt, to whom the treasury minister gave a copy of the handbook that he had brought back from Europe, promptly instructed the Secretary of Defense to withdraw it from circulation and to implement harsher measures against the defeated enemy.[56]

*

So as not to leave the Department of Defense in sole charge of dealing politically with the defeated Germans, Morgenthau's staff now began to devise a plan of their own, which had all the elements of a drastic scorched-earth post-war settlement: German heavy industry was to be dismantled, the Ruhr industrial region shut down, coalmines flooded, high-ranking party functionaries of the NSDAP incarcerated, and all Nazi leaders put before the firing squad. The aim was to create a stable peace order by completely expunging the aggressor. Admittedly, the Morgenthau Plan did not find favour among his colleagues in either the State Department or the Department of Defense. Even so, Morgenthau was determined to 'see this matter through to the bitter end' so long as he had the President's backing.[57] Others would only 'water down' the plan.[58] But even he was surprised when he was given the opportunity by Roosevelt at the Quebec Conference in mid-September 1944 to present his plan in person to Winston Churchill. Initially, Churchill welcomed the presence of the US Secretary of the Treasury, since Great Britain's application for a significant loan as part of the ongoing Lend–Lease Agreement with the US was to be resolved in Quebec. But then he realised that Morgenthau did not want to talk about financial support but instead discuss how Germany should be treated after the war.[59] Because Churchill's close advisor Frederick Lindemann got the distinct impression that the American administration was making the US$6.5 billion loan to the British contingent upon their approval of the US Treasury's proposals, Churchill reconsidered the objection that he had originally raised and finally ended up signing a hastily drafted paraphrase of the Morgenthau Plan jointly with the US President.[60] Roosevelt instructed the Department of Defense to adapt Directive JCS 1067 to the resolutions passed at the Quebec Conference. But then the press began to question Roosevelt's support for the Morgenthau Plan, after it emerged that he had forced it through in the face of a veto by most members of his cabinet.[61] From the furious reaction in the press, Roosevelt, who already had his sights set on the next presidential election, got a fore-taste of quite how explosive an issue his treasury minister's plan would be on the campaign trail, and so immediately began to row back from it. Secretary of State Cordell Hull was delegated to explain to journalists that no firm decisions had yet been taken regarding Germany's post-war economy. Roosevelt himself affirmed that it had never been his intention to turn Germany into farmland. What had motivated him to approve the Morgenthau Plan, he explained, was the disastrous state of Great Britain's economy. Five years of war had crippled the country. Roosevelt had calculated that, with the help of the Morgenthau Plan, Britain would take over the running of the Ruhr after the war and so recover from its depression.[62]

*

However, the real prize for Britain in 1944 was not the Morgenthau Plan; instead it came from the Warburg family, who in December of that year donated their cultural studies library to the University of London. In July 1936, when they had extended the contract with the Courtauld Institute, the German Warburgs had still thought that they would somehow be in a position to provide annual support to the tune of £1,000 from their side. During the compulsory purchase of his house on the Kösterberg, Max Warburg had been authorised by the foreign exchange bureau to use 100,000 Reichsmarks from the proceeds to buy books from German booksellers for the Warburg Library in London and to pay for orders placed with German printers in four annual instalments.[63] Even as a refugee, he had discharged his financial responsibilities. The remittances were sent by one remaining female employee at the Warburg offices in Hamburg. However, on the day that Great Britain declared war on Germany, permission to pay for the book purchases and printers' bills with funds from the blocked account was immediately revoked.[64] Orders for books that had been placed before 3 September 1939 could still 'on a case by case basis' and 'on production of the appropriate documentation' be paid from their account. But by the time the final payment was made in August 1940, not even the first of the four permitted annual instalments had been used up.[65] At the very time when the library was having to provide paid employment to an ever-increasing number of Jewish refugees, Fritz Saxl felt himself abandoned with his financial worries in a London constantly under the threat of German air attack. In this difficult situation, the art historian Edgar Wind, who had in the meantime been appointed as a lecturer at the New York Institute of Fine Arts, helped the Warburg Library raise its public profile by reviving its efforts to go global, which had been in abeyance since the death of Felix Warburg.[66] His idea of creating a group of American

Friends of the London Warburg Library met with the family's approval but unlike before, this time no one proceeded to take the next steps on their own initiative. The first preparatory discussion took place in the presence of all those involved; however, Wind first had to secure the agreement of respected institutes before Max Warburg encouraged his nephew Edward to become involved, with a substantial donation, in the still yet to be founded Association of the Friends of the Warburg Institute.[67] Yet Edgar Wind believed that the Warburg family could still be doing much more for the Warburg Library. In the interim, New York University had acquired Paul Warburg's former town house, which was used to accommodate the graduate programme of the Institute of Fine Arts. Walter Cook, the Institute's director, had fulfilled his end of the bargain by raising US$50,000 for the purchase of the Warburg books.[68] But the great patron of the arts Felix Warburg, who was supposed to contribute a further 50,000 dollars, was no longer alive and his family had so far only contributed half of the agreed sum. The other half was to be released as soon as the plan for London and New York to work together came to fruition, something which in wartime was now out of the question.[69] Edgar Wind believed that the family was still nonetheless obligated to settle this debt of honour, especially since Walter Cook was 'one of the most loyal helpers in this current crisis.'[70] Max Warburg dissuaded him from exerting moral pressure because that would only be harmful and achieve the complete opposite of what they intended.[71] Felix Warburg's son Edward had in the meantime been appointed chairman of the Joint's allocation committee. In view of the crises raging in Europe, the cultural studies library, which was well on the way to becoming independent, was not exactly top of his list of priorities requiring especially urgent help. As always, the views of individual family members needed to be sounded out; however, they had grown increasingly remote from the library. Yet the converse was also true: as a result of sheer physical distance, academic autonomy, war, and funding from outside the family, the library had shifted away from being a joint family project.[72] As early as May 1940, Max Warburg signalled to the director of the library that they would entrust the library to a foundation just as long as such an arrangement guaranteed the long-term funding of the work of the library and its employees.[73] Around Christmas 1944, Eric Warburg finally signed the deed of foundation in favour of the University of London, prompting *The Observer* to comment, in what was now Britain's fifth year of war against Germany, that the country's finest Christmas present that year had come from Hamburg.[74]

*

In the US sector of the Western Front, the Air Intelligence staff, which had originally consisted of ten officers and their men, was now increased by the addition of another five officers. As a lieutenant colonel, Eric Warburg was the commanding officer's right-hand man. There was a series of smaller mobile teams who enjoyed considerable freedom of movement. During the Ardennes Offensive, the area in which these units operated stretched from Maastricht in the north to Luxeuil-les-Bains in the south and from Châlons-sur-Marne in the west to the front.[75] From February 1945, German forces were irrevocably on the defensive. Eric Warburg's 'Prisoner of War Interrogation Units of the US Air Force' – or to give it its unwieldy military acronym, POW–IUUSAF – swarmed into German territory that the Allies had occupied with so-called 'T-forces'; this area now comprised the cities of the Ruhr, Cologne, Frankfurt, Stuttgart, Munich, Nuremberg, and many other towns in southern Germany. The T-forces were independently operating technical units that were under the direct command of the Anglo-American Combined Intelligence Operations Service (CIOS), a committee of experts that was made up of intelligence operatives from both countries.[76] The T-forces seized any intelligence material that the CIOS deemed to be top priority. It was only now that the Air Intelligence POW interrogation units were officially assigned to the USSTAF, the highest control-and-command centre of the United States Army Air Forces. By 15 April 1945 it was possible to move its headquarters to Wiesbaden. Now that a German defeat was assured, the war again Japan came to the fore. The USAAF combined intelligence operations that were vital for the war in the Pacific under the acronym LUSTY, which stood for 'Luftwaffe Secret Technology'. Among other things, the intelligence units were tasked with finding out how great the German lead was in the development of rockets, aircraft, and other weapons systems, and how much know-how the Germans had passed on to their allies, the Japanese.[77] Even as late as March 1945, the Junkers Aircraft and Engine Works in Dessau had played host to a delegation from Japan.[78] The documents that were in the possession of the Luftwaffe's Japanese translator when he was taken prisoner provided detailed information on how many aircraft had been manufactured in Japan between 1939 and 1945. These papers included a map of all Japanese factories that were making parts for the armaments industry.[79]

*

President Roosevelt died on 12 April 1945. Secretary of State Stimson was now counting on an about-turn in US policy toward Germany under Roosevelt's successor Harry S. Truman. Stimson let Truman know that he had considered earlier suggestions of punishing the Germans by allowing them to starve to be a serious mistake; although it was necessary to denazify and demilitarise Germany, at the same time it had to be stabilised economically.[80] Truman shared Stimson's view. Directive JCS 1067, which was further revised and adapted to current political circumstances, ultimately served at the Potsdam Conference as a strategy for American policy toward Germany. The long-term goal was now 'peaceful cooperation with Germany within the family of nations'.[81] Yet had it not been for Morgenthau's persistence, Directive JCS 1067 would have been issued to the military governors of Germany without the mandatory order requiring that all expropriated Jewish property should be handed back forthwith. It was also Morgenthau who had initiated the debate over what punishment should be meted out to Nazi war criminals – though his demand that they be summarily executed was replaced by the requirement that even those who were responsible for war crimes should be subject to due legal process.[82] When Eric Warburg saw the first photographs of the emaciated inmates of concentration camps at the beginning of May, he wrote to his parents: 'The faces of these people, who have gone through a living hell … tell their own tale for all eternity. Although these martyrs – each a mere twenty-five to thirty-five kilos of skin and bone – have in all likelihood not been focussing on this world in their thoughts for some considerable time now, I am certain that they would, insofar as they are able, demand that we never ever forget.'[83]

Warburg took stock after the German surrender: after the Normandy landings, he and his men had interrogated 8,000 Luftwaffe POWs. These included such high-ranking generals and commanders as Karl Koller, Walther von Axthelm, and Hugo Sperrle; the latter had been the commanding officer of the Condor Legion, which fought on the Nationalist side in the Spanish Civil War (1936–9) and in 1937 had carpet-bombed the Basque town of Guernica. The list of names that he supplied to the unit of the Ninth Air Force which interrogated him included those of well-known aircraft manufacturers and aeronautical engineers such as Willy Messerschmitt, the Horten brothers, and Ernst Heinkel.[84] Yet none of the interrogations were as comprehensive as those of the commander-in-chief of the German Luftwaffe, Reichsmarschall Hermann Goering, which Eric Warburg personally conducted. Immediately after his arrest on 10 May 1945 in Zell am See in Austria, Goering had been questioned by Carl Spaatz, the commander of US Strategic Air Forces in Europe.[85] By the time he came to be interrogated a few days later by Eric Warburg, the British Air Ministry and the intelligence section of the Ninth Air Force had compiled a dossier of 600 questions – primarily on air operations in the Third Reich. Unlike at his first questioning, Goering had no idea who his interrogator was. Eric Warburg spoke German and pretended to be of Swedish extraction. As a result of his many visits to Scandinavia before the war, his Swedish accent sounded genuine and natural. He also slipped a few smatterings of Swedish into the conversation, whereupon Goering, whose first wife had been from Sweden, became quite talkative. He would never have chatted in such a relaxed manner with a German Jew. The questioning was more of a history lesson than an interrogation. In the words of the British historian Richard Overy, it appealed to Goering's vanity that the enemy was asking him 'for help in understanding the system they had just defeated.'[86] The interview was conducted over several days; Eric Warburg spent a total of twenty hours talking to Goering.[87] He noted: 'Whenever the questioning began to falter somewhat, and one then began to address him as "Herr Reichsmarschall" a few times, things quickly picked up and proceeded smoothly again, just like squeezing a few drops of oil into a squeaky Singer sewing machine.'[88] A whole set of questions was devoted to the subject of Japan.[89] Warburg then drew up memoranda of the interviews and presented them to his superiors. After the interrogation, Goering was to be flown to Luxembourg on board a Piper J-3 Cub, a light aircraft with room for only four people. The image of this former Nazi bigwig waiting on the small airfield in his white rubberised raincoat with matching peaked cap – 'looking like a Berlin traffic policeman in the rain' – would be one that would remain with Eric Warburg especially vividly throughout the rest of his life. For Goering refused to board the plane. As a former fighter pilot during the First World War, he claimed he could tell the aircraft wasn't safe. Eric Warburg pondered how he should react. Should he have Goering physically manhandled into the cabin? He decided once more to try a diplomatically polite approach instead. He began by addressing Goering *sotto voce* as 'Herr Reichsmarschall' and then continued, audibly louder, 'We guarantee your safe arrival.' That did the trick. Goering gave him a crisp salute, turned on his heel, stepped up onto the tiny single-step footstool placed beside the plane, and with some difficulty squeezed himself through the cabin door. That was the last time Warburg set eyes on him.[90] Bruce Hooper, the official historian of the US Air Force, asked Eric whether he would like to be involved in writing the history of the American air war.[91] But he was eager to get back to his unit. The war was over, but not Operation Lusty.

*

In February 1945, at the Yalta Conference, it was decided that Thuringia and Saxony would in future be part of the Soviet occupation zone. Eric Warburg was at a loss to understand why the Allies were prepared to cede a third of occupied Germany to the Soviet Union. 'This will mean creating a situation in which a totally devastated country where Fascists were in power for twelve years is immediately brought into the sphere of influence of another totalitarian regime.'[92] The Yalta accords did not provide a firm basis for a peaceful post-war order; instead, they destroyed what had been created in August 1941 with the signing of the Atlantic Charter by the USA, Great Britain, and Russia: the right of nations to demo-cratic government and self-determination.[93] In his family, Eric Warburg had a very able interlocutor in the shape of his cousin James. The son of Paul Warburg, James had given up a career in banking in the 1930s. This former finance specialist became an expert on US foreign policy. On and off, James Warburg worked in the government: from 1934 as an economic advisor to Roosevelt and after 1941 as a propaganda specialist at the OSS. James Warburg shared his cousin's opinions: the demar-cation line that had been drawn at Yalta between the Russian sphere of influence and the West ran from Wismar to Trieste through Plzeň in western Bohemia, where the US Army, advancing from the West, had stopped on 6 May 1945 and left the liberation of Prague to the Red Army, despite the fact that General Patton's troops would have had ample time to do so themselves before the first Soviet soldiers arrived. Russia had proceeded to destroy democracy in Czechoslovakia, and consequently it ought not to be allowed to spread its influence any further.[94] Yet James Warburg was not always in agreement with the political U-turns that the United States had performed in the course of the war. For instance, after the fall of Mussolini, when the US government accepted the appointment of his former general chief of staff Pietro Badoglio as prime minister of the new post-Fascist administration, a man who had been responsible for serious war crimes during the Italian invasion of Ethiopia, and forbade its own propaganda department from continuing to refer to Badoglio as a fascist in radio broadcasts, James Warburg resigned his post in protest and curtailed his activities for the OSS in 1944.[95] He saw the pact with the reactionary Badoglio regime as a betrayal of the Allies' ideals – the very principles that had led him to welcome the USA's entry into the war in the first place. He also condemned the negotiations between the OSS head in Switzerland, Allen Welsh Dulles, and Karl Wolff, the highest-ranking SS officer in Italy, about a partial surrender – one which was dearly bought, since it came at the cost of exempting Wolff from prosecution at the Nuremberg Trials and destroying political trust between the Western Allies and Russia.[96]

*

American troops were meant to withdraw from Thuringia and Saxony before the official handover on 1 July 1945. At the end of May, the Air Intelligence interrogation units were transferred to Bad Kissingen, close to the future border region between the Western and Soviet occupation zones. Military installations and chemical laboratories were clustered in this region of central Germany. Magdeburg, Plauen, Jena, Dessau, and Leipzig were home to many factories that had formerly produced military equipment: tanks, field artillery, optical sighting devices, night vision equipment, rifles, steel helmets, aircraft engines, and so on. The original plan was to seize only construction plans, tools, and machinery. But during their searches Eric Warburg's men – alongside the T-forces – came across manufacturing facilities for rockets, weapons systems, and aircraft.[97] Interest began to shift from recovering technology and military hardware to securing military technological know-how, and Operation Lusty became Operation Overcast. In the chaos that reigned post-war, scientific experts were tracked down and, together with their entire families and sometimes even their dogs, cats, chickens, and bicycles, transported from Thuringia to Bad Kissingen, where the families were put up in the Wittelsbacher Hof Hotel, specially commandeered for the purpose. Not all the scientists were thrilled to learn that they and their families needed to be ready to leave within a matter of hours. However, in most cases the threat that the Russians would be arriving in a few days' time persuaded them to board jeeps and lorries and let themselves be driven to the American occupation zone.[98] Any question of the legitimacy of such evacuations was subordinated to the fact that the USA was still on a war footing and that the country's future national security depended upon securing the scientific expertise of these individuals. The estimated number of scientists and rocket technicians evacuated from the Soviet occupation zone has been put at around 1,800. At that time, the US Army was working on the assumption that it could find plenty of tasks for the German V-weapon engineers and aeronautical experts in its military research and development facilities – for in June 1945 the United States still found itself at war with Japan. After the interviews that were conducted by Eric Warburg at the Wittelsbacher Hof Hotel, the German scientists from various disciplines were required to hold themselves in readiness in case their services were needed.[99] They were not allowed to leave the American sector, as the French and Russian security services were also trying to lure the brightest and best scientists with promises of optimal working conditions. French attempts at enticing away boffins from the Americans bore fruit in the case of ballistics expert Hubert Schardin, one of the occupants of the Wittelsbacher Hof. In August 1945 the French set up a research institute for him in Saint Louis, where he and a several of his German colleagues were able to carry on their work. Among the scientific experts interned at the hotel were Theodor Zobel, Wolfgang Nöggerath, Gerhard Braun, and Rudolph Edse, four former colleagues from the Hermann Goering Aeronautical Research Institute, who on 19 September, in the company of a group of engineers and the V-2 designer Wernher von Braun, director of the Peenemünde rocket testing range, were flown out from Paris to the United States. While von Braun and his engineers resumed their work on rocketry for the USA at Fort Bliss, Texas, the final destination for the four aeronautical scientists was the US Air Force base of Wright Field, where another 260 scientists and engineers from Germany also arrived in the same year. One of their first assignments was to sort through and archive boxes and boxes of documents and other important items that had been impounded from German research and military installations.[100]

*

Eric Warburg frequently travelled from Bad Kissingen to Wiesbaden, where accommodation had been made ready for surviving resistance fighters associated with the 20 July Plot to kill Hitler who had agreed to appear as witnesses at the Nuremberg Trials.[101] There, he got to know Fabian von Schlabrendorff, one of the 20 July plotters who had been held in various concentration camps after the failed assassination. Schlabrendorff was one of more than 140 political prisoners whom the SS had transported from Dachau to the South Tyrol region at the end of the war to use as hostages. Freed from SS captivity by soldiers of the Wehrmacht, they were finally liberated by the Americans after the German Army in Italy surrendered.[102] None of Eric Warburg's friends in Germany who had been with the resistance had survived. Albrecht von Bernstorff, who had made no secret of his contempt for the Nazis, had been arrested in his flat in Berlin on 30 July 1943. On the night of 23–24 April 1945, along with two other prisoners he was removed by SS henchmen from his prison cell in Lehrter Straße jail, taken to one of the countless bombsites in the vicinity, and summarily executed.[103] His two fellow inmates were the Social Democrat politician Ernst Schneppenhorst and the landowner Karl Ludwig von und zu Guttenberg.[104] The bodies of the three men were never recovered. Those who were arrested and put to death after the 20 July Plot included Adam von Trott, the Werner brothers, and Hans Bernd von Haeften, whose parents were close friends of the Warburg family. John Rittmeister, the brother of Eric's boyhood friend Wolfgang and a member of the 'Rote Kapelle' (Red Orchestra) resistance movement, was put to death in Plötzensee Prison on 13 May 1943.

*

Wolfgang Rittmeister accompanied Eric Warburg when he revisited the Kösterberg for the first time in the summer of 1945. Over the preceding years, the grounds and the buildings had been used as a Wehrmacht hospital. The war had left its mark on the site. A bomb blast had destroyed a section of the 'Ark' and army huts had been erected on the lawns. Anti-aircraft gun emplacements and radar antennae had been mounted on top of the two water towers. The whole place would have to be renovated.[105] But now was not the time for that. Fritz Warburg's share in the property had been seized 'due to the war', and Eric Warburg's own share was confiscated as 'enemy property'. In 1938 they had established a General Management Company (AVG), which operated as a subsidiary of their expropriated banking house and acted as the landlord of their property portfolio. It was this agency that had signed the rental agreement with the German Army on behalf of the 'foreign' owners of the two parcels of land.[106] The share of the Kösterberg belonging to Eric's father, who had lived in exile in New York since 1938, had been compulsorily purchased and its status was still unsettled. But in order to ensure that, after the closure of the Wehrmacht hospital, the barracks and houses were not occupied by the British Army, Eric obtained permission from the British military administration, via the AVG, for the entire property to be placed at the disposal of the Joint. Since the German authorities raised no objection, this amounted to a de facto acceptance on their part of the return of his father's share of the land. To begin with, the Joint housed 150 displaced persons from the Terezin concentration camp on the Kösterberg.[107] And the three houses on the site once occupied by the Warburgs now provided temporary accommodation for around 100 orphans from the Bergen-Belsen camp, who were getting ready for their new life in Palestine.

The Japanese surrender on 2 September 1945 saw the winding up of Operation Overcast in Germany. The Supreme Headquarters of the Allied Expeditionary Force (SHAEF) in northern France, where the Wehrmacht High Command had signed the unconditional surrender of Germany on 7 May, had already been disbanded in mid-July. The closure of the CSDIC facility at Latimer House was due to follow in November. As Eric Warburg did not want to work in the American military administration,[108] the time had now come to end his involvement with Air Intelligence. In November he boarded a Liberty ship in Bremerhaven that was ferrying 1,600 troops back to the United States. The military mission was over, National Socialism was defeated, and service in the Army was at an end for most of the men. Eric Warburg had himself transferred to the reserves.[109] On board the ship, he made the acquaintance of Heinrich Kronstein, a naturalised German–American, who was returning from a US government mission. Kronstein was a specialist in competition law, and had left Germany in 1933. Since 1941, he had been working in the Anti-Trust division of the US Justice Department under Thurman Arnold, the most popular competition regulator in the USA, who had conducted the most legally far-reaching anti-trust campaign in the history of America. In 1940 he launched investigations into 180 US corporations that had entered into agreements with international and German concerns.[110] In March 1942 he brought a lawsuit against Standard Oil, which he accused of concluding a cartel agreement with IG Farben that had, he claimed, had the effect of delaying the development in the United States of synthetic gasoline and synthetic rubber (both production processes had been pioneered by IG Farben).[111]

Because Roosevelt feared that the investigations of the popular anti-trust campaigner might have detrimental implications for the US war economy, he transferred Arnold to the Federal Court of Appeal in 1943. Heinrich Kronstein had continued his work in the Anti-Trust division even after Arnold's departure. However, after the Potsdam Agreement enshrined demerger and decartelisation of German industry as one of the main objectives of the occupation government – alongside denazification, democratisation, and demilitarisation – the Department of Defense seconded him and sent him to the American zone of occupation at the end of July 1945. Here, the economic division of the Office of Military Government, United States (OMGUS), which was in the process of being formed, had already begun monitoring industrial output. Kronstein became the military government's German Agency Officer, and in this role was responsible for denazifying particular sectors of industry within the US occupation zone and for reorganising German industrial associations.[112] Kronstein visited factories, met leading industrialists, and learned about the problems arising from the denazification of industrial production. The conversations about this that he had with Eric Warburg made the long transatlantic crossing on the uncomfortable troopship more entertaining and thoroughly informative.

6

Returning in Stages

Immediately after the German surrender, Eric Warburg had made an excursion to Hamburg from Bad Kissingen in order to exonerate the two partners running their former banking operation. Thanks to the declaration he made to the British military administration, Rudolf Brinckmann and Paul Wirtz were immediately able to resume their business activities.[1] In view of the 'uncertain post-war situation' Max Warburg refrained from making use of a British order that would have given the bank – which had been 'Aryanised' in 1938 – its former name back. It seemed inappropriate to him to suggest, through the name Warburg, a family connection with the bank that no longer existed.[2] And so it was that, when the renowned financier Max Warburg died in exile in New York the following year aged seventy-nine, the bank he had presided over for almost thirty years bore the name of its current partners: Brinckmann, Wirtz & Co. In his final year, Max was able to witness his son's first steps in starting a family. Eric Warburg had got to know his future wife Dorothea Thorsch at his parents' house immediately after coming to America from Europe. Seated next to his mother at the tea table, she was the youngest daughter of Alfons and Marie Thorsch, a banking family from Vienna who were friends of the Warburgs; shortly before the Nazi annexation of Austria, they had emigrated to

Canada via England and Switzerland. Soon after their arrival, though, Marie died, followed a year later by her husband. Eric Warburg was captivated by the beautiful Marie and her air of refinement, which seemed to him reminiscent of the golden age of pre-war Europe, now lost forever, that Stefan Zweig described in his memoirs *The World of Yesterday*. She exuded sheer elegance. On this occasion he gave his parents no cause to fear that his interest would only extend as far as a brief fling. He was fortunate that his easy-going, cheerful demeanour struck a chord with Dorothea Thorsch. On 14 February 1946, barely three months after they first met, they got married. Presumably one of the reasons why they resolved to wed so quickly was Max Warburg's rapidly declining health. He did not live to see the birth of his first grandchild, Marie Warburg, who was born in 1947.

*

In August 1946, Eric Warburg was in Hamburg again to meet the representatives of the Joint and discuss the future of the children's home on the Kösterberg. Since his last visit, the grounds had been transformed into an educational and train-ing campus. The former hospital barracks were being used as workshops by tailors, leatherworkers, and mechanics. There was also a market garden and various cultural programmes. The managers of the children's home made sure that the children only spoke Hebrew to one another. Within two to three months they would receive their certificates of entry to Palestine, thereafter being in a position to communicate in Hebrew in daily life. The children's home was just a waystation. Eight thousand of Hamburg's Jewish community, which had once numbered some 20,000, had not survived the Holocaust.

Apart from a very small group of less than 1,000 people, most of them Eastern European refugees, after 1945 there were no Jews left in Hamburg.[3] Considering the enormity of the National Socialist atrocities, large sectors of the Jewish diaspora shunned any Jewish presence in the homeland of those who had perpetrated these crimes.[4] A project that included the option of a future in Germany would not have been supported by the Joint. As soon as the final group of children had departed for Palestine, the two villas on the Kösterberg would be renovated and made available to the small Jewish community as an old people's home. Eric Warburg planned to use the 'Noah's Ark' as a guest house. It transpired that he would be visiting Hamburg more often in the future.[5] But at this stage it seemed to be largely out of the question that his wife would ever accompany him on these trips. The very thought of it brought Dorothea Thorsch out in a cold sweat. After the Austrian *Anschluß*, the Gestapo and the paramilitary National Socialist Motor Corps (NSKK) could scarcely wait to get their hands on the stately Thorsch Palace. From one day to the next, the people of Vienna cast off all their inhibitions. The family's townhouse at Metternichstraße in the city was ransacked from top to bottom. Paintings, family photographs, the library, furniture, and even the silver tableware all disappeared, never to be seen again. No valuation reports on the valuables and artworks that had been stolen were attached to the official papers that the authorities issued to cover the theft. Only in the case of thirty paintings could it be established that they had been taken to the central depot for confiscated art collections at the Neue Burg on Heldenplatz in Vienna.[6] Eva, one of Dorothea's older sisters who stayed on in Vienna after the Nazi takeover, was thrown into a Gestapo prison cell and tortured to try to get her to reveal the whereabouts of the family's jewels after all the jewellery boxes were found to be empty when the house was looted. Weeks passed before they were able to secure her release; Eva was scarred for the rest of her life.[7] As such, Dorothea could not imagine ever setting foot on German soil again. For this reason too, Eric Warburg set his sights on a future in the United States. He went back to his working life at the bank and also began to get involved on the Council on Foreign Relations, where Allen Welsh Dulles had just taken over the chairmanship.

*

After Truman disbanded the OSS in October 1945, Dulles had returned to his civilian profession. Given the strategic upheaval the world was undergoing, he reckoned that his talents in the secret service realm would be in demand again soon enough. But in 1945, Truman still took the view that a democracy had no need of a foreign intelligence service in peacetime. Admittedly, in August he had suspended economic aid to the Soviet Union out of displeasure over the Soviets' policies in Eastern Europe, though he did not perceive in them a threat to the United States. He had no desire to lapse back into the old pre-war model, where virtually no contacts had existed between East and West at an intergovernmental level. But while the White House still entertained the possibility of cooperation with the Soviet Union, the direction of travel in the Council was already decidedly anti-communist. Where Europe was concerned, the internationalists on the Council believed that the US administration, thanks to its indecisive attitude, was once again charting an isolationist course. Eric Warburg was one of those who sounded alarm bells. He thought the plan to complete the withdrawal of

US forces from Europe just eighteen months after the end of the war was a huge mistake. Such a half-hearted occupation policy would, he believed, drive Germany into the arms of the Russians. Pro-Soviet leanings were already evident among some young people there. The Soviet Union was in the process of installing the first communist governments in Central Europe. Little wonder, then, that the evacuation of American forces from Thuringia and Saxony was seen by Germans as merely the first step towards further concessions by the USA to the 'stronger power'.[8]

*

The presence of Eric Warburg's name on the list of members of the Council on Foreign Relations was a clear indication that the US establishment now saw him as one of their own. Membership of the Council was by invitation only. Quite a few of the people whom Eric Warburg encountered there had sufficient financial means to be able to devote their time to a political agenda without needing to earn a living from it. One such full-time activist and foreign policy expert was Christopher Emmet. Since 1939, he had been presenting a fortnightly radio broadcast from New York, writing articles for American and German newspapers and publishing guest articles and letters to the editors of major press organs, in which he campaigned for the reconstruction of Germany. Emmet came from a wealthy and decidedly Germanophile East Coast Protestant family.[9] Like his many brothers and sisters, he had been born in Germany before the First World War, because his mother thought that antenatal care was far more advanced there than in America. As a result Christopher Emmet had repeatedly spent spells of several months living in small German towns and receiving private tuition from German teachers. After attending Harvard, he returned to Germany in the 1920s to continue his studies at several universities; his longest stay was in Berlin, where he witnessed the rise of the Nazis. He returned to the United States in 1933 as an opponent of the Nazis and a committed anti-communist.[10] The committees on which Emmet was active over the course of the years reflected his evolution into a cold warrior.[11] Having seen how great an influence the Communist Party had exerted over German workers in Weimar Berlin, he feared that after the country's defeat the German populace might be driven into the arms of the Soviets if America abandoned them to their own devices. Accordingly, he joined Eric Warburg in 1947 in calling for a halt to the dismantling of industrial facilities in the West German occupation zones.[12] If this could be achieved, it would put clear blue water between the policies of the West and the Soviets, who in their zone of occupation were pursuing a course of exacting harsh reparations. Hitherto, the Allied Control Council, to which the Soviets also belonged, had shown itself unable to reach effective decisions on fundamental questions of occupation policy – such as the creation of central administrative bodies as a prelude to economic harmonisation. As a consequence, in March 1946 a study group of the Council on Foreign Relations proposed that a policy confined to West Germany should be followed, if necessary without the involvement of the Soviet Union.[13] Soviet foreign policy, which was geared to the expansion of their sphere of influence, was sowing increasing mistrust in US government circles. The US diplomat George Kennan, who was stationed at the embassy in Moscow, warned the State Department in his famous 'Long Telegram' of 22 February 1946 of Soviet ambitions to become a global power, and advised the USA to confront it decisively with a policy of 'containment'. In the meantime, Truman too had decided on a change of policy towards Russia. Following repeated attempts by the Russians to interfere in the politics of Iran and Turkey, he resolved that he would no longer treat the former alliance partner with 'kid gloves'.[14] Germany therefore began to loom large in US foreign policy in 1946. In September of that year, in Stuttgart, US Secretary of State James F. Byrnes gave an address (the 'Speech of Hope'), in which he gave notice that the British and American zones of occupation would be combined into a 'Bizone', with the aim of ensuring 'the maximum possible unification'. In a speech to Congress in March 1947, President Truman announced a new direction in US foreign policy, later known as the 'Truman Doctrine', which saw the world as divided into Western democratic and Eastern communist systems.[15] A programme of aid and reconstruction for Europe began under Byrne's successor George C. Marshall.

*

Allen Welsh Dulles, whose OSS office in the Swiss city of Bern became a rallying point for opponents of Hitler during the war, published a book in the United States in 1947 entitled *Germany's Underground*, which told the story of the middle-class and conservative resistance to the National Socialist regime and alerted Americans to the fact that not all Germans were Nazis. The timing of its publication strongly suggested that it was a tactical move in a strategy aimed at changing the climate of opinion in the USA towards Germany.[16] Yet Dulles had started researching the book back in the summer of 1945.[17] With the assistance of Fabian von Schlabrendorff, he made contact with surviving relatives of the executed

German resistance fighters behind the 20 July Plot. Insofar as Schlabrendorff was able to find out the current addresses of these surviving opposition figures, Dulles visited them and got them to describe in great detail their lives in the National Socialist state. He then wrote the book on the basis of their eyewitness accounts. The list of survivors and their relatives that Schlabrendorff compiled contained the names of around 250 people.[18] Dulles sent them all a copy of the book after publication. Their responses led to the founding of the American Committee to Aid Survivors of the German Resistance, primarily to assist widows and young children, who even in the first years after the war were still regarded as the dependants of 'traitors' and 'oath-breakers'.[19] Eric Warburg got involved in this initiative alongside the theologians Paul Tillich and Reinhold Niebuhr and the philosopher Helmut Kahn. Because the well-known US journalist Dorothy Thompson was also active on the committee, its appeals reached willing donors right across the USA. The fate of the families of executed opposition members touched the American public, and welfare parcels and cash donations were dispatched to Germany – until in 1949 reports began to appear with growing frequency in the American press about a resurgent German nationalism that had no qualms about publicly defaming the murdered resistance fighters. Dulles attempted to account to the mayor of Hamburg, Max Brauer, for Americans' increasing reluctance to donate by explaining that it was very hard for them for properly appreciate the problem when Germany itself so undervalued the contribution of its resistance fighters that it offered almost no support to their surviving dependants. Brauer, who fled from the Nazis in 1933 and emigrated to the United States and only returned to his home city in 1946, had approached Dulles to seek help for Gertrud Oster. She was the widow of Major General Hans Oster, one of the most active opponents of Hitler, who had been involved in several attempts to topple the dictator and who was hanged for his part in the 20 July Plot to assassinate him. Brauer pondered how the city of Hamburg might help Gertrud Oster and the other dependants, and duly founded the July 20 1944 Relief Organisation. Eric Warburg was involved with this initiative too. He had returned to Germany again in May 1949 and planned on staying for several weeks.

*

When he arrived in the British occupation zone, the Restitution Law had just been passed. In this connection, the Jewish Joint Distribution Committee and the Jewish Agency had established legal successor organisations to the Reich Association of Jews in Germany. The successor in title in the American zone of occupation was the Jewish Restitution Successor Organization (JRSO). In the British zone, only the Jewish Trust Corporation (JTC) was officially recognised. In 1950 the JTC concluded a general agreement with the federal regions within the British zone which ruled that compensation should be paid across the board for all expropriations of property belonging to Jewish organisations, foundations, and communities that had taken place during the National Socialist period. The Israelite Hospital Foundation in Hamburg was one of the organisations affected by this ruling; for decades prior to its compulsory nationalisation in September 1939 it had been supported by the Warburg family. Until his arrest on the night of 9–10 November 1938 Fritz Warburg had been the head of the foundation. Felix Epstein, formerly an attorney at M. M. Warburg, stepped into his shoes. In 1942, Epstein was deported, survived detention in the Terezin concentration camp and returned to Hamburg, where he directed his energies toward reviving the foundation. However, the general agreement did not provide for the restitution of real estate, or for any resurrection of Jewish institutions or foundations; compensation for community property was only paid in the form of money. For on no account did Jewish organisations want to initiate the revival of Jewish community life in the land of the perpetrators. The reimbursed assets were intended to be invested in the formation of new communities in the destination countries for accelerated migration. Epstein took a different approach. He wanted to revive the old foundation on its original site in Hamburg. However, the hospital foundation on whose behalf he was acting was not recognised as a third negotiating partner in the restitution process alongside the JTC. As a result, there was little chance of success. It was only through Eric Warburg's mediation that talks between Epstein and the Hamburg Senate were set in motion, at which the possibility emerged of the Israelite Hospital being rebuilt. At a new location, the hospital would fulfil the original purpose of the foundation, which would mean that Jewish and Christian patients would be accepted on equal terms, a fact of which Fritz Warburg reminded all those concerned in a letter he wrote from Stockholm in 1946.[20] Fritz himself did not come back to Hamburg again; instead he and his wife moved to Israel, where Eva, their middle daughter, was already living with her family on a kibbutz.

*

By 1949 the number of children housed at the children's home on the Kösterberg had shrunk to twenty-five, and the

Jewish Joint Distribution Committee began making preparations to wind up the institution. The handing over of the plot to Eric and Fritz Warburg was scheduled to take place on 1 September.[21] Fritz Warburg wanted to leave the White Villa to the Red Cross, and Eric had something similar in mind for the villa that had belonged to his parents. In August, in the name of the former partners in the firm M. M. Warburg, he began negotiations with Brinckmann & Wirtz about the reallocation of their shares. Aside from himself, the group of expropriated shareholders included Fritz Warburg, Ernst Spiegelberg, and Siegmund G. Warburg. Eric's cousin Siegmund had emigrated to London in 1934, where in the same year he founded the New Trading Company, from which the London private banking firm of S. G. Warburg & Co. developed in 1946. Eric Warburg settled with the current partners of M. M. Warburg on a 25 per cent holding for their group as limited partners in Brinckmann, Wirtz & Co.

*

West Germany was granted a new Basic Law and statehood in 1949, events which might have suggested that the West Germans were once more looking to the future with greater optimism. Instead, on his visit during the summer of that year, Eric Warburg witnessed how the general mood was tipping over into nationalism and self-righteousness. In April, final judgment was reached in the Wilhelmstraße Trial, the eleventh in a series of twelve court cases that followed the Nuremberg Trials, in which leading members of the German Foreign Office who had operated within what was now the American zone were called to account for their actions during the Nazi dictatorship. The defendants, 185 individuals all told,

181

included members of SS death squads (*Einsatzgruppen*) and officers of the General Staff, who stood accused of mass shootings and other atrocities. The most well-known among them was Ernst von Weizsäcker; as a secretary of state, prior to 1945 he had been the most high-ranking official in the ministerial bureaucracy. In his defence, he claimed that he had remained in office in order to carry on clandestine resistance to the regime.[22] In a majority verdict, however, the three American judges found otherwise. Weizsäcker had been a signatory to a document authorising the deportation of 6,000 French Jews to Auschwitz in 1942. As a result, he was sentenced to seven years in jail for crimes against humanity. This verdict caused a huge public outcry. Weizsäcker, the very epitome of an educated *haut bourgeois*, was in the dock alongside Nazi mass murderers and SS henchmen.[23] 'A Diplomat On Trial' was how Margret Boveri entitled her report of the court proceedings, in which she contended that the three judges were incapable of reaching a fair verdict.[24] Anyone who saw his signature on anti-Jewish documents as proof positive that Ernst von Weizsäcker had colluded in Nazi war crimes was, she said, being naïve – a view shared by Marion Dönhoff.[25] This friend of the Weizsäcker family claimed that the condemned man had a proven track record of 'resistance'. As a diplomat of the old school he had, she maintained, found National Socialism abhorrent, made peace overtures behind Ribbentrop's back, sought dialogue with the West during the Sudetenland crisis, and only stayed in post in order to defend the old institution against the National Socialist interlopers. She pleaded for an amnesty for Ernst von Weizsäcker. Some of Dönhoff's colleagues chose to direct their fire against Weizsäcker's accuser Robert Kempner, a superior councillor in the Prussian Interior Ministry during the Weimar period, who was dismissed from his post in 1933 and driven into exile for being a Jew and a Social Democrat and who in the meantime had taken US citizenship. His adversaries used this to contest his right to level accusations at a German citizen who had made the sacrifice of remaining at his post throughout. Boveri, meanwhile, was adamant that the only people in a position to pass fair judgment on collaboration with the Nazis were those who had lived under the regime.[26] Ernst von Weizsäcker received the support first and foremost of journalists who worked at the newspaper *Die Zeit*. Hans Georg von Studnitz wrote: 'Anyone who has not himself breathed the atmosphere of a dictatorship, is not entitled to pass judgment.'[27] This passionate plea came from the pen of a journalist who before 1945 was employed in the press department of the Foreign Office, had been a card-carrying member of NSDAP since 1933, and who remained a dedicated National Socialist and anti-Semite to the last. There was no shortage of former career diplomats who came forward during the trial to attest to Ernst von Weizsäcker's resistance credentials and at the same to exonerate themselves from any blame. For students of contemporary history, the resistance narrative that was wheeled out in defence of Ernst von Weizsäcker forms part of the 'departmental myth-making' which set in at the very moment of Germany's surrender.[28] Likewise, the picture painted by Marion Dönhoff of a general aristocratic resistance against Hitler, which for decades represented the official line taken by the Federal Republic of Germany on domestic resistance to the Hitler regime, has meanwhile been subject to correction: in reality, it was only a 'tiny minority' of aristocratic figures who distinguished themselves by taking an opposing stance.[29] The overwhelming majority of aristocrats, especially those living east of the River Elbe, had become politically radicalised as a result of losing out from moves towards modernisation during the nineteenth century. Eric Warburg counted many of those representatives of the minority view among his friends. Yet Dönhoff also considered his close friend Albrecht von Bernstorff, who was murdered by the SS in the Lehrter Straße jail in the Moabit district of Berlin, to be a friend of hers. She said she had first met Bernstorff in 1933 in a Berlin café, when he had been sitting at an adjoining table and fearlessly proclaiming his repugnance for the National Socialists.[30] Warburg had known Bernstorff since their teenage years, and like Dönhoff he preferred the idea of a conservatively minded opposition to Nazi Germany. It fitted more easily into his anti-communist worldview.

*

In the summer of 1949, while broad swathes of the press were busy airing their resentment at the verdicts handed down in the Nuremberg Trials, at the Hotel Petersberg near Bonn the Allied High Commission began its work as the principal occupation authority in Germany. As early as March 1948, Great Britain, the United States, and France had agreed to transform the Bizone into a Trizone through the addition of the French zone of occupation. At the Conference of Foreign Ministers held in Washington in early April 1949, the 'treaty for the merger of the three Western zones of occupation' was signed.[31] From September 1949 an occupation statute would regulate the relationship between the future West German state and the Allied occupying powers, who even after the formation of the Federal Republic of Germany would initially retain certain rights of supervision and devolve these gradually to Germany over the years that followed. The military governor Lucius Clay was replaced in July 1949 by the civilian high commissioner John McCloy. *The New York Times* declared that this was finally a case of the right job for the man and the right man for the job.[32]

*

The verdict in the Wilhelmstraße Trial had still not been endorsed by Lucius Clay. Ernst von Weizsäcker's legal team used this factor to their advantage; Hellmut Becker, Weizsäcker's German attorney, took the view that there might be expectations, not just in Germany but also in the United States, of 'a decision in an altogether different spirit' from John McCloy, who was himself a lawyer.[33] Becker put it about that the Wilhelmstraße verdict was legally flawed. A record of cross-examination supposedly contained evidence that a witness for the prosecution – one Friedrich Gaus, a former legal advisor to the Foreign Office – had been intimidated by the prosecutor Robert Kempner.[34] It was certainly the case that, in a handwritten affidavit to the chief prosecutor Telford Taylor after the disputed questioning, Gaus had pronounced the whole of the German bureaucratic system guilty in the spirit of collective responsibility. The Munich *Neue Zeitung* newspaper printed Gaus' statement on its front page.[35] This was an attempt to suggest to the public that German collective guilt as a whole was on trial here, and that no distinction was now being made between supposedly blameless civil servants with a loyalty to the state and Nazi gangsters. However, the fact that Gaus' statement had not been factored into the verdict went unheeded. The argument that had broken out in America after the seventh follow-on case from the Nuremberg Trials concerning clear procedural shortcomings now reached Germany and provided Weizsäcker's lawyers with support.

Charles Wennerstrum, the presiding judge in the seventh trial – at which Wehrmacht generals stood accused of having caused the deaths of thousands of Yugoslavian and Greek civilians – had held forth to a reporter from the *Chicago Tribune* after the trial ended in February 1948 about how the whole concept of prosecution was 'vengeful' and tainted by 'personal ambitions'. It was significant, he claimed, that so many of those employed by the prosecuting authorities had only 'become Americans in the last few years.' Mired in 'prejudices and feelings of hatred', these people denied Germans any justice.[36] Everyone knew who he was referring to: Benjamin Ferencz, the prosecutor in the trial of the *Einsatzgruppen*, the ninth follow-on trial, which concerned the mass shootings of around a million Soviet Jews, and Robert Kempner in the Wilhelmstraße Trial. Those in Germany who suspected that a Jewish desire for revenge lay behind the verdicts felt vindicated by Wennerstrum's remarks.[37] Even before his arrival in Germany, therefore, John McCloy found himself assailed from several sides to reconsider the verdict. The US diplomat George Kennan asked for Weizsäcker to be pardoned, as did the theologian Reinhold Niebuhr.[38] And the accusation of 'victors' justice' also echoed around the corridors of the reparations authorities, whose civil servants were anything but cooperative. An opposition had formed from groups who considered themselves victims of the 'Jews and the restitution process', and it set about trying to hamper the programme of restitution. When that failed, campaigns from pressure groups began; there was even talk of a 'second expropriation', though no distinction was drawn between Nazi perpetrators and their victims.[39] While a loose confederation of the war criminals lobby and opponents of restitution complained loudly in Germany about Jewish victors' justice, all of a sudden the old

Sidney Warburg story was resurrected in the German press. This fictitious member of the Warburg family, who had allegedly amassed donations amounting to millions of dollars from British, American, and Dutch sponsors and channelled them to Hitler, who used them to bankroll his rise to power, was originally the invention of the Dutch forger J. G. Schoup. He had been exposed in 1933 when he tried to sell this concocted story to the Amsterdam publisher Van Holkema & Warendorf. In the 1940s a certain René Sonderegger appeared on the scene, who made minor changes to Schoup's fairytale and published it as 'financial global history' under the title *The Third Reich in the Service of International High Finance*. But Sonderegger did not stop there. In a subsequent work, *Spanish Summer* – which he published under the pseudonym Severin Reinhard – he spun the tissue of lies even further and attempted to substantiate the supposed existence of Sidney Warburg and the leading role played by the Warburgs in the worldwide Zionist conspiracy – albeit with invented sources.[40] Sonderegger claimed that the person behind Sidney Warburg was in fact James Warburg. The interest generated by his abstruse assertions prompted James Warburg to issue a sworn statement in 1949 that he was not the same person as Sidney Warburg.[41] Eric Warburg eventually secured a legal ruling that all newspapers that had retailed the story as fact should be forced to print a public retraction.[42] He was not after retribution, but justice. It was his firm conviction that civilised coexistence could only function properly on a legal basis. But now, in the trials that followed on from Nuremberg, the reputation of the American occupying power had been damaged precisely by legal procedural errors. His fear was that if nothing was done, it might discredit the whole system of the democratic administration of justice. He compared notes on this with Heinrich Kronstein, the lawyer whose acquaintance he had made four years before on the troopship. They asked themselves what Kronstein's former boss Thurman Arnold would have said about the accusation that the Allies had used methods in the Wilhelmstraße Trial which were unworthy of the Western side. Kronstein passed on to Arnold the record of cross-examination with Gaus' statements, which had come into Eric Warburg's possession via someone associated with Weizsäcker's defence team.[43] Arnold had meanwhile retired from politics, was practising as an attorney once more, and had founded a law firm with two partners. As expected, he was aghast at the dilettante style of questioning which in his view had deprived Weizsäcker of a fair hearing before a US military court. He got in contact with Weizsäcker's legal team and by contesting the verdict before the US military tribunal was ultimately able to get the term of imprisonment reduced to two years.[44]

*

It was in this summer of 1949 of all moments, when emotions were running high within the Nazi old-boy network and its auxiliaries in the German press, that the programme of dismantling German infrastructure which had been resolved four years previously – at the Potsdam Conference – began to be implemented in British-occupied Hamburg.[45] At the end of May, Günther Henle, one of the foremost representatives of the Rhineland and Westfalian iron and steel industry, approached the Hamburg mayor Max Brauer and asked him to use the contacts with the American trade unions that he had fostered during his time in exile to lobby for an end to the dismantling work. For in the last workers' council elections at the firm he owned – the Klöckner steelworks in Düsseldorf, which was one of the plants scheduled for disassembly in the Washington Agreement – the KPD (the German Communist Party) had greatly increased its representation.[46] In Hamburg, where just forty-one factories were on the list of industrial facilities to be dismantled, no such campaigns against the policy comparable to those in the Ruhr had been organised. Protests only erupted here too when, on 11 July, dynamiting of the slipways commenced at the Blohm & Voss shipyard. In order to destroy, over a length of around 250 metres, the two-metre-thick concrete base of the slipway, which was reinforced with iron and had been built to bear the bulk of ships weighing tens of thousands of tons during their launch, sixty controlled explosions were needed.[47] When the works council at the German Reiherstieg shipyard, which was also scheduled for demolition, set up a committee to oppose destruction and disassembly, Eric Warburg's fears that the KPD was also profiting from the dismantling programme and was gaining influence in workplaces in Hamburg too appeared to be realised.[48] Despite the fact that the restrictions imposed upon post-war German shipbuilding and the shipping industry were far more damaging to the economy of this major maritime city, at the sight of the ruined port installations, popular resentment was directed primarily at the policy of industrial demolition (although, in the case of the Reiherstieg yard, that damage was actually down to the war). On numerous occasions during the war, Eric Warburg had written to his family from the front to express his view that the mistakes of the Versailles peace agreement, which had been motivated by a desire for retribution, should never be repeated. For this was where the suffering of the German Jews had begun.[49] He was, he said, the very last person to forget what the Nazis had done and what an indescribable burden of blame they shouldered, but even so he questioned whether retribution was the answer. Sooner or later, people in the West would be deeply ashamed that 'we could ever have imagined that this was the better world we'd been fighting for.'[50] He found it unbearable to look at the destroyed slipways on which, when he was thirteen years old, the *Imperator* and her sister ships were constructed; at the time these ocean liners of the Hamburg America Line were the largest passenger vessels afloat, and made weekly voyages to New York.

*

With the images of Hamburg's dynamited shipyards fresh in his mind, Eric Warburg travelled to the town of Bad Homburg vor der Höhe on 24 August 1949. John McCloy, who had only arrived in Germany a few weeks before, had invited him to come and dine with him. The entry for that evening in the High Commissioner's office diary read: '8.00 Dinner at home Mr. Eric Warburg.'[51] According to the other entries for 24 August, McCloy's entire day had been taken up with discussions on the topic of dismantling German industry. He had had a meeting with Robert Haines from the European Recovery Program, better known as the 'Marshall Plan'. In addition, one of the staff members in his office was Norman Collission. In 1947 Collission was assigned the task of aligning the list of industrial plants to be dismantled, which at the time contained the names of 873 facilities, with the new direction of US policy.[52] Leaving aside the 335 armaments factories on the list, the Collission Commission struck through the names of one-third of the firms originally slated for demolition. In January 1948 the Humphrey Committee recommended sparing a further eight facilities on the list from dismantling. Finally, at the Washington Conference of Foreign Ministers in April 1949, the USA, Great Britain, and France set the number of factories to be demolished in the Trizone at 682.[53] This was still the state of play in August of that year. It must have come as something of a shock to McCloy that Eric, the cousin of his friends Freddy and Eddy Warburg, with whom he had been used hitherto to making pleasant small talk in the relaxed American country-club atmosphere of Woodlands, suddenly appeared at his table sounding like the West German politicians, trade union leaders, and employers who still considered the figure of 682 far too high. Eric Warburg did not beat about the bush but came straight to the point, describing the dismantling policy as a blunder. McCloy, whose job it was as high commissioner to represent the official position of the US State Department, and who was caught completely off guard by this visitor presenting the German position to him so bluntly, resorted to a somewhat curious comparison. In ancient times, he said, after defeat the Germanic tribes had been forced to witness their swords and spears being smashed to pieces before their very eyes. Eric Warburg replied that he was really surprised at the analogy. He had taken McCloy to be smarter than that. They weren't talking here about swords but industrial complexes. And besides, the Russians were just waiting for the West Germans to grow heartily sick of their shabby treatment by the occupying powers.[54] This kind of plain speaking got McCloy's dander up too, so much so that Eric Warburg began to worry that he had taxed the American's patience beyond breaking point. But by the time they parted company a short while later McCloy had reverted to his usual calm tone of voice, and announced that he would be prepared to halt the demolition if the future federal government came up with some alternative proposals. He had in mind specifically a declaration on security cooperation that would guarantee the incorporation of the Trizone into the Western alliance, plus he was also seeking an agreement regarding Germany's accession to the International Authority for the Ruhr (IAR). Before Eric Warburg left, McCloy asked him to give him the names of ten steelworks and fuel plants that he thought should be crossed off the demolition list. Three days later the names were on McCloy's desk. Six of the plants that Eric Warburg listed had already been identified by the Humphrey Committee as worthy of reprieve, including the Klöckner works. But the second name on Eric's list, directly below the August Thyssen steel mill in Hamborn, was Salzgitter AG, a German steelworks that came with hugely problematic political baggage. Founded in 1937 to produce steel purely for armaments, and as part of the Nazi Four-Year Plan, it was better known by the name Hermann Goering Imperial Works (*Hermann-Göring-Reichswerke*). From the beginning of the war, forced labourers had been employed there, and from 1942 on concentration camp inmates too. Neither Collission nor Humphrey would have dreamt of striking the Hermann Goering Imperial Works off the list. Had they done so, the French would on no account have agreed to link the common security policy towards Germany with their consent to the occupation statute and the new German constitution at the Foreign Ministers' Conference in Washington. The fate of Salzgitter AG may also have been the reason why the discussion over dinner at McCloy's became so heated. The dismantling of the Salzgitter works affected half of the coking plants, three-quarters of the blast furnaces, the steelworks and rolling mill, the foundry, the forge, and the central workshop.[55] Just a few days before Eric Warburg's meeting with John McCloy in Bad Homburg, the workers at Salzgitter had downed tools after learning that sections of their plant that had already been dismantled were about to be shipped abroad. The Church, unions, and municipal authorities all stood behind the workforce, and some 7,000 people took part in the protests. The local stakeholders demanded that at least the core of the works should remain intact – otherwise reconstruction, the stated aim of the parallel Marshall Plan, would no longer be possible. In essence, McCloy's attitude to the question of dismantling was not so very different from that of Eric Warburg. If destruction of industrial facilities were to resume more than four years after the cessation of hostilities, their policy was at risk of suffering great harm. McCloy also saw eye to eye with Eric Warburg in their analysis of the inter-war years. Back then, in the late 1920s and early 1930s, the republican administration, which had been overly concerned with rehabilitating Germany on the world stage, had not managed to integrate its own populace, materially or ideologically, into the structural shift towards democracy that the country was going through during the Weimar period, while the USA had spent too long refusing to make any concessions to the German government. Warburg had also added another point of criticism to the list that he prepared for McCloy: in the British zone, where Salzgitter was located, he complained that most of the industrial plants were not being dismantled but scrapped.[56] In his view, by constantly wheeling out the argument that the plants earmarked for demolition lacked profitability and were too expensive to maintain, the British were playing directly into the hands of the communists, yet public opinion in West Germany blamed the USA for this senseless destruction. McCloy could only agree on this point too. In view of the fact that Germany was one great sea of ruins and considering the high level of unemployment, tearing down factories that could have been redeployed for peaceful purposes was catastrophically bad optics.[57] However, in the case of the Hermann Goering Imperial Works, McCloy believed that the security concerns of the French had to take precedence. Although he saw himself as being firmly behind a halt to the dismantling programme, in this instance he thought that it would be unavoidable. An occupation statute that would gradually see West Germany achieve full sovereignty with a fully intact steel industry that was still capable of turning out war materiel would be unacceptable to the French. A halt to the dismantling programme was in any event premised upon Germany committing itself to security cooperation with the Western Allies and required that the country join the International Authority for the Ruhr, in order for controls to be imposed upon future German steel production. The new federal government just had to swallow the bitter pill that none of this was compatible with the preservation of Salzgitter AG.

*

On 1 September 1949, a week after Warburg and McCloy's reunion, Konrad Adenauer was elected as the first chancellor of the new Federal Republic of Germany. The journalist Marion Dönhoff, who was friends with Eric Warburg, conveyed McCloy's message to Adenauer. According to her, Adenauer could scarcely believe that Eric Warburg should have been able to bring about a change of mind in McCloy.[58] With the signing of the Petersberg Agreement on 22 November 1949, he assured the occupying powers in the three western zones that the German federal government would in future cooperate fully with the Western Allies on all security-related matters and also promised that the Federal Republic would accede to the IAR. In return, by devolving certain rights to the Federal Republic, the governments of the three occupying powers initiated the first steps towards it gaining full sovereignty as a nation state. In addition, the anticipated measures bringing economic relief were undertaken: alongside the revision of the dismantling programme, eighteen of the largest industrial facilities in Germany were struck off the demolition list – with the exception, however, of Salzgitter AG. For tactical reasons, though, Adenauer only announced this to the German parliament after signing the Petersberg Agreement. His speech has gone down in history primarily for the Social Democrat leader Kurt Schumacher's scathing description of Adenauer as the 'Allies' Chancellor', since this contractual tying-in of West Germany to the Western Bloc made any reunification with East Germany virtually impossible. Meanwhile, work began on dismantling Salzgitter AG.

*

Nevertheless, John McCloy made one final attempt to save the buildings in Salzgitter. He submitted proposals to Hubert Robertson and André François-Poncet, his colleagues in the British and French zones, on how the plant might be used for peaceful purposes. The British, however, offered no response.[59] Accordingly, dynamiting of the foundations in Salzgitter began in February 1950, at a time when demolition work in the rest of West Germany had all but come to a halt. The situation escalated in Salzgitter. On 7 March, workers occupied the facilities due for demolition. They disabled the drilling machines that were used to drill the holes in which explosive charges were placed. That same day, British military personnel appeared on the site. Hundreds of policemen were supposed to impose law and order, but the police sympathised with the protesting workforce. This stand-off ended on 17 March, when the dismantling work was provisionally halted. Politics in Washington had intervened.

*

One week previously, on 10 March, McCloy had been summoned to answer questions before a senate committee which approved the funding for the occupation. He was called upon to explain why the Salzgitter works in the British zone were being demolished at the same time as they were trying, with American taxpayers' money, to persuade the Germans of the democratic fairness of their system. French misgivings and British interests were of no concern to the Republican senator and minority leader Kenneth Wherry, who declared: 'Here we are appropriating millions and millions of dollars to build good will, and out there in this little community where they need work these buildings are being blown up in order to please a bunch of Communists over in France.' McCloy pointed out the limits of his own authority. Once a decision had been made at inter-Allied level, he said, his influence did not extend to getting that decision rescinded. But Senator Wherry wasn't about to let him get away with that, telling the committee: 'I do believe that if Mr. McCloy were to [say] … that he wants to make a review of that plant and have further demolition stopped until he does, I would guarantee that they would not blow up anything more.'[60] And so it was that, in the interplay between the occupying powers, the balance shifted for a moment on 17 March 1950 in favour of the workers in Salzgitter, because, with regard to approving aid amounting to 30 million dollars for the coming financial year, Senator Wherry reminded High Commissioner McCloy that it was his voters in Nebraska who provided the funds for his occupation budget. Also, the Allies' demands on security cooperation effectively made the West Germans partners, and as partners they had every right to expect greater concessions in many areas.

*

Social lobby groups in West Germany had already taken up position: in this moment they threw their weight principally behind the interests of convicted war criminals, with the 'unjust' Weizsäcker trial acting a blueprint in this regard. The most outspoken criticism came from a group of lawyers in Heidelberg, an alliance of advocates, judges, and legal scholars, which also included Weizsäcker's lawyer Hellmut Becker. But Germany's Protestant and Catholic bishops and cardinals were no less reticent in putting themselves forward as lobbyists for war criminals. They left no stone unturned in attempting to get the verdict re-examined. McCloy also received a plea for clemency from the Vatican, where Weizsäcker had been sent as ambassador in 1943.[61] And yet at this stage McCloy had already softened the previous US line by introducing the possibility of parole. In recognition of good conduct, five days every month would be remitted from prisoners' sentences. This provision had already seen the first sixty prisoners released just before Christmas. Emboldened by this, Weizsäcker's defence team encouraged proponents of a pardon in America to go public in calling for the immediate release of their client. In December a guest commentary by the publisher Victor Gollancz appeared in *The Times*, who maintained that there were sound humanitarian grounds to support a pardoning of Weizsäcker.[62] Gollancz, who until the Hitler–Stalin Pact had been a communist 'fellow-traveller', published a volume of essays entitled *Betrayal of the Left* in 1941, a work which in Great Britain signalled the break of the democratic Left with communism. For Gollancz, the verdict in the Wilhelmstraße Trial only served to encourage the idea of German collective guilt, which would discredit the West Germans as Western-alliance partners and drive them into the arms of the Soviet Union.[63] Marion Dönhoff may well have also had a hand in the fact that, just a few days after Gollancz's commentary piece appeared in *The Times*, Eric Warburg also sat down at his desk in New York to compose a letter to John McCloy. She went directly to Hellmut Becker to ask him to set out some substantive points that Eric Warburg could use for guidance. Becker, however, told her that the only thing required in this instance was to 'speak to McCloy in a way that moves him, and Warburg, who knows him well ... can do that far better than I can.'[64]

*

In his letter, Eric Warburg encouraged McCloy to be more decisive in dealing with the question of war criminals. He endorsed the release, as soon as possible, of all those prisoners who could not be regarded as 'Nazi criminals' but who rather numbered among the 'Weizsäckers'. He did not try to turn Weizsäcker into some clandestine resistance fighter or put him on a pedestal. Instead, he saw him as the prototype of a person who 'looking at the wrong Hindenburg example ... wrongly stayed on with the erroneous hope that they could prevent worse and who, in their subsequent efforts, were often too timid and too weak.'[65]

*

Eric Warburg's letter reached McCloy just before he left for the States on 20 January, where he hoped to assure himself of the public's backing for his policy on Germany, especially where the treatment of war criminals was concerned.[66] After he gave a speech in Boston, a commentary piece by Robert S. Marcus, political director of the World Jewish Congress, appeared in *The New York Times* on 10 February. Marcus wrote that Germany's far right would be jubilant if Ernst von Weizsäcker, who had been implicated in the deportation of 6,000 Jews to Auschwitz, was released in the context of a general amnesty.[67] The Weizsäcker legal team, which as well as Becker also included Weizsäcker's son Richard, who had interrupted his law studies at Göttingen in order to defend his father, began to grow nervous. The US military tribunal had only just reduced the duration of his term in prison from five to two years. But bad press in the USA reduced the chances of a pardon. Christopher Emmet advised the Weizsäcker team to seek a right of reply in the same newspaper. Ideally this would come from an American citizen who was well versed in this area and would be perceived as a 'neutral' by readers.[68] Accordingly, Weizsäcker's elder son, Carl Friedrich von Weizsäcker, turned to Eric Warburg. Carl Friedrich, a physicist, had accepted an invitation from the chancellor of the University of Chicago, Robert Hutchins, to come to the United States in the Goethe anniversary year of 1949. He was still in the States in February 1950 when he corresponded with Eric Warburg. Weizsäcker believed that Eric Warburg ought to publicly correct the representative of the World Jewish Congress, and do so moreover on the basis of the very verdict that Marcus himself had cited. Carl Friedrich von Weizsäcker even provided the text for Eric's correction: 'M. (sic) Marcus cited the case of W. But to be fair, the same court that convicted W. at the same time ... confirmed his resistance against Hitler.'[69] In the eyes of the readers, this would relativise Ernst von Weizsäcker's conviction for complicity in crimes against humanity; though the correction would significantly fail to mention that the judges had absolutely no doubt about Weizsäcker's guilt.[70] Carl Friedrich von Weizsäcker appeared to know exactly the favour he was asking of Eric Warburg here, for he almost apologised for the fact that Eric himself had put the idea in his head.[71] Eric had written to him in Chicago, attaching a clipping of the article from *The New York Times*. Although it was not definitely clear to Weizsäcker from this whether Eric Warburg was himself thinking of writing the open letter, the active role he was taking in this matter certainly admitted of that possibility. His 'neutrality' demonstrated that he had opted to take as unprejudiced a view as possible of the Weizsäcker case, namely a fair sense of justice, which was why he had personally put the Weizsäckers in touch with Thurman Arnold. For his aim was merely to restore justice, not to seek retribution.[72] He had in no way been seeking to suggest that the wrong people had been put in the dock at Nuremberg, however he allowed himself to be guided by the insight that he should be ready for a new beginning if he wanted to continue to remain in contact with his old homeland. It helped that he clearly harboured no feelings of revenge. But there was no way he would allow himself to be manipulated either. Nothing was further from his intention than to turn the Weizsäcker case into a public dispute between Jews. He showed no further interest in acting on Carl Friedrich von Weizsäcker's request. In weighing up the case of Ernst von Weizsäcker, the only point on which he concurred with his friend Marion Dönhoff's judgment was that Weizsäcker's case ought not to have been tried in the same arena as those of Nazi gangsters. Unlike Marion Dönhoff, he did not view Weizsäcker as a resistance fighter. It was clearly enough for her, his acutely class-conscious friend, that Ernst von Weizsäcker had been repelled by Hitler's vulgarity. As for Eric Warburg's views on this score, Carl Melchior had already perfectly encapsulated them in 1933: 'One should only put oneself at the service of one's government if it regards certain basic principles of humanity and justice as sacrosanct. Acquiescing in inhumane policies in order to supposedly guard against something worse is the road to perdition'.[73] Eric Warburg distinguished between the genuinely irreproachable characters who had paid for their resistance to Hitler with their lives and those who in all probability deluded themselves so as not to have to admit in their heart of hearts that they were too weak to resist. In his letter to McCloy, he described this latter group as '[those] whom you might refer to in the plural as the "Weizsäckers" (for he is a prototype of them).'[74] Carl Friedrich von Weizsäcker was not content to let this judgment on his father stand. He claimed that his father's actions represented 'one of the greatest sacrifices a person can make, regardless of how it may be judged legally or politically. It would have been so much easier for him to have stood aloof and kept his hands clean.'[75] But Eric Warburg did not dispute that. Anyone who was a representative of the so-called elite, or who by dint of their socially elevated position operated one of the levers of power within the state, was positively obliged to display civil courage, especially if that state was an unjust regime of the worst kind.[76] But what Ernst von Weizsäcker considered resistance had in fact been a moral failure on the part of a decision-maker which had been so banal – when measured against the high standards that representatives of a bourgeois elite (albeit a self-appointed one) like Ernst von Weizsäcker set for their own conduct – that in Eric Warburg's opinion 'the fact that some infamous papers carry their signature ... [along] with imprisonment and the ordeal of trial seems to me punishment enough.'[77] He did not advocate an immediate amnesty but instead expressed sympathy with the view that the right moment to pardon the 'Weizsäckers' had not yet come. 'Looking back at this whole chapter in years to come,' he prophesied, 'it will – I think – reflect great political wisdom to have left this path open by postponing the confirmation of these sentences.'[78]

*

For Ron Chernow, the biographer of the Warburg dynasty, after 1945 Eric Warburg seemed to be revisiting the fascination he had had since his childhood in the German Second Empire with the military and the aristocracy. With the result, he says, that of all the identities that were in conflict within Eric – the German, the Jew, and the American – the German ultimately won out again.[79] But was that really the case? Certainly, Eric Warburg's letter to McCloy in December 1949 about the political wisdom of keeping the possibility of pardon open might seem to suggest this,[80] but in saying this he was surely thinking of the political decisions that were now on the agenda. The Germans were to be compelled through a statute of occupation to restore all Jewish property that had been 'Aryanised'. Perhaps Eric Warburg was imagining that pardoning the 'Weizsäckers' among the war criminals might enable McCloy to be all the more inflexible towards the Germans when demanding an appropriate reparations policy.[81] They could expect a strong pushback. For even the military laws that had constituted the legal basis for restitution in the occupation zones had been passed in the face of opposition from local German politicians.[82] John McCloy and his British colleague Ivone Kirkpatrick now made it clear to the prime ministers of the regions within their zones of occupation that where the ongoing process of restitution was concerned they would insist upon the contractual obligation of the Federal Republic.[83] In 1951 Konrad Adenauer announced that he was prepared to enter into talks with Israel and representatives of the Jewish diaspora about material reparations measures. As a body to represent their common interests, international Jewish organisations convened the Jewish Claims Conference (JCC), which began negotiations with representatives of the Federal Republic in 1952 in the Dutch town of Wassenaar.[84] In 1953 Ben Ferencz took over the leadership of the JCC for Germany and in this capacity implemented reparations agreements with the Federal Republic.

*

Within the Weizsäcker circle, the Shoah was treated merely as a procedural matter, as for example when Marion Dönhoff in her newspaper articles excused Weizsäcker's signing of documents that directly harmed Jews as a necessary concession to his cover story.[85] Or when they attempted to seek out German Jews as 'neutral' advocates to aid their defensive strategy. No true awareness of the Shoah was in evidence, however. Eric Warburg underestimated the depth of involvement with the Nazis of individual members of this circle. Weizsäcker's German attorney Hellmut Becker hushed up his membership of the NSDAP. And it was not only Ernst von Weizsäcker who retrospectively recast the conformist attitude he had displayed before 1945 as oppositional. Immediately after the end of the war, during his internment at Farm Hill, a British stately home that had been converted into an interrogation centre, his son Carl Friedrich, who until 1945 had worked as a physicist on the German project to enrich uranium, explained that they had never followed through on the plan to build an atomic bomb during the war because of their moral integrity: 'If we had wanted Germany to win the war, we would have succeeded in building an atom bomb.'[86] Thanks not least to this 'whitewashing' of his past, which began even in 1945, Weizsäcker was able to reconnect with the international scientific community after the war.[87] It was only in the mid-1980s that he rowed back on his earlier statement. Contrary to what he claimed immediately after the war, he now said that he had been perfectly prepared to work with the National Socialist regime and was interested in discussing with Hitler the development of an atomic bomb.[88] It would presumably have come as no surprise to Eric Warburg that Weizsäcker found the idea of a Europe under German leadership and immune from any attack very attractive.[89] For it was precisely this prospect that had induced Eric to fight against the Nazis on the American side. In the meantime, however, National Socialism had been neutralised as a real political threat. After the outbreak of the Korean War, a Bolshevik Europe under Russian leadership suddenly appeared a much more realistic scenario. Among the partners in the banking firm Brinckmann & Wirtz too, fear of a Russian invasion had been rife ever since the Berlin Airlift in 1948–49 and had been the catalyst to the bank's acquisition of the pilot schooner *Atalanta*. This vessel was fully equipped to make a fast getaway in such an event. On his visits to Hamburg, Eric Warburg was able to observe as an outsider how the increasingly tense international situation was affecting the general mood. Perhaps he believed that concessions would have to be made and that not too many demands be placed upon people lest West Germany's social stability be jeopardised once more. The route of conciliation involving all social groups, via which Eric Warburg himself was now reaching a rapprochement with Germany, revealed its shortcomings in the public reception of the cases that followed the Nuremberg trials. They were widely seen as having failed after McCloy granted early release to the 'Weizsäckers' who had been convicted as war criminals – a total of seventy-nine out of the ninety cases he had presided over. What was intended as a gesture of reconciliation was seen by those who had traduced the trials from the very beginning as Jewish revenge justice as a vindication of their stance.[90]

*

Looking back, the day on which the transatlantic dialogue entered Eric Warburg's life can be pinpointed exactly: 24 August 1949, when he met John McCloy for dinner in Bad Homburg vor der Höhe. McCloy had set aside ninety minutes for his guest that evening. They immediately began discussing US policy on Germany. Three years later the conversation between the two men assumed institutional form in the sister organisations of the American Council on Germany and the *Atlantik-Brücke* (Atlantic Bridge) organisation in Germany. After his mission in Germany ended in 1952, McCloy returned to work in the private sector in the USA, while continuing as an éminence grise of the US establishment to advise American administrations on geostrategic questions and foreign policy matters relating to Germany. By virtue of his position and contacts, he remained the most important link in the German–American network, whose most significant driving force was Eric Warburg.

McCloy's recognition of Eric Warburg as a key figure in German–American rapprochement at the same time lent particular importance to Eric's role as the contact person to the Jewish community. The strategy of creating channels of cooperation in their own interest, which also benefitted the non-Jewish side, had proved its worth for the non-Zionist Jewish community in the USA in the twentieth century. The charismatic Felix Warburg used such channels, as did Lewis Strauss in his work with Herbert Hoover.[91] For his part, with the ACG and the *Atlantik-Brücke*, Eric Warburg alongside McCloy now established the most important German–American channels of communication that had existed thus far in the post-war period, and which also reaped rewards for the Jewish community in the Federal Republic.

*

Directly after the war the American Jewish Committee (AJC) had been the only international Jewish organisation to resume dialogue with Germany, where 20,000 Holocaust survivors had decided to remain.[92] In 1947 a survey conducted by the Frankfurt Institute for Social Research, whose director Max Horkheimer was advising the AJC about conditions in Germany, found that a higher than average proportion of Germans, namely more than 60 per cent, still held racist and anti-Semitic views.[93] The American Jewish Committee devised a re-education scheme, supported by John McCloy, the central element of which was to be a programme for German teachers, journalists, and politicians to visit the United States.[94]

*

McCloy tried to impress upon the Senate appropriations committee that was responsible for setting the US occupation budget why he regarded it as crucial that the Germans, who had lived for so many years in isolation, heard nothing but propaganda and had no opportunity to leave the country, should now come into contact with the rest of the world.[95] Yet US senators' enthusiasm for the exchange programme had its limits.[96] McCloy did not receive the level of funding that would have allowed him to make the scheme a fixture within the occupation authority.[97] Presidential elections were pending in the United States in 1952. Since 1950, the USA had been involved in another war, in Korea, which began on 25 April of that year with an attack by North Korea on its southern neighbour, and developed into a proxy war with the intervention of the USA and China. Senator Robert Taft, one of the Republican Party's two candidates, wanted to take the United States out of NATO. However, the other candidate, the former US supreme commander in the Second World War, Dwight Eisenhower, won out in the primaries and then went on to take the presidency. As president, he expanded the international role of the USA. But there had been a brief moment of uncertainty when signs of waning US interest in Europe had become apparent. These doubts were a major factor behind the idea of a transatlantic bridge that would make German–American relations more robust on both sides of the

Atlantic in the face of a changing political climate: it would be built on the basis of personal contacts, cross-party meetings, exchange programmes, and conferences. The Germans would learn about American politics, and the Americans would be shown the democratic face of the Federal Republic. The instigators of this scheme among Eric Warburg's close circle of friends included not only Christopher Emmet and Marion Dönhoff but also the journalist Ernst Friedlaender and the Christian Democrat politician Erik Blumenfeld. Ernst Friedlaender, who had spent the Nazi period in Lugano and Liechtenstein, where his career as a journalist began, was initially appointed the acting editor-in-chief of *Die Zeit* on his return to Hamburg before becoming a radio commentator. Erik Blumenfeld, the son of a Jewish shipowner and coal importer, survived Auschwitz and Buchenwald and spent the final days of the Third Reich hiding out in Hamburg.

*

Meanwhile, in the USA Eric Warburg's cousin James had become one of the most outspoken critics of a foreign policy that since the Truman Doctrine of 1947 had been exclusively aimed at containment. This would, he contended, enable the Soviet Union to exploit the yearning for a new and better future that was taking hold throughout the world for its own purposes.[98] The creation of a German–American network was also a response to the fact that the American policy of containment alienated many social groups. The visiting programme of the American Council on Germany was aimed at the chief representatives of these groups, including union leaders, journalists, and academics. The idea was to win them round to the more attractive social model that the West was offering as an alternative to Soviet communism. Eric Warburg fundamentally espoused the views of his cousin. Yet while James Warburg linked the vision of a better future with the role of the United Nations, his Hamburg cousin put his money on the transatlantic partnership with the USA.

*

Since 1946 Eric Warburg had been making trips to Germany almost on a yearly basis. On these occasions, his wife remained at home in the USA with their three children – their daughter Erica was born in 1952. They lived on the Woodlands estate in a cottage that Frieda Warburg had made available to them. When their relatives made over the estate to the Greenburgh municipality in the 1950s, they relocated to Norwalk, Connecticut.[99] Since the death of her husband, Eric's mother Alice Warburg had been living in the New York apartment that she had shared with Max during their final years together. The whole family's life was centred around the USA. No one except Eric had gone back to Hamburg since the end of the war. But Eric Warburg wanted to show his children the place where he had spent his own childhood, which loomed large in his memory as a time of unalloyed happiness. In 1954 Dorothea Warburg was finally able to bring herself to accompany her husband to Hamburg with their children. He had more or less refurbished the 'Noah's Ark' to make it suitable for a family to occupy. The Kösterberg park, which in the post-war period had been just a hotchpotch of barracks, were blooming gardens once more. Eric taught his children how to sail on board the *Kong Bele*. The cutter that he had used to leave Germany in 1938 had been mothballed during the war years in a Swedish dry dock. Eric Warburg ensured that his wife only came into contact with those who had proved their loyalty to the antifascist cause during the Nazi period. The family travelled back to the USA at the end of the summer holidays. A compromise appeared to have been reached: occasional family holidays on the Kösterberg, but home would remain the USA. But just two years later Eric Warburg informed his wife that he was going to join Brinckmann, Wirtz & Co. as a partner. And to do this, they would need to move to Hamburg. This decision, which he took on his own, came totally out of the blue to Dorothea. Eric, on the other hand, had had ten years to mull it over and could not be dissuaded. He did not find his regular job in New York fulfilling any longer. For sure, the bank was doing well enough to sustain its employees and his family; as the representative of Brinckmann, Wirtz & Co., it had secured both Volkswagen and Ferrostaal as clients after 1945.[100] Yet the status that M. M. Warburg had in Hamburg could not be matched in New York. There, E. M. Warburg was just one of many similarly sized Wall Street banks. Only in the 1950s, when John Vogelstein and Lionel Pincus joined as partners and transformed the banking house into one of the first private equity firms, did it begin to grow. By that stage, however, Eric Warburg had already mentally made the leap across to Hamburg.

*

The fact that a member of the prominent Warburg dynasty was returning to the land of the perpetrators was greeted with incomprehension by many Jewish organisations. The Jewish community in America explained Warburg's behaviour by concluding that he was more of a German than an American.[101] Yet at first even Dorothea could not understand her husband's desire to live in Germany again. 'Let's not call the place Germany but Central Europe,' her spouse suggested. He was adamant that Jews should be able to live in Central Europe again after the Holocaust.[102] He was firmly convinced that his father, if he had lived longer, would also have tried to make a fresh start in Germany again in his shoes.[103] But if Eric Warburg was now enthused by the idea of taking decisions in the same way his father had done, then this surely also reflected the need he felt to add one further chapter to the family history that since the eighteenth century had been inextricably linked with Hamburg. He, who as a young man could only be persuaded with difficulty to return to Germany at all and fulfil his designated role as a banker after a three-year sojourn in the United States, had ironically found his feet in that role only after being forced to emigrate. His wife and children's day-to-day existence continued to play out in Connecticut, while he now spent most of the year in Hamburg. It was only in 1960 that Dorothea relinquished her place of residence in Connecticut and followed her husband to Germany with their three children.[104] They were joined by Alice Warburg, who died in Hamburg that same year at the age of eighty-seven.

7

Changing Times

In 1982 Eric Warburg published his memoirs in a private printing, intended solely for his children, grandchildren, and friends. One chapter was devoted to the 'evening discussion' he had with John McCloy on that far-off day in Bad Homburg in August 1949. Looking back over a span of thirty-four years, it seemed to Warburg that McCloy had, on his arrival in Germany, started out by representing the views of US Secretary of the Treasury Henry Morgenthau Jr. and had only become an opponent of the dismantling of German industry as a result of that conversation over dinner with him. McCloy, who received a copy of the book from Warburg directly after publication, wrote him a letter emphatically denying this. He claimed that what Eric had said in his memoirs about his attitude to the Morgenthau Plan was 'dead wrong'. He, McCloy, had dismissed it out of hand the minute he and his colleagues in the Department of Defense learnt about the agreements that Churchill and Roosevelt had made at the Second Quebec Conference in September 1944. That could be verified from the memos that Henry Stimson, his boss at the time, had published in his autobiography *On Active Service* in 1948.[1] 'I wrote all the early memos attacking it,' McCloy maintained.[2] 'I have just come across added contemporaneous proof of these facts the other day when I turned up some of my notes on a visit to Churchill's home in Kent in 1947 when he referred to my early attack on the Morgenthau Plan and [Churchill's advisor] Lindemann's rather sordid attempt to gain U.S. Government postwar credits for Germany. Churchill then repudiated it as Roosevelt had before him and he spoke of Lindemann and Morgenthau as "those two Shylocks" who had concocted the whole scheme.' McCloy was angered by Churchill's choice of words on that occasion. 'Was Lindemann a Jew?' he asked Warburg. Because, he said, he had no idea himself. 'I do not think Churchill had any anti-Semitism in his character but he did use the term "Shylocks" when speaking of Lindemann to me.'[3] At this point McCloy made the connection to his own current situation: 'I am sure if I published my contemporaneous note on my visit to Churchill in 1947 now, as things are going, I would be accused of anti-Semitism.'[4] In June 1983, when McCloy wrote this, he was at the centre of a controversy concerning the refusal of the US military in 1944 to accede to the requests of Jewish organisations to bomb the gas chambers at Auschwitz. He had been involved in these events, but in 1983, four decades after they had taken place, a public row erupted over the extent to which he bore responsibility for them.

*

In 1978 the Holocaust researcher David Wyman had been the first to raise the question of why Auschwitz had not been bombed, despite the fact that the US Air Force had carried out raids against the Buna industrial complex run by IG Farben, just 4 miles to the east, on several occasions between July and December 1944. In the *Commentary*, a monthly journal published by the American Jewish Committee,

Wyman had reconstructed, on the basis of documents that had crossed McCloy's desk at the Department of Defense, the wall of deafening silence with which the US government had reacted when news came to it about the extermination of Europe's Jews. In February 1983 the Harvard historian Alan Brinkley responded to the result of Wyman's investigation with a defence of McCloy, who was firmly in the crosshairs of Wyman's criticism: his position within the government apparatus, wrote Brinkley, had not been sufficiently important that he could be held responsible for decisions taken by the administration.[5] Student representatives at Harvard took a different view. When the university announced a scholarship programme funded by the Volkswagen Foundation that was to bear McCloy's name, they demanded that it be renamed.[6] In an interview with McCloy in the *Washington Post* in April 1983, journalist Morton Mintz broached Wyman's question once more. McCloy replied that the matter had been nothing more than a brief episode for him during his time at the Department of Defense, which he had not thought about much over the ensuing decades, until the first articles on the debate surrounding the bombing of Auschwitz began to appear in 1978. McCloy did himself no favours with these offhand remarks. For now it appeared to his academic adversaries to be an open-and-shut case that the bombing of the gas chambers would have been technically feasible but that he, McCloy, had vetoed it. In his letter to Eric Warburg in 1983, McCloy complained that historical fact was being skewed to accord with their latest preconceptions, and deplored the new spirit of the age which all of a sudden had begun to weigh up in terms of morality matters that for him had been simple *realpolitik*. He found himself facing criticism from people who had not even been born when the events in question

215

unfolded, and exclaimed wearily: 'Alas, there are too many around who never knew Moses.'[7] At Harvard, meanwhile, the political scientist Guido Goldman had spoken up in his defence, claiming that a distortion of history was at work here.[8] For not a word had been said in the whole debate about how much support McCloy had given the Jewish Restitution Successor Organization during his time as high commissioner; operating in the American occupation zone, the JRSO had focussed on finding evidence of dispossessed Jewish property and seeking restitution. As the son of Nahum Goldman(n), the founder and long-serving president of the World Jewish Congress, Guido Goldman's objection carried considerable weight.

*

McCloy searched among the old newspaper cuttings that he had assiduously kept for ones that corroborated this support-ive stance. In November 1983 he sent Eric Warburg an article which had appeared in *The New York Times* on 10 August 1949, under the heading 'McCloy Orders Aid to Nazis' Victims', and noted; 'I do not know that I can trace all of the records which would give evidence of the continuity of my efforts to obtain adequate compensation to the victims of the Nazi persecution. But the records are there, as this article indicates, and as Mr. Ferencz [the head of the JRSO at the time in the American occupation zone] has frequently testified.'[9] McCloy gave no more interviews. He turned down requests from the BBC, which wanted to quiz him as an eyewitness to history, and the filmmaker Claude Lanzmann, who asked for an interview with McCloy for his documentary *Shoah* (1985).[10] McCloy felt that the image he wished to see associated with himself was slipping away from him. The only way of wresting back control of the narrative was to publish his own collection of interviews, in which he would tell a group of handpicked interlocutors about his role in US government decisions. In the form of a series of table talks with top-level US diplomats, he envisaged himself taking stock of his career and thereby providing authorised source material for future historians that would be free of the distortions of the current debate. In a chapter entitled 'Restitution and Reparation', Ben Ferencz would take the part of his interlocutor. In the end, however, the volume of interviews was never completed, though McCloy did manage to arrange some of them, including the one with Ferencz. Ferencz strongly urged him to talk on the subject of the bombing of Auschwitz. As high commissioner, Ferencz said, he had done everything properly. But that too had to do with Auschwitz. The topic simply had to be addressed; the readers of his book would expect it. Otherwise people would say he was skipping over this part of his life story and running away from the facts. 'Say that the prime objective was to win the war, and that all other problems could be resolved thereafter.' That was the plain truth of the matter, said Ferencz, but it really needed to be spelt out.[11]

*

Throughout his working life, the security of the USA had been·paramount for McCloy. All of the decisions he took were subordinated to the question of how something might impact the future security of the country. Even as a college student – when President Woodrow Wilson was still steering a neutral course – he had joined the Preparedness Movement and volunteered for officer training at summer camps in 1915 and 1916. It was Theodore Roosevelt in person who had sworn in the volunteers, who pledged to take up arms to defend American values. This experience imbued John McCloy with a view of the world that saw the US military as the guarantor of peace and democracy.[12] The New York businessmen and bankers who financed the Preparedness Movement were clients of the Cravath law firm. Paul Cravath was one of its founders, together with Henry Stimson, McCloy's future boss at the Department of Defense. Before McCloy left the department in 1945, he was involved in shaping the new direction of US security and defence policy. After the attack on Pearl Harbor, the realisation dawned that oceans no longer provided reliable geostrategic protection.[13] Before the new direction in US defence and security policy could take legislative form in the National Security Act of 1947, the Cold War had already begun and President Truman had reconsidered his attitude regarding the necessity of a foreign intelligence service. The newly created Central Intelligence Agency was placed under the direction of the National Security Council.

*

Eric Warburg sent a memo to McCloy for his planned collection of interviews; this was the customary way the two men communicated with one another. He recalled the military assignment of the Allied air forces, which was to destroy German industry both within Germany and in the territories the Germans had occupied. He took the view that there was only a very slim chance that, during a bomb drop, the 'individual buildings where the Holocaust took place' would have been hit with pinpoint accuracy.[14] In one of the interviews that he conducted for his planned book, McCloy had his interlocutor Herbert Okun – at the time US ambassador to the German Democratic Republic – read out excerpts from Eric Warburg's memo, so that it would be recorded in the transcript. At a later point in this same interview, he said: 'We didn't know as much about Auschwitz as we later did.'[15] But in his first essay on the theme of the 'Auschwitz Bombing', which was published in 1978, Wyman had established that McCloy had been briefed both about the camp and the extermination of the Jews, but that he had remained sceptical.[16] In a private discussion he had in December 1944 in his office at the Pentagon with Leon Kubowitzki of the World Jewish Congress, McCloy assured Kubowitzki that no one else was listening in and asked him to give an honest response to the question: 'Do you really believe that all these dreadful things have happened?'[17]

*

Now, almost forty years later he was sitting opposite Herbert Okun in his office at 1 Chase Manhattan Plaza, greatly agitated by a debate in which the subject of Auschwitz suddenly threatened to discredit his entire life's work, although as far as he was concerned Auschwitz had had nothing to do with his remit back then. But because none of those responsible from the government team at the time were still alive, the eighty-eight-year-old McCloy saw that he would have to shoulder the burden of defending himself. Forced into a corner, it was at this critical juncture that his flair for finding the right words deserted him, as he declared that he attached little importance to 'things like Auschwitz and these other things'. At best, he said, they constituted 'little footnotes to history'.[18] At that moment he seemed not to realise that he had just said something utterly monstrous. By making confessions like this, he confirmed all the reservations of his current critics and adversaries, who saw him as the embodiment of the dark side of *realpolitik*. In their view, if it was lacking in any morality, the primacy of security that he so extolled was just what one would find in a fascist dictatorship. McCloy's response was that he didn't know what he had to apologise for.[19] He wanted to go down in history as a 'positive fellow', and as someone whose constructive contribution had helped further the global security of the USA. The reconstruction of West Germany had, he maintained, been one such contribution. Indeed, he had only taken on the post of high commissioner in 1949 in the first place in order to ensure that the *vae victis* attitude of the Morgenthau Plan did not prevail when the occupation statute was drafted – this was how he explained the situation to Maurice Matloff, who as chief historian of the US Army was one of the selected interlocutors for his book project.[20] McCloy felt unfairly criticised, but with his self-righteous way of defending himself suddenly came across as totally divorced from his age. This was no longer the man whom Eric Warburg and Ben Ferencz had credited with a great capacity to learn, who as high commissioner had behaved decently after 1945, and whose personal achievement had in their opinion been to elevate the interests of the Jewish victims of the Holocaust into a key element of his post-war security structure.[21]

*

For some of Eric Warburg's American relatives, his return to Germany was a journey back into a past that no longer existed.[22] Since 1960 he had been living in Hamburg with his wife and family. In 1969, the renewed significant involvement of the family was once more recognised in the name of the bank, which now traded under the name of M. M. Warburg, Brinckmann & Wirtz. It would finally revert to its original name in 1990.[23]

But even now, in 1982, in the figure of his son Max, the sixth generation of Warburgs took over the running of the bank. Dorothea Warburg had come to terms with her life in Germany. She and her husband were still living at the 'Noah's Ark' on the Kösterberg. Their grown-up daughters Marie and Erica had long since flown the nest. The two other family villas continued to be rented out to the Red Cross. Wolfgang Rittmeister, Eric's friend from his schooldays, had moved into the apartment above the garage. He lived there with his wife, surrounded by bookshelves laden down with books from the GDR on the communist resistance to the Nazis. For Wolfgang Rittmeister was researching the life of his brother John, who had been executed in Plötzensee Prison because of his membership of the *Rote Kapelle* (Red Orchestra) resistance movement. In 1980, Ingrid Warburg-Spinelli, Fritz Warburg's eldest daughter, had paid a visit to her cousin Eric for the first time. She was surprised by the make-up of the residential community on the Kösterberg.[24]

Nothing about Eric Warburg's life was backward-looking. Granted, he set great store by the family's history and was passionate about upholding traditions. And he liked to show visitors to the banking house on Ferdinandstraße the old historic photographs of previous generations of Warburgs that hung on his office walls. But politically and socially he still continued, in the ninth decade of his life, to be primarily interested in the future, for which a new course now had to be set in the American Council on Germany and the *Atlantik-Brücke*. For after the disaster of the Vietnam War, a security policy understood in purely military terms was no longer acceptable to sections of the American public. The same development was evident in West Germany, where relations with the United States had soured. It was the beginning of the Reagan era. After a policy of rapprochement had set in in Germany over the previous decade, people now felt that the current US leadership was not in a position to sustain a constructive East–West dialogue. As he did almost every day, Eric Warburg prepared a memo on which he noted the most important points he wanted to talk about at his next meeting with McCloy. Dialogue had continued unbroken between the two men for over thirty years: they agreed that the North–South conflict had to be seen as a global political challenge and not just a subdivision of the conflict between East and West. For young people in Germany had begun to perceive NATO and the European Union as merely a military alliance. The USA would therefore need to signal that it too was interested in contributing to improved East–West relations. It would have to start showing a greater interest in Europe and Germany again. As he jotted down this note to himself, Eric Warburg added a bold exclamation mark.[25]

Epilogue

Historical images show the Warburg Library at different times in diverse locations and occupying a variety of buildings. In Hamburg, it was initially housed in the home of the academic Aby Warburg and then, from 1926 onwards, immediately next door in a purpose-built library building. After its transfer to London, for the first three years it found a home at Thames House, which at the time was a newly built office complex on the Embankment, boasting a neoclassical facade with many features reminiscent of the British Empire. In 1938 it moved into the Imperial Institute Building, a Victorian edifice which originally served as an exhibition space to showcase the global aspirations of the British Commonwealth and which had latterly been used by the University of London as an administrative block. And after a further twenty years it took up residence again in new quarters, as the Warburg Institute finally came to occupy its own dedicated building on Woburn Square in Bloomsbury. The library's frequent change of location appears like some object lesson from the interpretative method that Aby Warburg introduced into art history, involving the study of pictorial elements from antiquity that then resurface in a series of ever-changing visual motifs as they migrate, so to speak, across the ages and through different countries. In this way, while taking into consideration all non-pictorial sources, the historical dimension of a work of art is explored. A photographic portrait of Eric Warburg hangs in the lobby of the Warburg Archive on the fourth floor of the present-day Warburg Institute on Woburn Square. His clear gaze falls on the observer, to whom he presents himself as a thirty-eight-year-old in the prime of his life – the dedication beneath the picture gives its date as September 1938 – standing against a neutral background with his arms crossed self-confidently as a kindred spirit among kindred spirits. In the family council, his was the voice of the one-vote majority that from the outset had always spoken in favour of the London solution for the library. At the time when he had the photo of himself taken, a long period of uncertainty for the employees of the library had just come to an end. Eric Warburg dedicated the portrait to them on the occasion of their taking occupancy of the Imperial Institute Building in West Kensington – as a symbol of his firm commitment to the institution. As for Eric himself, this marked the beginning of the period he spent as an émigré.

*

In Eric Warburg's German–Jewish odyssey, the struggle of the 'good European' to uphold the values of the Enlightenment – a subject that Aby Warburg had examined closely in historical terms in the symbolic forms and pictorial motifs of art – continued to resonate. Except that Eric Warburg, who was a banker and not a humanities scholar, fought with the weapons of a robust democrat and – at least sometimes – took a stand on the side of the cold warriors. Because he had the knack of taking something positive from even the most difficult situations, he managed to turn the bad hand that fate dealt him into the driving force behind a development that made him into a staunch champion of Germany's integration into the Western alliance. In around 1990, 'politics' as the subject of scholarly art-historical interest, in the form of the Political Iconography Research Unit, found a home in the building in Heilwigstraße in Hamburg that Eric had saved from demolition in 1938. The building had survived the war unscathed and over decades had seen a variety of owners and uses, until the city of Hamburg finally acquired it in 1993 and restored it to its original condition. Around the same time Thames House, where the library had been housed for the first three years after its transfer, became the property of the British government. It set up the headquarters of the domestic security service MI5, the agency whose brief memorandum in November 1933 had ensured a future in London for the KBW and its employees. It is intriguing to speculate what Eric Warburg would have thought of this.

Bibliography

Aby M. Warburg zum Gedächtnis. Worte zur Beisetzung von Professor Dr. Aby M Warburg. Privatdruck. O. O., o. J. 1929.

Amenda, Lars: '"Welthafenstadt" und "Tor zur Welt": Selbstdarstellung und Wahrnehmung der Hafenstadt Hamburg 1900–1970', in: *Deutsches Schiffahrtsarchiv*, Vol. 29 (2006), pp. 137–58.

Anderl, Gabriele: 'Emigration und Vertreibung', in: Weinzierl, Erika/ Kulka, Otto D. (eds.): *Vertreibung und Neubeginn. Israelische Bürger österreichischer Herkunft.* Bohlau, Vienna/Cologne/Weimar 1992, pp. 167–337.

Andrews, Henry M. (Victor Gollancz): 'To the Editor of *The Times*', in: *The Times* (19.12.1949).

Anzenberger, Robert J.: *The Eagle and the Bear: US–Finnish Relations from 1917–1946.* Thesis. Master of Arts. Texas State University. December 2020.

Arnold, Thurman: 'Due Process in Trials', in: *The Annals of the American Academy of Political and Social Science*, Vol. 300, No.1, Internal Security and Civil Rights (July 1955), pp. 123–30.

Asmussen, Nils: 'Hans-Georg von Studnitz. Ein konservativer Journalist im Dritten Reich und in der Bundesrepublik', in: *Vierteljahrshefte für Zeitgeschichte*, 45. Jhg. (1997), H.1, pp. 75–119.

Baldwin, Nicholas: 'Notiz', in: *Vierteljahrshefte für Zeitgeschichte*, 36. Jhg. (1988), H.4, pp. 793–5.

Bauer, Friedrich L.: *Entzifferte Geheimnisse. Methoden und Maximen der Kryptologie.* Springer, Munich 2000.

Beck, Jürgen (ed.): *Die Schlachten des Winterkrieges in Finnland.* 2 vols. Jazzybee Verlag, Altenmünster 2019.

Becker, William H./McClenahan Jr., William M.: *The Market, the State and the Export-Import-Bank of the United States, 1934–2000.* Cambridge University Press, Cambridge 2003.

Bednarz, Dieter: 'Der große Basar', in: *Spiegel Special* 2/2005, pp. 135–7.

Beevor, Antony: *Ardennes 1944: Hitler's Last Gamble.* Viking, London 2015.

Bell, Falko: *Britische Feindaufklärung im Zweiten Weltkrieg. Stellenwert und Wirkung der 'Human Intelligence' in der britischen Kriegführung 1939–1945.* Schöningh, Paderborn 2016.

Bender, Cora/Hensel, Thomas/Schüttpelz, Erhard (eds.): *Schlangenritual. Der Transfer der Wissensformen vom Tsu'ti'kive der Hopi bis zu Aby Warburgs Kreuzlinger Vortrag.* Akademie Verlag, Berlin 2007.

Benz, Wolfgang/Paucker, Arnold/Pulzer, Peter (eds.): *Jüdisches Leben in der Weimarer Republik / Jews in the Weimar Republic.* Mohr Siebeck, Tübingen 1998.

Benz, Wolfgang: 'Wirtschaftsentwicklung von 1945 bis 1949', in: *Informationen zur politischen Bildung.* Heft 259. Bundeszentrale für politische Bildung. 13.7.2005.

Berger, Deidre: *AJC and Germany. History in the Making 1945–2020.* AJC, Berlin 2020.

Berghahn, Volker R.: 'John J. McCloy, Shepard Stone und die deutsch–amerikanischen Beziehungen während des Kalten Krieges', in: Lorenz: *Transatlantik*, pp. 167–78.

Binswanger, Ludwig/Warburg, Aby: *Die unendliche Heilung. Aby Warburgs Krankengeschichte.* ed. by Chantal Marazia and Davide Stimilli. Diaphanes, Zurich/Berlin 2007.

Bird, Kai: 'Deutschlands Prokonsul 1949. McCloy und die entstehende Bundesrepublik', in: Lorenz: *Transatlantik*, pp. 123–55.

Bird, Kai: *The Chairman. John J. McCloy & the Making of the American Establishment.* Simon & Schuster, New York 1992.

Birmingham, Stephen: *In unseren Kreisen. Die großen jüdischen Familien New Yorks.* Ullstein, Berlin/Frankfurt am Main 1969.

Birmingham, Stephen: The Jews in America Trilogy: *Our Crowd, The Grandees*, and *The Rest of Us*. Open Road Media, New York 2016.

Bohme, Hartmut: 'Aby M. Warburg (1866–1929)', in: Michaels: *Klassiker der Religionswissenschaft*, pp. 133–56.

The Bomber's Baedeker. Guide to the Economic Importance of German Towns and Cities. Enemy Branch, London 1944 (First edition 1943).

Bommarius, Christian: *1949. Das lange deutsche Jahr*. Droemer, Munich 2018.

Boveri, Margret: *Der Diplomat vor Gericht*. Minerva, Berlin/Hanover 1948.

Bredekamp, Horst: *Aby Warburg, der Indianer. Berliner Erkundungen einer liberalen Ethnologie*. Wagenbach, Berlin 2019.

Bredekamp, Horst/Buschendorf, Bernhard/Hartung, Freia/Krois, John Michael (eds.): *Edgar Wind. Kunsthistoriker und Philosoph*. Akademie Verlag, Berlin 1998.

Bredekamp, Horst: 'Falsche Skischwünge. Winds Kritik an Heidegger und Sartre', in: Ibid.: *Edgar Wind*, pp. 207–26.

Bredekamp, Horst: *Aby Warburg and America – The Art Historian as Ethnographer*. Bard Graduate Center, New York 2023.

Breidecker, Volker: 'Einige Fragmente einer intellektuellen Kollektivbiographie der kulturwissenschaftlichen Emigration', in: Reudenbach: *Erwin Panofsky*, pp. 83–108.

Breitfeld, Oliver (ed.): *Albert Renger-Patzsch. Parklandschaften. 60 Fotos für die Warburgs*. Conference Point Verlag, Hamburg 2005.

Breunung, Leonie/Walther, Manfred: *Die Emigration deutschsprachiger Rechtswissenschaftler ab 1933. Ein bio-bibliographisches Handbuch*. De Gruyter, Berlin/Boston, MA 2012.

Burger, Reiner: *Theodor Heuss als Journalist. Beobachter und Interpret von vier Epochen deutscher Geschichte*. LIT, Münster 1999.

Buscher, Frank M.: 'Bestrafen und erziehen. "Nürnberg" und das Kriegsverbrecherprogramm der USA', in: Frei: *Transnationale Vergangenheitspolitik*, pp. 94–139.

Cara (Council for Assisting Refugee Academics): *Defending Academic Freedom since 1933. 80th Anniversary*. London 2013.

Chernow, Ron: *The Warburgs: The Twentieth-Century Odyssey of A Remarkable Jewish Family*. Vintage, New York 2016.

Condon, Richard W.: *The Winter War: Russia against Finland*. Ballantine Books, London 1972.

Conze, Eckart: 'Aufstand des preußischen Adels. Marion Gräfin Dönhoff und das Bild des Widerstands gegen den Nationalsozialismus in der Bundesrepublik Deutschland', in: *Vierteljahrshefte für Zeitgeschichte*, 51. Jhg. (2003), H.4, pp. 483–508.

Conze, Eckart/Frei, Norbert/Hayes, Peter/Zimmermann, Moshe: *Das Amt und die Vergangenheit. Deutsche Diplomaten im Dritten Reich und in der Bundesrepublik*. Blessing, Munich 2010.

Conze, Eckart: '"Es wurde ganz wacker Widerstand geleistet." Geschichtsbilder und Personalpolitik im Auswärtigen Amt nach 1945', in: Schulte: *Widerstand und Auswärtiges Amt*, pp. 271–85.

Conze, Eckart: 'Kein Hort des Widerstands. Das Auswärtige Amt im Zweiten Weltkrieg', in: Mehlhorn: *Gewissheit im Widerstand*, pp. 87–106.

Czempiel, Ernst-Otto: *Das amerikanische Sicherheitssystem, 1945–1949. Studie zur Außenpolitik der bürgerlichen Gesellschaft*. De Gruyter, Berlin 1966.

Die Kabinettsprotokolle der Bundesregierung online: Das Alliierte Sicherheits- und Kontrollsystem.

Dietrich, John: *The Morgenthau Plan: Soviet Influence on American Postwar Policy*. Algora Publishing, New York 2002.

Diner, Dan: 'Im Zeichen des Banns', in: *Die Welt*, 15.9.2012.

'Direktive an den Oberbefehlshaber der US-Besatzungstruppen in Deutschland (JCS 1067) (April 1945)', in: *Deutsche Geschichte in Dokumenten und Bildern*. Vol. 8: *Die Besatzungszeit und die Entstehung zweier Staaten* (1945–1961). https://germanhistorydocs. ghi-dc.org/sub_document.cfm?document_id=2297.

Dönhoff, Marion Grafin: 'De Nobilitate', in: Reventlow: *Albrecht Bernstorff*, pp. 48–52.

Dönhoff, Marion Grafin: 'Leben heißt, sich verpflichtet wissen. Zum 80. Geburtstag von Eric Warburg', in: *Die Zeit*, No.16, 11.4.1980.

Dönhoff, Marion Gräfin: 'Ohne Rachegefühle die Geschichte erlebt und mitgestaltet', in: Kulturforum Warburg: *Warburg*, pp. 123–7.

Doerries, Reinhard R.: 'Individualist und Diplomat. Albrecht Graf von Bernstorff', in: Schulte: *Widerstand und Auswärtiges Amt*, pp. 35–49.

Doerries, Reinhard R.: 'Transatlantic Intelligence in Krieg und Frieden: Die Rolle von Nachrichtendiensten in den deutsch–amerikanischen Beziehungen', in: Berg, Manfred/Gassert, Philipp (eds.): *Deutschland und die USA in der Internationalen Geschichte des 20. Jahrhunderts. Festschrift für Detlef Junker*. Franz Steiner Verlag, Stuttgart 2004, pp. 279–302.

Döscher, Hans-Jürgen: *Seilschaften. Die verdrängte Vergangenheit des Auswärtigen Amts*. Propylaen, Berlin 2005.

Dünzelmann, Anne E. *... keine normale Reise. Eva Warburg und die Kinder/Jugendalijah in Schweden*. Books on Demand, Norderstedt 2017.

Dulles, Allen Welsh: *Germany's Underground*. Da Capo Press, Boston 2000 (1947).

Duve, Thomas: '"Idee Europa" bei Albrecht Mendelssohn Bartholdy und in der ersten Nachkriegszeit', in: Repgen, Tilman (ed.): *Europa als Idee*. Nomos, Baden-Baden 2016, pp. 13–34.

Eisermann, Daniel: *Außenpolitik und Strategiediskussion. Die Deutsche Gesellschaft für Auswärtige Politik 1955 bis 1972*. De Gruyter Oldenbourg, Berlin 1999.

Embden, Heinrich: 'Anamnese. Warburg', in: Binswanger: *Heilung*, pp. 260–2.

Ferguson, Niall: *Paper and Iron: Hamburg Business and German Politics in the Era of Inflation 1897–1927*. Cambridge University Press, New York 1995.

Foerster, E./Commentz, C./Dahlmann, W./Kielhorn, C./Schwarz, T. (eds.): *Praktischer Stahlschiffbau. Ein Hilfsbuch für Werft, Reederei und Lehrstätte*. Springer, Berlin 1930.

Foreign Crops and Markets. United States Department of Agriculture. Office of Foreign Agricultural Relations. United States Foreign

Trade in Agricultural Products. Wartime Exports to the United Kingdom. July–January 1940–1941. Washington DC.

Foreign Relations of the United States. Diplomatic Papers, 1940, Volume I. General. Department of State. Historical Division, Bureau of Public Affairs, 1959.

Foreign Relations of the United States. Diplomatic Papers, 1941, General, The Soviet Union, Vol.1. Relations between Finland and the Soviet Union, and the attempts of the United States to persuade Finland not to participate in the war against the Soviet Union in association with Germany (Documents 1–115).

Franke, Holger: *Leonard Nelson: Ein biographischer Beitrag unter besonderer Berücksichtigung seiner rechts- und staatsphilosophischen Arbeiten.* Verlag an der Lottbek, Ammersbek bei Hamburg 1991.

Franz, Manuel: *'Fight for Americanism' – Preparedness-Bewegung und zivile Mobilisierung in den USA 1914–1920.* Transcript, Bielefeld 2021 (PDF 2020).

Fraschka, Mark A.: *Franz Pfeffer von Salomon. Hitlers vergessener Oberster SA-Führer.* Wallstein, Göttingen 2016.

Frei, Norbert (ed.): *Transnationale Vergangenheitspolitik. Der Umgang mit deutschen Kriegsverbrechern in Europa nach dem Zweiten Weltkrieg.* Wallstein, Göttingen 2006.

Frei, Norbert: *Vergangenheitspolitik. Die Anfänge der Bundesrepublik und die NS-Vergangenheit.* dtv, Munich 1999.

Frey, Marc: 'Deutsche Finanzinteressen an den Vereinigten Staaten und den Niederlanden im Ersten Weltkrieg', in: *Militärgeschichtliche Mitteilungen,* Vol. 53 (1994), H.2, pp. 327–53.

Fry, Helen: *The Walls Have Ears: The Greatest Intelligence Operation of World War II.* Yale University Press, New Haven, CT/London 2019.

Gantzel, Klaus Jürgen (ed.): *Kolonialrechtswissenschaft. Kriegsursachenforschung. Lntemationale Angelegenheiten.* Nomos, Baden-Baden 1983.

Gantzel-Kress, Gisela: 'Zur Geschichte des Instituts für Auswärtige Politik: von der Gründung bis zur nationalsozialistischen

Machtübernahme', in: Gantzel: *Kolonialrechtswissenschaft*, pp. 23–88.

Gatzke, Hans W.: *Germany and the United States: A 'Special Relationship'?* Harvard University Press, Cambridge, MA/London 1980.

Geiss, Imanuel: 'Die manipulierte Kriegsschuldfrage', in: *Militärgeschichtliche Zeitschrift*, Vol. 34 (1983), H. 2, pp. 31–60.

Geyelin, Philip: 'John McCloy's Good Name', in: *The Washington Post* (29.6.1983).

Gimbel, John: 'U.S. Policy and German Scientists: The early Cold War', in: *Political Science Quarterly*, Vol. 101, No.3 (1983), pp. 433–51.

Goldenstedt, Christiane: *'Du hast mich heimgesucht bei Nacht' – Die Familie Kuhn im Exil*. Books on Demand, Norderstedt 2013.

Goodman, David: *Radio's Civic Ambition: American Broadcasting and Democracy in the 1930s*. Oxford University Press, Oxford 2011.

Goschler, Constanti/Böick, Marcus/Reus, Julia (eds.): *Kriegsverbrechen, Restitution, Prävention. Aus dem Vorlass von Benjamin B. Ferencz*. Vandenhoeck & Ruprecht, Göttingen 2019.

Gosztony, Peter: *Die Rote Armee. Machtfaktor der Weltpolitik*. Goldmann, Munich 1983.

Greiner, Bernd: *Die Morgenthau-Legende. Zur Geschichte eines umstrittenen Plans*. Hamburger Edition, Hamburg 1995.

Grindrod, Muriel K.: 'The Institut für Auswärtige Politik, Poststrasse 19, Hamburg', in: *International Affairs* (Royal Institute of International Affairs 1931–1939), Vol. 10, No. 2 (March 1931), pp. 223–9.

Hacke, Jens: *Existenzkrise der Demokratie. Zur politischen Theorie des Liberalismus in der Zwischenkriegszeit*. Suhrkamp, Berlin 2018.

Haltet das Tor offen! [Kurt Sieveking], Trautmann, Hamburg 1931.

Hansen, Knut: *Albrecht Graf von Bemstorff. Diplomat und Bankier zwischen Kaiserreich und Nationalsozialismus*. Peter Lang, Frankfurt am Main 1996.

Hauser, Dorothea: 'Banking on Emigration: Reconsidering the Warburg Bank's Late Surrender, Schacht's Protective Hand,

and Other Myths about Jewish Banks in the "Third Reich"', in: Kreutzmüller: *Dispossession*, pp. 148–65.

Hauser, Dorothea/Kreutzmüller, Christoph: 'Max Warburg. 1867–1946', in: Pohl: *Deutsche Bankiers*, pp. 419–32.

Hauser, Dorothea: 'Zwischen Gehen und Bleiben. Das Sekretariat Warburg und sein Netzwerk des Vertrauens 1938–1941', in: Heim: *Wer bleibt*, pp. 115–33.

Hearings before the Committee on Appropriations, United States Senate. Eighty-First Congress. Second Session. Making Appropriations for Foreign Aid for the Fiscal Year Ending June 30, 1951, and for Other Purposes. U.S. Government Printing Office, Washington, DC 1950.

Heideking, Jurgen: 'Politisches Kalkül und Menschlichkeit: Allen W. Dulles, Gero von Schulze-Gaevernitz und der deutsche Widerstand nach dem 20. Juni 1944', in: Wala: *Gesellschaft und Diplomatie*, pp. 235–54.

Heim, Susanne/Meyer, Beate/Nicosia, Francis R. (eds.): *'Wer bleibt, opfert seine Jahre, vielleicht sein Leben'. Deutsche Juden 1938–1941.* Wallstein, Göttingen 2010.

Heinrich Kronstein's Documents and Publications. Preface to Report on Conditions in Germany, ca. 1945. International Law Institute. Nr.22.

Heise, Carl Georg: *Persönliche Erinnerungen an Aby Warburg*. Edited and with a commentary by Björn Biester and Hans-Michael Schäfer. Harrassowitz, Wiesbaden 2005.

Henke, Klaus-Dietmar: *Die amerikanische Besetzung Deutschlands*. De Gruyter Oldenbourg, Berlin 1995.

Herrmann, Manfred: 'Project Paperclip: Die Anwerbung deutscher Wissenschaftler nach dem Zweiten Weltkrieg als Waffe im Kalten Krieg?', in: Wala: *Gesellschaft und Diplomatie*, pp. 255–72.

Hersh, Burton: *The Old Boys: The American Elite and the Origins of the CIA*. Scribner's, New York 1992.

Herwig, Helger H.: 'Clio Deceived. Patriotic Self-Censorship in Germany after the Great War', in: *International Security*, Vol. 12 (1987), No. 2, pp. 5–44.

Historical Note from Herbert Hoover. Register of the Finnish Relief Fund records. Hoover Institution Library and Archives. Online Archive.

Hockerts, Hans Günter/Kuller, Christiane (eds.): *Nach der Verfolgung: Wiedergutmachung nationalsozialistischen Unrechts in Deutschland?* Wallstein, Göttingen 2003.

Hofmann, Gunter: *Marion Dönhoff. Die Gräfin, ihre Freunde und das andere Deutschland.* C. H. Beck, Munich 2019.

Hoover, Jennifer A.: *Secrets in Switzerland: Allen W. Dulles' impact as OSS station chief in Bern on developments of World War II & U.S. dominance in post-war Europe.* Undergraduate Honors Thesis. Williamsburg, VA 2009.

Horn, Karen: 'Von Versailles über Lausanne ins Verhängnis: Im Schicksal des jüdischen Juristen Carl Melchior spiegelt sich das deutsche Drama des 20. Jahrhunderts', in: *Neue Zürcher Zeitung* (22.6.2019).

Huizinga, Johan: *Briefe II (1928–1945).* Wilhelm Fink, Paderborn 2017.

Hunt, M.: 'La rafle des savants allemands ou l'operation "Lusty"', in: *Revue Militaire Suisse*, Vol. 98 (1993), H.8, pp. 396–407.

Huwart, Olivier: *Du V2 à Véronique. La naissance des fusées françaises.* Marines éditions, Rennes 2004.

'Im Gespräch: Richard von Weizsäcker. Es geht hier nicht um meinen Vater', in: *Frankfurter Allgemeine Zeitung* (25.10.2010).

Jacobsen, Annie: *Operation Paperclip: The Secret Intelligence Program That Brought Nazi Scientists To America.* Little, Brown & Co., New York 2015.

Jähnicke, Burkhard: *Washington und Berlin zwischen den Kriegen. Die Mixed Claims Commission in den transatlantischen Beziehungen.* Nomos, Baden-Baden 2003.

Jenss, Harro et al. (eds.): *Israelitisches Krankenhaus in Hamburg – 175 Jahre.* Hentrich und Hentrich Verlag, Berlin 2016.

Jewish Telegraphic Agency (JTA): '$3,000,000 Left to Charity by Mrs. Warburg; Last Will Made Public', in: *Daily News Bulletin* (New York), Vol. XXV, No.181 (September 23, 1958), p. 3.

Jünger, David: *Jahre der Ungewissheit. Emigrationspläne deutscher Juden 1933–1938*. Vandenhoeck & Ruprecht, Göttingen/Bristol, CT 2016.

Kaplan, Marion/Meyer, Beate (eds.): *Jüdische Welten: Juden in Deutschland vom 18. Jahrhundert bis in die Gegenwart*. Wallstein, Göttingen 2005.

Karras, Steven (ed.): *The Enemy I Knew: German Jews in the Allied Military in World War II*. Zenith Press, Minneapolis 2009.

Kellerhoff, Sven Felix: '1922 ruinierten US-Zölle die Weltwirtschaft', in: *Die Welt* (4.1.2021).

Keynes, John Maynard: Two Memoirs: *Dr Melchior: A Defeated Enemy* and *My Early Beliefs*. Hart-Davis, New York 1949.

Kieffer, Fritz: *Judenverfolgung in Deutschland – eine innere Angelegenheit? Internationale Reaktionen auf die Flüchtlingsproblematik 1933–1939*. Franz Steiner Verlag, Stuttgart 2002.

Kilton, Thomas D./Birkhead, Ceres (eds.): *Migrations in Society, Culture and the Library. WESS European Conference, Paris, France, 22–26 March 2004*. American Library Association, Chicago 2005.

Kimminich, Otto: 'Die Entwicklung des internationalen Flüchtlingsrechts – faktischer und rechtsdogmatischer Rahmen', in: *Archiv des Völkerrechts*, Vol. 20, No. 4 (1982), pp. 369–410.

Kinzer, Stephen: *The Brothers: John Foster Dulles, Allen Dulles, and their Secret World War*. Times Books, New York 2013.

Kleßmann, Eckart: *M. M. Warburg & Co. 1798–1998*. Dölling und Galitz, Hamburg 1999.

Klingler, Erika: 'The Warburg Institute: 1933–1936', in: Kokorz: Übergänge, pp. 263–80.

Knoll, Michael: 'Schulreform durch "Erlebnispädagogik". Kurt Hahn – ein wirkungsmächtiger Pädagoge', in: *Pädagogisches Handeln. Wissenschaft und Praxis im Dialog*, Vol. 5 (2001), H. 2, pp. 65–76.

Knoll, Michael (ed.): Kurt Hahn. *Reform mit Augenmaß. Ausgewählte Schriften eines Politikers und Pädagogen*. Klett-Cotta, Stuttgart 1998.

Koebner, Thomas/Sautermeister, Gert/Schneider, Sigrid (eds.):

Deutschland nach Hitler. Zukunftspläne im Exil und aus der Besatzungszeit 1939–1949. Westdeutscher Verlag, Opladen 1987.

Koebner, Thomas: Die Schuldfrage.Vergangenheitsverweigerung und Lebenslügen in der Diskussion 1945–1949', in: Koebner: *Deutschland nach Hitler*, pp. 301–29.

Köhler, Ingo: *Die 'Arisierung' der Privatbanken im Dritten Reich. Verdrängung, Ausschaltung und die Frage der Wiedergutmachung.* C. H. Beck, Munich 2005.

Kokorz, Gregor/Mitterbauer, Helga (eds.): Übergänge und Verflechtungen. Kulturelle Transfers in Europa. Peter Lang, Bern 2004.

Kopper, Christopher: 'Wirtschaftliche Selbstbehauptung im sozialen Ghetto. Jüdische Wirtschaftsbürger im "Dritten Reich"', in: Ziegler: *Großbürger und Unternehmer*, pp. 204–14.

Kramer, Alan: *Die britische Demontagepolitik am Beispiel Hamburgs 1945–1950.* Verein für Hamburgische Geschichte, Hamburg 1991.

Krammer, Arnold: *Die internierten Deutschen. 'Feindliche Ausländer' in den USA 1941–1947.* Universitas Verlag, Tübingen 1998.

Krapf, Isolde: 'Bad Kissingen. Geheimakte "Paperclip"', in: *Mainpost* (19.9.2011).

Kreis, John F. (ed.): *Piercing the Fog: Intelligence and Army Air Forces Operations in World War II.* Bolling AFB, Washington, DC 1996.

Kreutzmüller, Christoph/Zatlin, Jonathan R. (eds.): *Dispossession: Plundering German Jewry, 1933–1953.* The University of Michigan Press, Ann Arbor MI 2020.

Krohn, Helga: *Die Juden in Hamburg. Die politische, soziale und kulturelle Entwicklung einer jüdischen Großstadtgemeinde nach der Emanzipation 1848–1918.* Hans Christians Verlag, Hamburg 1974.

Krumm, Christian: *Johan Huizinga, Deutschland und die Deutschen. Begegnung und Auseinandersetzung mit dem Nachbarn.* Waxmann Verlag, Münster 2011.

Krusenstjern, Benigna von: 'Der Widerstandskämpfer. Adam von Trott zu Solz und das Auswärtige Amt', in: Schulte: *Widerstand und Auswärtiges Amt*, pp. 169–78.

Kulturforum Warburg (ed.): *Warburg und die Warburgs*. Hermann
Hermes Verlag, Warburg 1988.

*Kulturwissenschaftliche Bibliographie zum Nachleben der Antike. Erster
Band. Die Erscheinungen des Jahres 1931*. In Gemeinschaft mit
Fachgenossen bearbeitet von Hans Meier, Richard Newald, Edgar
Wind. Teubner, Leipzig/Berlin 1934.

Kuratorisches Statement des Hauses der Kulturen der Welt (HKW)
zu 'A Kind of World War'. *Ein Filmessay von Anselm Franke und
Erhard Schüttpelz*. Bilderatlas Mnemosyne.

Kurowski, Franz: *Alliierte Jagd auf deutsche Wissenschaftler. Das
Unternehmen Paperclip*. Kristall bei Langen Müller, Munich 1982.

Lackmann, Thomas: *Albrecht Mendelssohn Bartholdy. Völkerrechtler
und Pionier der deutschen Friedensforschung*. Hentrich und
Hentrich Verlag, Berlin 2015.

Lebensgeschichtliches Interview mit Benjamin Ferencz, 2.12.2013,
in: *Quellen zur Geschichte der Menschenrechte*, herausgegeben vom
Arbeitskreis Quellen zur Geschichte der Menschenrechte, https://
www.geschichte-menschenrechte.de/personen/benjamin-ferencz.

Lehmann, Axel: *Der Marshall-Plan und das neue Deutschland.
Die Folgen amerikanischer Besatzungspolitik in den Westzonen*.
Waxmann Verlag, Münster 2000.

Lembke, Ulrike/Valentiner, Dana-Sophia: 'Magdalene Schoch –
die erste habilitierte Juristin in Deutschland', in: *Hamburger
Rechtsnotizen* (Zeitschrift der Fakultät für Rechtswissenschaft der
Universität Hamburg) (2012), H.2, pp. 93–100.

Leonhard, Jörn: 'Erwartung und Überforderung. Die Pariser
Friedenskonferenz 1919', in: *Aus Politik und Zeitgeschichte*
(Bundeszentrale für politische Bildung), 69. Jhg. (8.4.2019),
No.15,pp. 4–11.

Lepsius, M. Rainer: 'Johannes Lepsius und Kurt Hahn', in: www.
lepsiushaus-potsdam.de.

Lewallen, Robert D.: *The Winter War: The United States and the
Impotence of Power*. Alyssiym Publications/Lulu.com 2010.

Liedtke, Rainer: 'Zur mäzenatischen Praxis und zum kulturellen
Selbstverständnis der jüdischen Wirtschaftselite in Deutschland:

Die Hamburger Warburgs im ersten Drittel des 20. Jahrhunderts',
in: Ziegler: *Großbürger und Unternehmer*, pp. 187–203.

Lillteicher, Jürgen: 'Die Rückerstattung in Westdeutschland. Ein
Kapitel deutscher Vergangenheitspolitik?', in: Hockerts: *Nach der
Verfolgung*, pp. 61–77.

Lingen, Kerstin von: 'Immunitätsversprechen. Wie
SS-Obergruppenführer Karl Wolff der Strafverfolgung entging', in:
Militärgeschichtliche Zeitschrift, Vol. 68 (2009), H. 2, pp. 379–421.

Lorenz, Ina/Berkemann, Jörg: *Die Hamburger Juden im NS-Staat 1933
bis 1938/39*. 7 vols. Wallstein, Göttingen 2016.

Lorenz, Ina: 'Ein Heim für jüdische Waisen. AJDC Warburg
Children Health Home Blankenese (1946–1948)', in: Kaplan:
Jüdische Welten, pp. 336–58.

Lorenz, Sebastian/Machill, Marcel (eds.): *Transatlantik. Transfer von
Politik, Wirtschaft und Kultur*. Westdeutscher Verlag, Wiesbaden
1999.

Lubenow, William C.: *Learned Lives in England, 1900–1950:
Institutions, Ideas and Intellectual Experience*. Boydell Press,
Woodbridge 2020.

Ludicke, Lars: 'Offizier und Diplomat. Ernst von Weizsäcker in
Kaiserreich, Weimarer Republik und "Drittem Reich"', in:
Schulte: *Widerstand und Auswärtiges Amt*, pp. 225–49.

Lutz, Hermann: 'Fälschungen zur Auslandsfinanzierung Hitlers', in:
Vierteljahrshefte für Zeitgeschichte, 2. Jhg. (1954), H. 4, pp. 386–96.

Machtan, Lothar: *Prinz Max von Baden. Der letzte Kanzler des Kaisers.
Eine Biographie*. Suhrkamp Verlag, Berlin 2013.

Malinowski, Stephan: *Vom König zum Führer. Sozialer Niedergang und
politische Radikalisierung im deutschen Adel zwischen Kaiserreich
und NS-Staat*. Akademie Verlag, Berlin 2003.

Malinowski, Stephan: 'From King to Führer: German Nobility and
National Socialism', in: *German Historical Institute London*, Vol.
XXVII/1 (2005), pp. 5–28.

Marcus, Robert S.: 'Letters to the Editor of *The New York Times*.
McCloy's Speech. Status of War Criminals Discussed in
Democratizing of Germany', in: *New York Times* (7.2.1950).

'Marion Dönhoff wird 75 Jahre alt. Widersprüche aushalten, Spannungen leben', in: *Die Zeit*, No. 49 (30.11.1984).

Marx, Christian: *Paul Reusch und die Gutehoffnungshütte. Leitung eines deutschen Großunternehmens*. Wallstein, Göttingen 2013.

Matloff, Maurice/Snell, Edwin M.: *Strategic Planning for Coalition Warfare. 1941–1942*. Historical Division, Department of the Army, Washington, DC 1953.

Mattenklott, Gert: 'Jüdische Identität und deutsche Nation', in: Koebner: *Deutschland nach Hitler*, pp. 30–38.

Mauer, Victor: *Brückenbauer. Großbritannien, die deutsche Frage und die Blockade Berlins 1948–1949*. De Gruyter Oldenbourg, Berlin 2018.

Mayer, Milton: *They Thought They Were Free: The Germans, 1933–45*. University of Chicago Press, Chicago 2017.

McDonald, James G.: *Advocate for the Doomed: The Diaries and Papers of James G. McDonald 1932–1935*. Indiana University Press, Indiana 2007.

McEwan, Dorothea: 'Due missioni politiche di Aby Warburg in Italia nel 1914–15', in: *Schifanoia*, 42/43. 2012 (2013), pp. 57–80.

McEwan, Dorothea: *Fritz Saxl. Eine Biografie. Aby Warburgs Bibliothekar und erster Direktor des Londoner Warburg Institutes*. Bohlau, Vienna/Cologne/Weimar 2012.

McEwan, Dorothea: *Studies on Aby Warburg, Fritz Saxl and Gertrud Bing*. Routledge, Abingdon-on-Thames 2023.

Mehlhorn, Ludwig (ed.): *Gewissheit im Widerstand. Adam von Trott zum 100. Geburtstag*. LIT, Berlin/Münster 2011.

Mendelssohn Bartholdy, Albrecht: 'Europäische Politik', in: *Europäische Gespräche*, 1. Jhg. (1923), pp. 13–22.

Mendelssohn Bartholdy, Albrecht: 'Rede zur Eröffnung des Instituts für Auswärtige Politik', in: Gantzel: *Kolonialrechtswissenschaft*, pp. 89–96.

Mendelssohn Bartholdy, Albrecht: 'Vom Völkerbund und der öffentlichen Meinung', in: *Europäische Gespräche*, 1. Jhg. (1923), pp. 288–301.

Michaels, Axel (ed.): *Klassiker der Religionswissenschaft. Von Friedrich Schleiermacher bis Mircea Eliade.* C. H. Beck, Munich 1997.

Michels, Karen: *Aby Warburg. Im Bannkreis der Ideen.* C. H. Beck, Munich 2007.

Michels, Karen: *'Es muß besser werden!' Aby und Max Warburg im Dialog über Hamburgs geistige Zahlungsfähigkeit.* Hamburg University Press, Hamburg 2020 (2015).

Mintz, Mortin: 'Why Didn't We Bomb Auschwitz?', in: *The Washington Post* (17.4.1983).

Mixed Claims Commission (United States and Germany). Reports of International Arbitral Awards. Recueil des Sentences Arbitrales (1 November 1923–30 October 1939). Vol. VII, pp. 1–391. https://legal.un.org/riaa/cases/vol_VII/1–391.pdf.

'Neuanfang: Von Schuld und Sühne', in: *Stern* (15.2.2001).

Nicosia, Francis R.: *Zionismus und Antisemitismus im Dritten Reich.* Wallstein, Göttingen 2012.

Niemetz, Daniel: '1945: Kriegsende in Mitteldeutschland', MDR Zeitreise (4.2.1920), 22.05 Uhr.

Oller, John: *White Shoe: How a New Breed of Wall Street Lawyers Changed Big Business and the American Century.* Dutton, New York 2019.

Oschlies, Wolf: 'Finnlands Juden zwischen Russland und Deutschland', in: *Zukunft braucht Erinnerung.* Das Online-Portal zu den historischen Themen unserer Zeit (13.7.2016). www.zukunft-braucht-erinnerung.de/finnlands-juden-zwischen-russland-und-deutschland/.

Overy, Richard: *The Bombing War: Europe 1939–1945.* Allen Lane, London 2013.

Overy, Richard: 'Instructive for the Future: the interrogation of the major war criminals in Germany, 1945', in: Andrew, Christopher/Tobia, Simona (eds.): *Interrogation in War and Conflict: A Comparative and Interdisciplinary Analysis.* Routledge, Abingdon-on-Thames 2014, pp. 93–109.

Panter, Sarah: 'Transnationale Netzwerke und Fragen der Zugehörigkeit. Ein Briefwechsel zwischen Jacob Schiff und Max

Warburg im Ersten Weltkrieg', in: *Hamburger Schlüsseldokumente zur deutsch–judischen Geschichte* (7.3.2017).

'Paul M. Warburg. Begründer des amerikanischen Federal Reserve Board', in: Kulturforum Warburg: *Warburg*, pp. 73–9.

Peters, Jurgen: 'Der Kampf gegen die Demontage und für die Erhaltung der Reichswerke in Salzgitter'. Rede auf dem Salzgitter-Forum, 5/6.3.2010.

Pfleiderer, Doris: *Deutschland und der Youngplan*. Dissertation. Universität Stuttgart 2002.

Poensgen, Ruprecht: 'Die Schule Schloss Salem im Dritten Reich', in: *Vierteljahrshefte für Zeitgeschichte*, 44. Jhg. (1996), H.1, pp. 25–54.

Pöppmann, Dirk: '"Im Amt geblieben, um Schlimmeres zu verhüten". Ernst von Weizsäckers Opposition aus Sicht der US-Anklage', in: Schulte: *Widerstand und Auswärtiges Amt*, pp. 251–68.

Pohl, Hans (ed.): *Deutsche Bankiers des 20. Jahrhunderts*. Franz Steiner Verlag, Stuttgart 2008.

Potthoff, Jürgen / Schmid, Ingobert C.: *Wunibald I. E. Kamm. Wegbereiter der modemen Kraftfahrtechnik*. Springer, Berlin 2012.

Press Releases. United States Department of State. Weekly Issue No. 119. Saturday, January 9, 1932. Publication No. 271.

Priemel, Kim Christian: *Flick. Eine Konzerngeschichte vom Kaiserreich bis zur Bundesrepublik*. Wallstein, Göttingen, 2nd edn. 2008.

Prittwitz, Cornelius: 'Anmerkungen zu Vergangenheit, Zukunft und Essenz der deutsch–amerikanischen Beziehungen', in: Lorenz: *Transatlantik*, pp. 97–108.

Pyta, Wolfram: 'Franz Pfeffer von Salomon. Begabt zu sein macht's nicht allein', in: *Frankfurter Allgemeine Zeitung* (10.4.2017).

Quack, Sigrid: 'Internationale Wirtschaftskanzleien im Spannungsfeld von Wandel und Kontinuität des Rechts', in: Dörrenbacher, Christoph (ed.): *Modelltransfer in multinationalen Untemehmen: Strategien und Probleme grenzüberschreitender Konzernintegration*. Edition Sigma, Berlin 2003, pp. 173–98. https://www.econstor.eu/bitstream/10419/122764/1/209604.pdf.

Raulff, Ulrich: 'Die sieben Häute der Schlange. Oraibi, Kreuzlingen und zurück: Stationen einer Reise ins Licht', in: Cestelli Guidi, Benedetta/Mann, Nicholas (eds.): *Grenzerweiterungen. Aby Warburg in Amerika 1895–1896*. Dölling und Galitz, Hamburg/ Munich 1999, pp. 64–74.

Reiling, Johannes: *Deutschland: Safe for Democracy?*. Franz Steiner Verlag, Stuttgart 1997.

Reudenbach, Bruno (ed.): *Erwin Panofsky. Beiträge des Symposiums Hamburg 1992*. Akademie Verlag, Hamburg 1994.

Reus, Julia: 'A Plea of Humanity to Law. Benjamin B. Ferencz' langer Weg von Nürnberg nach Den Haag', in: *Mimeo* (5.12.2019). https://mimeo.dubnow.de/a-plea-of-humanity-to-law/.

Reventlow, Elly Gräfin (ed.): *Albrecht Bemstorff zum Gedächtnis*. Altenhof 1952.

Richardi, Hans-Günter: *SS-Geiseln in der Alpenfestung. Die Verschleppung prominenter KZ-Häftlinge aus Deutschland nach Südtirol*. Edition Raetia, Bozen 2015.

Roberts, Priscilla: 'Paul D. Cravath, The First World War, and the Anglophile Internationalist Tradition', in: *Australian Journal of Politics and History*, Vol. 51, No. 2 (2005), pp. 194–215.

Roeck, Bernd: 'Die Warburgs', in: Reinhardt, Volker (ed.): *Deutsche Familien. Historische Portraits von Bismarck bis Weizsäcker*. C. H. Beck, Munich 2005, pp. 275–306.

Roß, Marlis: *Der Ausschluss der jüdischen Mitglieder 1935. Die Patriotische Gesellschaft im Nationalsozialismus*. Patriotische Gesellschaft von 1765, Hamburg 2007.

Rothfels, Hans: 'Zur 25. Wiederkehr des 20. Juli 1944', in: *Vierteljahrshefte für Zeitgeschichte*, 17. Jhg. (1969), H.3, pp. 237–53.

Rust, Christian: *Deutschland und die Nachkriegsordnung. Großbritannien, die Vereinigten Staaten und die Grundlagen einer Friedensregelung mit Deutschland in Paris 1919 und Jalta/Potsdam 1945*. Freie Universität Berlin Dissertation 2001. https://refubium. fu-berlin.de/handle/fub188/3754.

Samuel, Wolfgang W. E.: *American Raiders: The Race to Capture the Luftwaffe's Secrets*. University Press of Mississippi, Jackson MS 2004.

Saxl, Fritz: 'Die Geschichte der Bibliothek Aby Warburgs', in: Wuttke: *Aby M. Warburg*, pp. 335–46.

Saxl, Fritz: 'Die Kulturwissenschaftliche Bibliothek Warburg in Hamburg', in: Wuttke: *Aby M. Warburg*, pp. 331–4.

Saxl, Fritz: 'Warburgs Besuch in Neu-Mexico', in: Wuttke: *Aby M. Warburg*, pp. 317–26.

Schild, Georg: 'Wie der Jahrhundertkonflikt begann. Die USA und die russische Oktoberrevolution', in: *Die Politische Meinung* (Konrad-Adenauer-Stiftung), 62. Jhg. (27.10.2017), No. 546, pp. 113–17.

Schirach, Richard von: *Die Nacht der Physiker. Heisenberg, Hahn, Weizsäcker und die deutsche Bombe*. Berenberg, Berlin 2012.

Schnitter, Joachim: '"Ein gleichbleibend sicherer Bezugspunkt in allen Wirrnissen": Zu Geschichte und Denkmalwert von Warburgs Garten auf dem Kösterberg', in: Fischer, Hubertus/Wolschke-Bulmahn, Joachim (eds.): *Gärten und Parks im Leben der jüdischen Bevölkerung nach 1933*. Meidenbauer, Munich 2008, pp. 385–413.

Schoell-Glass, Charlotte: *Aby Warburg und der Antisemitismus. Kulturwissenschaft als Geistespolitik*. S. Fischer, Frankfurt am Main 2014.

Schulte, Jan Erik/Wala, Michael (eds.): *Widerstand und Auswärtiges Amt. Diplomaten gegen Hitler*. Siedler, Munich 2013.

Schwartz, Thomas Alan: *America's Germany: John J. McCloy and the Federal Republic of Germany*. Harvard University Press, Cambridge MA and London 1991.

Schwartz, Thomas Alan: 'Die Begnadigung deutscher Kriegsverbrecher. John McCloy und die Häftlinge von Landsberg', in: *Vierteljahrshefte für Zeitgeschichte*, 38. Jhg. (1990), H.3, pp. 375–414.

Schwarzer, Alice: *Marion Dönhoff. Ein widerständiges Leben*. Kiepenheuer & Witsch, Cologne 2017.

Sears, Elizabeth: 'Keepers of the Flame: Bing, Solmitz, Klibansky, and the Continuity of the Warburg Tradition', in: Despoix, Philippe/Tomm, Jillian (eds.): *Raymond Klibansky and the Warburg Library Network: Intellectual Peregrinations from Hamburg to London and*

Montreal. McGill-Queen's University Press, Montreal/Kingston/
London/Chicago 2018, pp. 29–57.

Sebestyen, Victor: *1946. Das Jahr, in dem die Welt neu entstand.*
Rowohlt Berlin, Berlin 2015.

Shafir, Shlomo: *Ambiguous Relations: The American Jewish Community
and Germany since 1945.* Wayne State University Press, Detroit
2018.

Skidelsky, Robert: *John Maynard Keynes: Fighting for Britain 1937–
1946.* Macmillan, London 2001.

Smith, Bradley F.: *Der Jahrhundertprozess. Die Motive der Richter von
Nürnberg. Anatomie einer Urteilsfindung.* S. Fischer, Frankfurt am
Main 1977.

Smith, Bradley F.: *The Shadow Warriors: OSS and the Origins of the
CIA.* André Deutsch, London 1983.

Smith, Bradley F.: *Reaching Judgement at Nuremberg.* Basic Books,
New York 1977.

Stark, William F.: *Das letzte Mal ums Horn. Das Ende einer Legende,
erzählt von einem, der dabei war.* Piper, Munich/Zurich 2004.

Stelzl-Gallian, Anita: 'Alfons Thorsch', in: *Lexikon der österreichischen
Provenienzforschung* (online). Verfasst am 6. Jänner 2019.

Stimson, Henry L./Bundy, McGeorge: *On Active Service in Peace and
War.* Harper and Brothers, New York 1948.

Strauss, Lewis L.: *Men and Decisions.* Macmillan, London 1963.

Streb, Jochen: 'Der transatlantische Wissenstransfer auf dem Gebiet
der Synthesekautschukforschung in Krieg und Frieden. Freiwillige
Kooperationen und erzwungene Reparationen (1929–1954)', in:
Technikgeschichte, Vol. 71 (2004), H. 4, pp. 283–303.

Strupp, Christoph: *Johan Huizinga. Geschichtswissenschaft als
Kulturgeschichte.* Vandenhoeck & Ruprecht, Göttingen 2000.

Stutterheim, Kurt von: *Die Majestät des Gewissens. In Memoriam
Albrecht Bernstorff.* Hans Christians Verlag, Hamburg 1962.

Süddeutsche Zeitung Photo: *Dossier Demontage und Reparationen,
1945–1949* (online). 53 Bilder.

Swaine, Robert T.: *The Cravath Firm and its Predecessors 1819–1947.*
Vol. II. Ad Press, New York 1948.

Tanner, Vaino: *The Winter War: Finland against Russia 1939–1940*. Stanford University Press, Stanford CA 1957.

Parkinson, Justin: 'Kurt Hahn: The man who taught Prince Philip to think', *BBC News (25.2.2016)*.

Thompson, Dorothy: *Kassandra spricht. Antifaschistische Publizistik 1932–1942*. Kiepenheuer, Leipzig/Weimar 1988.

'"Tönerner Koloß ohne Kopf". Die Rote Armee im finnisch–sowjetischen Winterkrieg 1939/40', in: *Der Spiegel*, No. 27, 28.6.1981, pp. 132–40.

Tüngel, Richard: 'Abermals: Robert Kempner. Einem Schädling muß das Handwerk gelegt werden', in: *Die Zeit*, No. 38, 20.9.1951.

Ulrich, Keith: 'Industriefinanzierung in Deutschland. Die Bedeutung jüdischer Privatbankhäuser in der Weimarer Republik', in: Benz: *Jüdisches Leben*, pp. 65–86.

Wala, Michael (ed.): *Gesellschaft und Diplomatie im Transatlantischen Kontext. Festschrift für Reinhard R. Doerries zum 65. Geburtstag*. Franz Steiner Verlag, Stuttgart 1999.

Wala, Michael: *Weimar und Amerika. Botschafter Friedrich von Prittwitz und Gaffron und die deutsch–amerikanischen Beziehungen von 1927 bis 1933*. Franz Steiner Verlag, Stuttgart 2001.

Wala, Michael: *Winning the Peace. Amerikanische Außenpolitik und der Council on Foreign Relations, 1945–1950*. Franz Steiner Verlag, Stuttgart 1990.

Warburg, Aby: *Schlangenritual. Ein Reisebericht*. Mit einem Nachwort von Ulrich Raulff. Wagenbach, Berlin 2011.

Warburg, Aby: 'A Lecture On Serpent Ritual', in: *Journal of the Warburg Institute* Vol. 2, No. 4 (Apr., 1939), pp. 277–92.

Warburg, Eric M.: 'Die Rettung der Bibliothek Warburg in Hamburg durch Emigration nach London', in: Kulturforum Warburg: *Warburg*, pp. 33–40.

Warburg, Eric M.: 'Max M. Warburg – ein erfahrener Bankier mit Engagement', in: Kulturforum Warburg: *Warburg*, pp. 47–72.

Warburg, Eric M.: *Zeiten und Gezeiten. Erinnerungen*. Selbstverlag, Hamburg 1982.

Warburg, Eric M.: 'The transfer of the Warburg Institute to England in 1933', appendix to the annual report of the Warburg Institute, 1952–53.

Warburg, Eric: *Times and Tides: A Log-Book*. N.p., Hamburg 1983.

Warburg, Eric: *A Bridge Over the Atlantic*. Atlantik-Brücke E.V., Hamburg 2009.

Warburg, James P.: *Deutschland – Brücke oder Schlachtfeld*. Franz Mittelbach, Stuttgart 1949.

Warburg, Paul M.: *The Federal Reserve System: Its Origin and Growth*. 2 vols. Macmillan, New York 1930.

Warburg Spinelli, Ingrid: *Erinnerungen. 'Die Dringlichkeit des Mitleids und die Einsamkeit, nein zu sagen'*. Luchterhand, Hamburg/Zurich 1991.

'Warum Hitler die Bombe nicht baute', in: *Die Zeit*, No.18 (24.4.1992).

Warnke, Martin: 'Die Kulturwissenschaftliche Bibliothek Warburg', in: Bollenbeck, Georg/Golz, Jochen/Knoche, Michael/Steierwald, Ulrike (eds.): *Weimar – Archäologie eines Ortes*. J. B. Metzler, Stuttgart 2001, pp. 74–9.

Weber, Regina: 'Raymond Klibansky', in: Spalek, John M./ Feilchenfeldt, Konrad/Hawrylchak, Sandra H. (eds.): *Deutschsprachige Exilliteratur seit 1933*. Vol. 3: USA. Supplement 1. De Gruyter, Berlin 2010, pp. 93–124.

Weigel, Sigrid: 'Aby Warburg's Schlangenritual: Reading Culture and Reading Written Texts', in: *New German Critique* 65 (1995), pp. 135–53.

Weinke, Annette: *Die Nürnberger Prozesse*. C. H. Beck, Munich 2015.

'Weizsaecker gets Porter, Arnold Aid; U.S. Lawyers to Fight 7-Year Sentence Imposed on Nazi by American Tribunal', in: *New York Times* (14.12.1949).

Wentling, Sonja P.: 'The Engineer and the Shtadlanim: Herbert Hoover and American Jewish non-Zionists 1917–28', in: *American Jewish History*, Vol. 88, No.3 (September 2000), pp. 377–406.

Wentling, Sonja P.: 'Prologue to genocide or epilogue to war? American perspectives on the Jewish question in Poland

1919–1921', in: *Journal of the Historical Society*, Vol. 8, No. 4 (2008), pp. 523–44.

Werner, Frank: 'Marion Gräfin Dönhoff. "Nürnberg war falsch"', in: *Die Zeit*, No.19 (6.5.2021).

Wilmes, Annette: 'Vor 50 Jahren: Der Wilhelmstraßenprozess. Ehemalige Diplomaten und Beamte des Auswärtigen Amtes in Nürnberg vor Gericht.' DeutschlandRadio Berlin, Wortspiel, 19.11.1998, 19.05 Uhr.

Wind, Edgar: 'Einleitung', in: *Kulturwissenschaftliche Bibliographie*, pp. V–XVII.

Witcover, Jules: *Sabotage at Black Tom. Imperial Germany's Secret War in America, 1914–1917*. Algonquin Books, Chapel Hill, NC 1989.

Wrede, Rabbe Axel: 'Finnland und seine Nachbarn', in: *Europäische Gespräche*, 1. Jhg. (1924), pp. 1–11.

Wuttke, Dieter (ed.): *Aby M. Warburg. Ausgewählte Schriften und Würdigungen*. Verlag Valentin Koerner, Baden-Baden 1979.

Wuttke, Dieter: 'Die Emigration der Kulturwissenschaftlichen Bibliothek Warburg und die Anfänge des Universitätsfaches Kunstgeschichte in Großbritannien', in: *Artibus et Historiae*, Vol. 5, No.10 (1984), pp. 133–46.

Wyman, David S.: *Das unerwünschte Volk. Amerika und die Vernichtung der europäischen Juden*. S. Fischer, Frankfurt am Main 1989.

Wyman, David S.: 'Why Auschwitz was never bombed', in: *Commentary*, Vol. 65 (May 1978), pp. 32–46.

Wyman, David S.: *Abandonment of the Jews: America and the Holocaust 1941–1945*. The New Press, New York 2007.

Zetsche, Anne: 'Eric M. Warburg', in: *Transatlantic Perspectives*, Retrieved March 25, 2020, from Transatlantic Perspectives: http://www.transatlanticperspectives.org/entry.php?rec=156.

Zetsche, Anne: *The Quest for Atlanticism: German–American Elite Networking, the Atlantik-Brücke and the American Council on Germany, 1952–1974*. Doctoral Thesis, Northumbria University, Newcastle 2016. http://nrl.northumbria.ac.uk/31606/.

Ziegler, Dieter (ed.): *Großbürger und Unternehmer. Die deutsche*

Wirtschaftselite im 20. Jahrhundert. Vandenhoeck & Ruprecht, Göttingen 2000.

Ziemke, Earl F.: *The U.S. Army in the Occupation of Germany 1944–1946.* Center of Military History, United States Army, Washington, DC 1990.

Zilliacus, Benedict: *Wilhelm Wahlforss.* Wartsilä, Helsinki 1984.

Zimmerman, David: 'The Society for the Protection of Science and Learning and the Politicisation of British Science in the 1930s', in: *Minerva*, Vol. 44, No. 1 (2006), pp. 25–45.

With thanks to the following archives:
Amherst College Archives, John J. McCloy Papers
Stiftung Warburg Archiv/Warburg Archive Foundation, Hamburg
The Warburg Institute Archive, London

Notes

Introduction

1   Letter from Max Warburg to Erich Warburg, 6.2.1935. F–20140, Stiftung Warburg Archiv.

2   Letter from Nina Grunenberg to Eric Warburg, 28.10.1981. F–10489, Stiftung Warburg Archiv.

3   I am indebted to Dorothea Hauser for this information.

Chapter 1

1   Schnitter, 'Ein gleichbleibend sicherer Bezugspunkt'.

2   Chernow, *Die Warburgs*, p. 428.

3   Oller, *White Shoe*.

4   Ibid.; 'Cravath', founded in 1819 by R. M. Blatchford, became Guthrie, Cravath & Henderson in 1901; then Cravath, Henderson & de Gersdorf in 1906; since 1944 it has been known as Cravath, Swaine & Moore (see Swaine, *The Cravath Firm* (I), p. VII).

5   See Quack, 'Internationale Wirtschaftskanzleien'.

6   Quoted in Sarah Panter, 'Transnationale Netzwerke und Fragen der Zugehörigkeit. Ein Briefwechsel zwischen Jakob Schiff und Max Warburg im Ersten Weltkrieg'. In: *Hamburger Schlüsseldokumente zur deutsch-jüdischen Geschichte*, 7.3.2017.

7   Attributed to Cicero: *Si vis pacem para bellum*.

8   See Franz, *Fight for Americanism*.

9   See Panter, 'Transnationale Netzwerke'.

10 See Warburg, E., *Zeiten und Gezeiten*, pp. 45, 49.

11 Erich Warburg to Aby Warburg. 22.4.1918. WIA, FC.

12 Aby Warburg to Eric Warburg. 15.7.1918. WIA, FC.

13 Aby Warburg to Eric Warburg. 15.7.1918. WIA, FC.

14 Quoted in Michels, *Aby Warburg*, p. 85; McEwan, 'Due missioni'.

15 Michels, *Aby Warburg*, p. 85.

16 Ibid.

17 Quoted in: www.frankfurt1933-1945.de.

18 Michels, *Es muß besser werden*, p. 70.

19 Kleßmann, *M. M. Warburg*, p. 51.

20 Frey, 'Deutsche Finanzinteressen', p. 334.

21 Max Warburg, 'Aufzeichnungen', quoted in Michels, *Aby Warburg*, p. 82.

22 Panter, 'Transnationale Netzwerke'; Michels, *Es muß besser werden*, p. 73. Embden, 'Anamnese. Warburg'.

23 However, Paul Warburg's suggestion was only heeded after the 'Great Panic' of 1907, a financial crisis that led to the collapse of more than 20,000 private, state, and national banks in the United States. The Panic of 1907 began with bad speculation on a grand scale by the 'Copper King' Otto Heinze, who bought up large quantities of the shares in the United Copper Company; he mistakenly speculated on the fact that a large number of the shares of the United Copper Company had been borrowed and sold short by speculators – in other words, that the short sellers had disposed of the shares in the belief that the price would drop, but would now be forced to repurchase them from him at a hugely increased cost. However, after it transpired that the amount of shares traded had by no means been artificially inflated, Heinze himself now had a problem: he had purchased more shares than he could afford. When this became known, within a matter of hours shares in the United Copper Company fell through the floor and Heinze found himself sitting on a mountain of debt. Initially the problem only affected the banks that had lent him the funds to purchase the shares. The fact that a panic could ensue from this was down to the very general liquidity problem of New York banks at the time. For Wall Street had siphoned off capital to the west of the country to fund the reconstruction of the city of San Francisco

after the devastating earthquake it had suffered the year before. Accordingly a run on the banks now ensued, since savers no longer trusted that their deposits were covered. In 1913 Paul Warburg's project assumed tangible form in the Federal Reserve Act, which laid the foundations for the US central banking system, the Federal Reserve Board.

24 Warburg, E., *Zeiten und Gezeiten*, p. 55.
25 Hansen, *Bernstorff*, p. 95f; quoted in Wala, *Weimar and America*, p. 20.
26 Burger, *Theodor Heuss*, p. 223.
27 Lepsius, 'Johann Lepsius and Kurt Hahn'; Woodrow Wilson delivered his 'Peace Without Victory' speech on 22.1.1917.
28 Horn, 'Von Versailles über Lausanne'.
29 Leonhard, 'Erwartung'.
30 Ibid.
31 Geiss, 'Kriegsschuldfrage', p. 33.
32 Lackmann, *Albrecht Mendelssohn Bartholdy*, p. 37.
33 Cravath quoted in Swaine, *The Cravath Firm* (Volume 2), p. 257.
34 Roberts, 'Paul D. Cravath'.
35 Eisermann, *Außenpolitik*, p. 52.
36 Cf. Pfleiderer, *Deutschland und der Youngplan*, p. 35.

Chapter 2

1 Machtan, *Prinz Max von Baden*; Lepsius, 'Johann Lepsius and Kurt Hahn'.
2 See Michael Knoll timeline: www.mi-knoll.de.
3 Lembke, 'Magdalene Schoch'.
4 Knoll, *Kurt Hahn*, pp. 12–18.
5 Erich Warburg to Aby Warburg. 22.4.1918. WIA, FC.
6 Erich Warburg to Aby Warburg, 11.6.1921. WIA, FC.
7 Franke, 'Leonard Nelson', p. 226.
8 Max Warburg to Aby Warburg, 2.11.1920. WIA, FC. Erich's cousin Siegmund George Warburg arrived in London in 1934 with barely £5,000 in his pocket, but within a few years had risen to become one of the city's principal private bankers.

9   See also 'Der Prozess Warburg-Fritsch' in: Schoell-Glass, *Aby Warburg*.

10   Michels, *Aby Warburg*, p. 77.

11   Ibid.

12   Kiesselbach: Autobiographische Skizze: 7. Handakte Staatsarchiv Hamburg.

13   Max Warburg, 'Aufzeichnungen', quoted in Michels, *Aby Warburg*, p. 82.

14   Michels, *Aby Warburg*.

15   Doerries, 'Individualist und Diplomat', p. 40.

16   See Ulrich, 'Industriefinanzierung', p. 70.

17   Ibid.

18   Warburg, E., *Zeiten und Gezeiten*, p. 91.

19   See the Wikipedia entry on the German aristocratic family of Ballestrem (https://en.wikipedia.org/wiki/Ballestrem).

20   Max Warburg to Aby Warburg, 4.12.1923. WIA, FC.

21   Kleßmann, *M. M. Warburg*, p. 67.

22   Max Warburg to Aby Warburg, 4.12.1923. WIA, FC.

23   Ibid.

24   Max Warburg to Aby Warburg, 2.11.1920. WIA, FC.

25   Warburg, E., *Zeiten und Gezeiten*, p. 76.

26   Kellerhof, '1922 ruinierten…' In *Die Welt*. 4.1.2021.

27   It was decided that the reparations instalments to be paid by Germany would only be raised to 2.5 billion gold marks from 1928 onwards. Even so, the level of reparations payments should remain linked to the German economic performance; half of these payments would be taken from budget measures tailored to it – for example customs and excise duties.

28   Swaine, *The Cravath Firm* (Volume 2), p. 307.

29   https://www.kredite.de/Wiki/dawes-anleihe.

30   Ulrich, 'Industriefinanzierung', p. 71.

31   Ibid., p. 72.

32   Aby Warburg only came to formulate his impressions in 1923 – thirty years after his actual journey to the US Southwest – in the form of a lecture he delivered during his stay at the clinic in

Kreuzlingen. This lecture, which is regarded as the key source document for Aby Warburg's thinking, evolved into one of the 'most commented-upon texts of the 20th century on aesthetics'. Quoted in: https://www.hkw.de/de/programm/projekte/2020/aby_warburg/bilderatlas_mnemosyne_start.php. See also: Raulf: Afterword, in Warburg, A., *Schlangenritual*; Bredekamp, *Aby Warburg*; 'Bender', *Schlangenritual*; Weigel, 'Aby Warburgs Schlangenritual'.

33 Warburg, E., *Zeiten und Gezeiten*, p. 73f.

34 Ibid., p. 90f.

35 Letter from Paul Warburg to Erich Warburg. 29 October 1924. F-10506. Stiftung Warburg Archiv.

36 Kinzer, *Brothers*.

37 Press Releases. United States Department of State.

38 Kinzer, *Brothers*, p. 52; Hersh also mentions the office in Hamburg; Hersh, *Old Boys*, p. 54.

39 See Michels, *Es muß besser werden*.

40 Quoted in Warnke, 'Bibliothek', p. 74.

41 Transcript of the agreement signed on 29.8.1929. F–20140, Stiftung Warburg Archiv.

42 Breitfeld, *Renger-Patzsch*, pp. 80, 106.

43 Letter from Aby Warburg to Erich Warburg, 13.12.1928. WIA, FC.

44 Kleßmann, *M.M. Warburg*, p. 77.

45 Hansen, *Bernstorff*, p. 150.

46 Ibid., p. 151.

47 Kleßmann, *M. M. Warburg*, p. 77.

48 Warburg, E., *Zeiten und Gezeiten*, p. 100.

49 Ibid., p. 101f.

50 Letter from the parents to their children, New York, 25.4.1946. F–10483, Stiftung Warburg Archiv; Kleßmann, *M.M. Warburg*, pp. 75, 77.

51 Aby S. (1864–1933) was a son of Siegmund Warburg (resident on the Alsterufer), who in turn was a brother of Moritz Warburg (resident in Mittelweg, and later also on the Kösterberg). The

male descendants of the Alsterufer Warburgs all have to 'S.' for 'Siegmund' as their second Christian name, whereas those from the Mittelweg Warburgs have the initial 'M.' for 'Moritz'. Erich's cousin Siegmund G. Warburg belonged to the Alsterufer Warburg line. The 'G.' stood for George, the name of his father, who was a brother of Aby S. Warburg.

52 Hauser, 'Banking on Emigration', p. 152.
53 Letter from Erich Warburg to Aby Warburg, 31.5.1926. WIA FC.
54 Böhme, 'Aby M. Warburg', p. 133.
55 Max Warburg quoted in Michels, *Es muß besser werden*, p. 5.
56 *Aby M. Warburg zum Gedächtnis*: 'Worte zur Beisetzung von Prof. Dr. Aby Warburg'.
57 Although before the crisis the bank had assets to the value of 400 million Reichsmarks, at the lowest point of the crisis in late 1932, these had dwindled to 275 million Reichsmarks. Hauser, 'Banking on Emigration', p. 151.
58 Information provided by Dorothea Hauser.
59 Information provided by Dorothea Hauser.
60 Chernow, *Die Warburgs*, p. 408.
61 Letter from Mary Warburg to Frede Warburg, 6.2.1932. WIA FC.
62 Letter from Max Warburg to Ernst Cassirer, 8.4.1931, quoted in McEwan, *Fritz Saxl*, p. 139.
63 Chernow, *Die Warburgs*, p. 492.
64 Letter from Mary Warburg to Frede Warburg, 6.2.1932. WIA FC.
65 Hauser, 'Banking on Emigration', p. 151.

Chapter 3
1   Quoted in Knoll, *Kurt Hahn*, p. 166.
2   McDonald, *Advocate*, p. 78.
3   In June 1933 Kurt Hahn emigrated to England.
4   Letter from Fritz Saxl to Raymond Klibansky, 13.3.1933. WIA, GC.
5   McDonald, *Advocate*, Diary entry 4.4.1933, p. 38.

6   Ibid.

7   McDonald, *Advocate*, Diary entry 8.4.1933.

8   McDonald, *Advocate*, Diary entry 4.4.1933.

9   Ibid.

10 McDonald, *Advocate*, Diary entry 1.4.1933.

11 McDonald, *Advocate*, Diary entry 4.4.1933.

12 McDonald, *Advocate*, Diary entry 12.4.1933.

13 Kinzer, *Brothers*, p. 57.

14 Ibid., p. 52.

15 Frey, 'Deutsche Finanzinteressen', p. 330f.

16 On the Briefcase Affair, see Reiling, *Deutschland*, pp. 216–242.

17 Transcript of the agreement of 29 August 1929; signed in
    Hamburg by Prof. Dr. A. Warburg, Max M. Warburg for
    himself and Felix, Paul M. Warburg, F. M. Warburg (Fritz).
    F-20140, Stiftung Warburg Archiv.

18 Transcript of the agreement of 6.5.1933. Signed by Max Warburg
    and F. M. Warburg. F–20140, Stiftung Warburg Archiv.

19 Ibid.

20 Transcript, signed by Max W. Warburg and F. M. Warburg,
    Hamburg, May 1933 (no specific date given). F–20140, Stiftung
    Warburg Archiv.

21 Letter from the American Consul General, George S.
    Messersmith, to Erich Warburg, M. M. Warburg & Co.
    Postschließfach 744, Hamburg 1, Berlin, Germany, 10 May 1933.
    WIA, FC.

22 Information provided by Dorothea Hauser.

23 Letter from Fritz Saxl to Raymond Klibansky, 13.3.1933. WIA,
    GC.

24 Information provided by Dorothea Hauser.

25 Bernstorff to Elly Reventlow. Quoted in Hansen, *Bernstorff*, p.
    192.

26 Quoted in Ibid., p. 196.

27 Ibid., p. 197.

28 Quoted in Ibid., p. 196.

29 M. M. Warburg had adapted the conditions of loan repayment

to the prevailing circumstances and drawn up a restructuring plan for the department store.

30 Hauser, 'Banking on Emigration', p.151f.

31 Ibid., pp. 152, 153.

32 In 1934 the levies and taxes amounted to 56 per cent; by 1939 the proportion of confiscated assets had risen to 96 per cent of a person's total estate; see Hauser, 'Banking on Emigration', p. 156.

33 See the profile 'Felix Warburg' in McDonald, *Advocate*.

34 On the Haavara Agreement, see Anderl, Emigration.

35 Note from Erich Warburg to Fritz Saxl, 16.6.1933. WIA FC.

36 Quoted in Chernow, *Die Warburgs*, p. 492.

37 Zimmerman, 'Society'.

38 Krumm, *Huizinga*, p. 195.

39 *Cara*, p. 7; Baldwin, 'Notiz', p. 794; Memorandum drafted by Erich Warburg on 17 November 1933. WIA FC.

40 Statement for visit of … Ross, Gibson, 1933. p. 4. WIA FC.

41 Ibid., p. 2.

42 Ibid., p. 4f.

43 Strupp, *Huizinga*, p. 40; Letter from Saxl to Huizinga.

44 Lubenow 2020: 141f.

45 Letters from Gertrud Bing to Eric Warburg, 28.9.1933 and 21.10.1933. WIA FC.

46 Letter from Gertrud Bing to Eric Warburg, 21.10.1933. WIA FC.

47 Letters from Gertrud Bing to Eric Warburg, 28.9.1933 and 21.10.1933. WIA FC.

48 Letter from Erich Warburg to Lord Lee. 27.10.1933. WIA FC.

49 Copy of a letter from Lord Lee to Mr. Max Warburg. London 28 October 1933. F–20140, Stiftung Warburg Archiv. The letter is also reprinted in Eric Warburg's account of the transfer of the Warburg Library to England. F–10508, Stiftung Warburg Archiv. Sonderdruck Poiesis 4.

50 Letter from Erich Warburg to Lord Lee. 27.10.1933. WIA FC; Memorandum drafted by Erich Warburg, 17.11.1933. WIA FC.

51 Erich Warburg: Note regarding KBW Hamburg, 4 November

1933. WIA FC; Memorandum, Erich Warburg, 4.11.1933. WIA FC.

52 Memorandum, Erich Warburg, 4.11.1933. WIA FC.

53 Roß, *Ausschluss*, p. 49; Letter from Max Warburg to Dr. von Kleinschmit, 28.11.1933. F–20140, Stiftung Warburg Archiv.

54 Letter from Max Warburg to Dr. von Kleinschmit, 28.11.1933. F–20140, Stiftung Warburg Archiv.

55 Paul Ruben himself, however, did not manage to get out of Germany before the outbreak of war. His poor state of health did not permit him to be deported to Terezin in 1942. He died in Hamburg in 1943.

56 Letter from Max Warburg to Dr. von Kleinschmit, 28.11.1933. F–20140, Stiftung Warburg Archiv; Letter from Kleinschmit to Max Warburg, Hamburg, 11.12.1933, Rathaus. F–20140, Stiftung Warburg Archiv

57 Klingler, The Warburg Institute, p. 273

58 Ibid., p. 270; the librarians Otto Fein, Hans Meier, Gertrud Bing, and the library's director Fritz Saxl emigrated with the Warburn Library to London.

59 Letter from Kleinschmit to Max Warburg, Hamburg, 11.12.1933, Rathaus. F–20140, Stiftung Warburg Archiv.

60 Erich Warburg's account of the transfer of the Warburg-Bibliothek to England. F–10508, Stiftung Warburg Archiv. Sonderdruck Poiesis 4.

61 Kopper, Wirtschaftliche Selbstbehauptung, p. 214.

62 Letter from Erich Warburg to Fritz Saxl, 22.11.1933. WIA FC; in *The New York Times* 22.11.1933: 'Hamburg Will Lose Warburg Library'. Erich Warburg to Saxl, 22.11.1933. WIA GC.

63 Max Warburg to Fritz Saxl, 26.11.1933, quoted in Klingler, 'The Warburg Institute', p. 265.

64 McDonald, *Advocate*, Diary entry 21.11.1933.

65 Ibid, p. 78.

66 Kimminich, 'Entwicklung', p. 383.

67 Germany's formal exit from the League of Nations took place on

19 October 1933, three days after the high commission was set up.

68 Thompson, *Kassandra spricht*, p. 65.

69 McDonald, *Advocate*, Diary entry 29.12.33.

70 Ibid.

71 McDonald, *Advocate*, Diary entry 5.1.34, p.247.

72 See 'Educational Clearing' Hauser, 'Banking on Emigration', p. 155.

73 Letter from Fritz Saxl to Erich Warburg, 17.11.1933. WIA FC.

74 Memorandum, drafted by Erich Warburg, 17.11.1933. WIA FC.

75 Telegram 17.11.1933. Warburg & Co. Hans Maier to Erich Warburg. WIA FC.

76 Within the group of German art historians belonging to the Warburg circle, Erwin Panofsky, Raymond Klibansky, and Edgar Wind *inter alia* were given research assignments financed with funds from the AAC.

77 Letter from Erich Warburg to Fritz Saxl, 5.12.1933, 31 Pine Street New York. WIA. FC.

78 Note from Erich Warburg to Fritz Saxl. 16.6.1933. WIA FC.

79 Warburg, E., *Zeiten und Gezeiten*, p. 73f.

80 McDonald, *Advocate*, p. 78.

81 Warburg, E., *Zeiten und Gezeiten*, p. 109.

82 Michels, *Aby Warburg*, p. 110f.

83 Ibid., p. 112.

84 Wind 1934: 'Einleitung', quoted in Breidecker, 'Einige Fragmente', p. 85.

85 Letter from Max Warburg to Erich Warburg, 6.2.1935, F–20140, Stiftung Warburg Archiv.

86 Weber, Klibansky, p. 106.

87 Ibid.

88 Letter from Max Warburg to Erich Warburg, 6.2.1935, F–20140, Stiftung Warburg Archiv.

89 McDonald, *Advocate*, Diary entry 5.2.1934.

90 Letter from James McDonald to Felix Warburg, 14.9.1933; quoted in McDonald, *Advocate*; Philipp Scheidemann and

Rudolf Breitscheid had already left the country at the beginning of March 1933; Walter Rathenau was murdered by right-wing extremists in 1922; while Friedrich Ebert and Gustav Stresemann had died of natural causes in the 1920s.

91 Letter from Erich Warburg to Felix Warburg, 1009 Fifth Avenue, 11 January 1935. F–20140, Stiftung Warburg Archiv.

92 Handwritten comment on a letter from Sol. N. Stroock to Max Warburg, ?.1935. F–20140, Stiftung Warburg Archiv.

93 Bibliothek Warburg. 16.9.1935. F–20140, Stiftung Warburg Archiv.

94 Letter from Erich Warburg to Edward Warburg, 8.2.1935. F–20140, Stiftung Warburg Archiv.

95 Letter from Erich Warburg to Felix Warburg, 14.2.1935. F–20140, Stiftung Warburg Archiv.

96 Letter from Erich Warburg to Edward Warburg, 8.2.1935. F–20140, Stiftung Warburg Archiv.

97 McDonald, *Advocate*, Diary entry 21.11.1933.

98 Chernow, *Die Warburgs*, p. 521.

99 Max Warburg: Erinnerungen, excerpts reprinted in Lorenz, *Hamburger Juden*, p. 121.

100 Jünger, *Jahre der Ungewissheit*, p. 360.

101 Warburg, E., *Zeiten und Gezeiten*, p.113.

102 Kinzer, *Brothers*, p.53.

103 Bibliothek Warburg – 16.9.1935. F–20140, Stiftung Warburg Archiv.

104 Quoted in: Bibliothek Warburg – Memorandum– 16.9.1935. F–20140, Stiftung Warburg Archiv.

105 Bibliothek Warburg – 16.9.1935. F–20140, Stiftung Warburg Archiv.

106 Ibid.

107 Letter from Erich Warburg to Max M. Warburg. 23 January 1935. F-20140, Stiftung Warburg Archiv.

108 Jünger, *Jahre der Ungewissheit*.

109 Ibid., p. 283.

110 Sears, 'Keepers', p. 30; Jünger, *Jahre der Ungewissheit*, p. 290.

111 Jünger, *Jahre der Ungewissheit*, p. 283.

112 Quoted in Ibid., p. 285.

113 Kieffer, *Judenverfolgung*.

114 Jünger, *Jahre der Ungewissheit*, p. 306; Kieffer, *Judenverfolgung*, p. 58.

115 *The Times,* quoted in Kieffer, *Judenverfolgung*, p. 109.

116 From the protest resolution passed by the Second World Jewish Congress, Geneva, September 1933, quoted in: Kieffer, *Judenverfolgung*, p. 89.

117 Jünger, *Jahre der Ungewissheit*, p. 314.

118 McDonald, *Advocate*, p. 55.

119 See the profile 'Felix Warburg' in McDonald, *Advocate*.

120 Felix Warburg to Samuel Untermyer, 4.6.1935, quoted in Kieffer, *Judenverfolgung*, p. 94.

121 McDonald, *Advocate*, p. 55.

122 Letter from Erich Warburg to Max Warburg, 5.12.1935. F–20140, Stiftung Warburg Archiv.

123 Ibid.

124 Letter from Erwin Panofsky to Felix Warburg, 12.12.1935. F–20140, Stiftung Warburg Archiv.

125 Letter from Fritz Saxl to Erich Warburg; London, 16.12.35. F–20140, Stiftung Warburg Archiv.

126 Letter from Gertrud Bing to Erich Warburg, 16.12.1935. F–20140, Stiftung Warburg Archiv.

127 Letter from Erwin Panofsky to Felix Warburg, 12.12.1935. F–20140, Stiftung Warburg Archiv.

128 Felix Warburg telegram 28.1.1936. F–20140, Stiftung Warburg Archiv.

129 McDonald, *Advocate,* Diary entry 20.6.1933, p. 74.

130 Letter from Carl Georg Heise to Erich Warburg, 31.1.1936. F–20140, Stiftung Warburg Archiv.

131 Letter from Erwin Panofsky to Max Warburg, 20.9.1935. F–20140, Stiftung Warburg Archiv.

132 Erich Warburg to Max Warburg, 5.12.1935. F–20140, Stiftung Warburg Archiv.

133 Letter from Erich Warburg to Fritz Saxl, 31. Januar 1936. F–20140, Stiftung Warburg Archiv.

134 Telegram from Erich Warburg to Felix Warburg, 4.2.1936. F–20140, Stiftung Warburg Archiv.

135 Letter from Max Warburg to Felix Warburg, 2.2.1936. F–20140, Stiftung Warburg Archiv.

136 Letter from Gertrud Bing to Erich Warburg, 24.3.1936. F–20140, Stiftung Warburg Archiv.

137 Letter from Gertrud Bing to Erich Warburg, 24.3.1936. F–20140, Stiftung Warburg Archiv.

138 Hauser, Zwischen Gehen und Bleiben, p. 129.

139 Chernow, *Die Warburgs*, p. 530f.

140 Pyta, 'Salomon'.

141 Fraschka, *Salomon*. On Pfeffer's role at the Munich negotiations with the American delegation, see pp. 472–6.

142 Doerries, 'Transatlantic Intelligence', p. 292.

143 Bird, *Chairman*, p. 90.

144 Fraschka, *Salomon*, p. 471.

145 Fraschka, *Salomon*.

146 Marx, *Paul Reusch*, p. 395; Priemel, *Konzerngeschichte*, p. 372f.

147 Quoted in Ibid., p. 379.

148 Marx, *Paul Reusch*, p. 395; Priemel, *Konzerngeschichte*, p. 372f.

149 Priemel, *Konzerngeschichte*, p. 381.

150 Ibid.

151 Hauser, 'Banking on Emigration', p. 156.

152 Warburg, E., *Zeiten und Gezeiten*, p. 122f.

153 Klingler, 'The Warburg Institute', p. 274.

154 Reichsbank main branch to M. M. Warburg, 24.4.1937, F-20140, Stiftung Warburg Archiv.

155 Klingler, 'The Warburg Institute', p. 277f.

156 Note, re: Warburg Library. According to the statement made by Mr. Erich M. Warburg, Hamburg, 24.8.1936. F–20140, Stiftung Warburg Archiv.

157 Draft Agreement, 21.7.1936; Letter from Erich Warburg to Gertrud Bing, 19.9.1936. F–20140, Stiftung Warburg Archiv.

158 Letter from Max Warburg to Fritz Saxl, 18.10.1936. F–20140, Stiftung Warburg Archiv.

159 Letter from Erich Warburg to Max Warburg, 22.7.1936. F–20140, Stiftung Warburg Archiv.

160 McDonald, *Advocate*: profile of Felix Warburg (ebook position 1501).

161 Letter from Erich Warburg to Peter Paul Braden, 18.8.1938. F–20140, Stiftung Warburg Archiv.

162 Ibid.

163 Heise, *Persönliche Erinnerungen*, p.114; Communication from Sieveking to Solmitz, 3 August 1939. See also the correspondence of the Foreign Exchange Board in Hamburg with the firm M. M. Warburg & Co. 29.6.1939. F–20140, Stiftung Warburg Archiv.

164 Roß, *Auschluss*, p. 50.

165 Letter from Erich Warburg to Peter Paul Braden, 18.8.1938. F–20140, Stiftung Warburg Archiv.

166 Ibid.

167 Note from Erich Warburg to Hans Meier, 18.9.1835. F–20140, Stiftung Warburg Archiv.

168 Letter from Max Warburg to Alfred Hirschberg, 12.1.1938. F–20140, Stiftung Warburg Archiv.

169 Wind, 'Einleitung'. Quoted in Breidecker, 'Einige Fragmente'.

170 Max Warburg: Erinnerungen. Excerpts reprinted in Lorenz and Berkemann, *Hamburger Juden*, p. 120.

171 19 March 1938: Aryanisation negotiations, M. M. Warburg & Co., Hamburg; reprinted in Lorenz, *Hamburger Juden*, pp. 125–126.

172 Aby S. Warburg and Carl Melchior both died on 30.12.1933; Siegmund G. Warburg had already left Germany in 1934, acquired British citizenship and founded the New Trading Company in London. Thereafter, his involvement in M. M. Warburg was confined to a sleeping partnership (see Kleßmann, *M. M. Warburg*, p. 98).

173 Comprising properties at Ferdinandstraße 67 and Bei den

Mühren, in addition to shares in the residence on Mittelweg in the Hamburg suburb of Rotherbaum.

174 Kleßmann, *M. M. Warburg*, p. 99.

175 Warburg, E., *Zeiten und Gezeiten*, p. 128.

176 Ibid., p 114.

177 Ibid.

178 Max Warburg: Erinnerungen. Excerpts reprinted in Lorenz, *Hamburger Juden*, p. 121f.

179 For a detailed description of the Warburg office, see Hauser, 'Zwischen Gehen und Bleiben'.

180 Dünzelmann, *...keine normale Reise*.

181 Hauser, 'Banking on Emigration', p. 155.

182 Warburg, E., *Zeiten und Gezeiten*, p. 96f.; 'Summer 1938, Mariehamn, Aland Islands, Finland. Gustav Erikson.' F–10436, Stiftung Warburg Archiv.

183 Michels, *Aby Warburg*, p.18.

184 Warburg, E., *Zeiten und Gezeiten*, p. 129.

Chapter 4

1 Goodman, *Radio's Civic Ambition*, p. 200f.

2 Hauser, 'Zwischen Gehen und Bleiben', p. 119.

3 Ibid., p. 127f.

4 Warburg Spinelli, 'Erinnerungen', p. 153.

5 Dünzelmann, *...keine normale Reise*.

6 Ibid.

7 Goodman, *Radio's Civic Ambition*, p. 200f.

8 Warburg, E., *Zeiten und Gezeiten*, p. 129; see also Kaltenborn 'I Broadcast the Crisis', New York 1938, quoted in: Goodman, *Radio's Civic Ambition*, p. 221.

9 Swaine, *The Cravath Firm*, p. 457.

10 Chernow, *Die Warburgs*, p. 617.

11 Kieffer, *Judenverfolgung*, p. 468.

12 Warburg, E., *Zeiten und Gezeiten*, pp. 122–4.

13 Ibid., p. 113.

14 Warburg, 'Erinnerungen', p. 280f.

15 Ibid; Roeck, 'Die Warburgs', p. 305.

16 Warburg, E., *Zeiten und Gezeiten*, p. 156.

17 Roberts, Paul D. Cravath, p. 213; Swaine, *The Cravath Firm*, p. 457.

18 Swaine, *The Cravath Firm*, p. 458.

19 Strauss, *Men and Decisions*, p. 62f.

20 Anzenberger, *Eagle*, p. 31.

21 https://www.hoover.org/news/herbert-hoovers-travels-finland; by the time he visited Helsinki, Hoover's presidency was already five years in the past.

22 Zilliacus, *Wahlforss*, p. 156.

23 Memorandum 5.10.1939, quoted in Anzenberger, *Eagle*, p. 43.

24 Lewallen, *Winter War*, p. 18.

25 Gosztony quoted in '"Tönerner Koloß ohne Kopf". Die Rote Armee im finnisch-sowjetischen Winterkrieg 1939/40', *Der Spiegel* 27, 1981, pp. 132–40.

26 Strauss, *Men and Decisions*, pp. 65–6.

27 Historical Note from Herbert Hoover. Register of the Finnish relief Fund records. Hoover Institution Library and Archives. Online Archive of California.

28 Strauss, *Men and Decisions*, p. 66.

29 Lewallen, *Winter War*.

30 See Wentling, 'The Engineer'.

31 See Ibid.; Wentling, 'Prologue'.

32 Ibid.

33 Ibid.

34 See Wentling, 'The Engineer'.

35 See Strauss, *Men and Decisions*, pp. 160–70.

36 Ibid., p. 68.

37 Gosztony quoted in '"Tönerner Koloß ohne Kopf"…', pp. 132–40.

38 *Haltet das Tor offen*, 8; https://johanneum-hamburg. de/index.php/schola-nostra/schule-mit-geschichte/ beruehmte-alumni/70-kurt-sieveking.

39 Amenda, Welthafenstadt, p. 142f.

40 Zilliacus, *Wahlforss*, p. 152

41 Lewallen, *Winter War*, p. 47f.

42 'The Secretary of State to the Finnish Minister (Procopé), Washington, February 8, 1940'. In: *Foreign Relations of the United States*. Diplomatic Papers 1940, Volume 1. General. Department of State. Historical Division, Bureau of Public Affairs, 1959.

43 Lewallen, *Winter War*, p. 54.

44 Ibid.

45 Franklin D. Roosevelt Library: http://www.fdrlibrary.marist. edu/_resources/images/psf/psfc0022.pdf.

46 Warburg, E., *Zeiten und Gezeiten*, p. 156.

47 Ibid.

48 Strauss, *Men and Decisions*, p. 70.

49 Ibid.

50 Gosztony, *Rote Armee*, p. 168.

51 Russia lost 150,000 men in the invasion. The Finns, who only had a few dozen tanks of their own, were nonetheless able to destroy almost 2,000 Soviet armoured vehicles. To do this they used hand-thrown petrol bombs, which they called 'Molotov Cocktails' after the Soviet foreign minister at the time; Oschlies, *Finnlands Juden.*

52 Oschlies, *Finnlands Juden.*

53 Warburg, E., *Zeiten und Gezeiten*, p. 156.

54 Swaine, *The Cravath Firm*, p. 458.

55 Ibid.

56 Stimson/Bundy, *On Active Service.*

57 *Foreign Crops and Markets 1940–1941*, p. 377.

58 'The Minister in Finland (Schoenfeld) to the Secretary of State. Helsinki July 4, 1941.' https://history.state.gov/ historicaldocuments/frus1941v01/d61.

59 *Foreign Relations of the United States*. Diplomatic Papers, 1941.

60 'The Minister in Finland (Schoenfeld) to the Secretary of State. Helsinki July 4, 1941.' https://history.state.gov/ historicaldocuments/frus1941v01/d61.

61 Ibid.

62 Oschlies, *Finnlands Juden.*

63 Quoted in Ibid.

64 See Ibid.

65 'The Finnish Minister (Procopé) to the Secretary of State. Washington, December 8, 1941.' In: *Foreign Relations of the United States.*

66 Information from Max M. Warburg; see also Swaine, *The Cravath Firm*, p. 672.

Chapter 5

1   William Friedmann and Leo Rosen.

2   Goldberg Alfred: WWII and General Interview with John McCloy. Box 51, Folder No. 69. John J. McCloy Papers. Amherst College Archives.

3   Bird, *Chairman*, p. 137.

4   Bauer, *Entzifferte Geheimnisse*, p. 149f.

5   Krammer, *Die internierten Deutschen*, p. 9.

6   See Kinzer, *Brothers*, p. 60f.

7   Ibid., p. 63.

8   Kreis, *Piercing the Fog*, p. 126.

9   Ibid., p. 127.

10 Warburg, E., *Zeiten und Gezeiten*, p. 165.

11 Hoover, *Secrets in Switzerland*, p. 12; Kinzer, *Brothers*, p. 67.

12 Fry, *The Walls Have Ears*, p. 150f.

13 Ibid., p. 96.

14 Ibid.

15 See Warburg E., *Zeiten und Gezeiten*, p. 166f.

16 Ibid., p. 168.

17 Ibid.

18 Bell, *Britische Feindaufklärung*, p. 80.

19 Warburg, E., *Zeiten und Gezeiten*, p. 170.

20 See 'Confidential' 26.7.1945, p. 2. F–10476, Stiftung Warburg Archiv.

21 Warburg, E., *Zeiten und Gezeiten*, pp. 176; 179.

22   Ibid, p. 175.

23   Ibid.

24   Ibid, p. 178.

25   Ibid, p. 171.

26   Ibid, p. 179.

27   'Confidential', p. 5. F–10476, Stiftung Warburg Archiv.

28   Ibid.

29   See Warburg, E., *Zeiten und Gezeiten*, p. 181.

30   Ibid, p. 184.

31   See 'Confidential', 26.7.1945, S. 2. F–10476, Stiftung Warburg Archiv.

32   Stimson/Bundy, *On Active Service*, p. 342.

33   Goldberg, Alfred: WW II and General Interview with John McCloy. p.51. Box 51, Folder No. 69. John J. McCloy Papers. Amherst College Archives.

34   *The Bomber's Baedeker* (Part 2), p. 445

35   https://www.ln-online.de/Lokales/Luebeck/Eine-Tafel-fuer-den-Retter-Luebecks; 16.6.2017

36   Warburg, E., *Zeiten und Gezeiten*, pp. 185–187

37   'Life War artist killed in crash', CBI Roundup, 16 December 1943. https://www.cbi-theater.com/roundup/roundup121643.html.

38   Bednarz, Der große Basar, p. 137.

39   Wentling, Prologue.

40   Wyman, *Das unerwünschte Volk*, p. 222f.

41   Ibid., p. 333.

42   Quoted in ibid., p. 334.

43   Ibid., p. 342f.

44   'A review has demonstrated that such an operation could only be carried out by drawing upon significant air power resources that are currently indispensable to the success of our forces that are engaged in decisive operations elsewhere.' (Quoted in: Wyman, *Das unerwünschte Volk*, p. 339).

45   WWII and general interview with Herbert Okun. 6.5.1983. p.

6. Box 51; Folder 68. John J. McCloy Papers. Amherst College Archives.

46   Bird, *Chairman*, p. 213; Wyman, *Das unerwünschte Volk*, p. 337.

47   Air Prisoners of War Intelligence Unit.

48   See 'Confidential', p. 6. F–10476, Stiftung Warburg Archiv.

49   Confidential Annex A. F–10476, Stiftung Warburg Archiv. Air P/W Interrogaton Unit United States Air Forces in Europe; EMW/wf/APWIU 8 September 1945. F–10476, Stiftung Warburg Archiv.

50   Ibid.

51   See 'Confidential', p. 7. F–10476, Stiftung Warburg Archiv.

52   See Beevor, *Ardennes 1944*, 'Chapter 3: The Battle for Aachen', pp. 28–40.

53   Eric Warburg to Mr. & Mrs. Max M. Warburg, 18 October 1944, 'Somewhere in Belgium'. F–10476, Stiftung Warburg Archiv.

54   See the following resources used when preparing this chapter: Stimson/Bundy, *On Active Service*; Smith, *Jahrhundertprozess*; Gatzke, *Germany and the United States*; Wyman, *Das unerwünschte Volk*; Henke, *Besetzung*; Greiner, *Morgenthau-Legende*; Rust, *Deutschland*.

55   Smith, *Jahrhundertprozess*, p. 34f.; Greiner, *Morgenthau-Legende*.

56   Quoted in Rust, *Deutschland*, p. 590.

57   Quoted in Greiner, *Morgenthau-Legende,* p. 174.

58   Quoted in Ibid., p. 176.

59   Dietrich, *Morgenthau Plan*, p. 61.

60   Summary of developments at the Quebec Conference in Ibid. pp. 58–69.

61   Stimson/Bundy, *On Active Service*, p. 580.

62   Ibid.

63   Communication from the chief Finance Officer in Hamburg (Foreign Exchange Board) to the firm of M. M. Warburg & Co. 29 June 1929. F–20140, Stiftung Warburg Archiv.

64   Attachment to the application for the granting of permission for payment of RM. 60.30 from the blocked account of Mr. Max

M. Israel Warburg. 18 July 1940. F–20140, Stiftung Warburg
Archiv.

65 Communication from Carl Jönsson, tax advisor and accountant,
to Messrs. Max M. Israel Warburg and Dr. Fritz M. Israel.
Warburg, Sekretariat, Hamburg 13, Mittelweg 17; 2 August 1940.
F-20140. Stiftung Warburg Archiv.

66 Letter from Edgar Wind to Erich Warburg, 6.3.1940. F–20140,
Stiftung Warburg Archiv.

67 Re. Warburg-Institute. New York, 11.3.1940. F–20140, Stiftung
Warburg Archiv.

68 Letter from Edgar Wind to Max Warburg, 4.3.1940. F–20140,
Stiftung Warburg Archiv.

69 Bibliothek Warburg – London. Memorandum Erich Warburg.
30 September 1938. F–20140, Stiftung Warburg Archiv.

70 Letter from Edgar Wind to Max Warburg, 4.3.1940. F–20140,
Stiftung Warburg Archiv.

71 Letter from Max Warburg to Edgar Wind, 8.3.1940. F–20140,
Stiftung Warburg Archiv.

72 Re. Warburg-Institute. New York, 11.3.1940. F–20140, Stiftung
Warburg Archiv.

73 Letter from Max Warburg to Fritz Saxl, 28.5.1940. F–20140,
Stiftung Warburg Archiv.

74 *The Observer*: 'A Present from Germany', 24.12.1944. Quoted in:
Wuttke, Emigration, p. 133.

75 See 'Confidential', p. 6. F–10476, Stiftung Warburg Archiv.

76 Henke, *Besetzung*, p. 746.

77 Gimbel, U.S. Policy, p. 436.

78 Henke, *Besetzung*, p. 744

79 See 'Confidential', p. 8. F–10476, Stiftung Warburg Archiv.

80 Stimson/Bundy, *On Active Service*, p. 583.

81 Quoted in Rust, *Deutschland*, p. 597.

82 Smith, *Jahrhundertprozess*, p. 37

83 Quoted in Chernow, *Die Warburgs*, p. 644.

84 Air P/W Interrogation Unit United States Air Forces in
Europe. To: Lt. Col. B. C. Burnam, C, Director of Intelligence,

Headquarters, Ninth Air Force, APO 696. US Army. Signed by Eric M. Warburg. Lt. Col. A.C., Commanding. F–10476, Stiftung Warburg Archiv.

85 Quoted in Overy, *The Bombing War: Europe 1939–1945*, p. 410.

86 Ibid., p. 75.

87 Warburg, E., *Zeiten und Gezeiten*, p. 226; Overy, *The Bombing War*, p. 93

88 Warburg, E., *Zeiten und Gezeiten*, p. 227f.

89 See Ibid., p. 226f; Source: 'Subject: Enemy Intelligence Summeries', 25 S., signed by Eric M. Warburg, Lt. Col., A.C. Commanding. 1 June 1945.

90 Warburg, E., *Zeiten und Gezeiten*, p. 233f.

91 Quoted in Overy, *The Bombing War*, p. 595.

92 Warburg, E., *Zeiten und Gezeiten*, p. 215.

93 Warburg, J., *Deutschland*, p. 254.

94 Ibid., p. 268.

95 Chernow, *Die Warburgs*, p. 625f.

96 Von Lingen, *Immunitätsversprechen*, p. 381

97 Henke, *Besetzung*, p. 748; Niemetz, Daniel, '1945: Kriegsende in Miteldeutschland', MDR Zeitreise, 4.2.20, 22:05 Uhr; Hunt, *La rafle des savants allemands*.

98 Ibid.

99 Henke, *Besetzung*, p. 753; Gimbel, *U.S. Policy*; Pothoff and Schmid, *Wunibald I. E. Kamm*, p. 273.

100 Ibid.; Samuel, *American Raiders*; Kurowski, *Allierte Jagd*, p. 14; Huwart, *Du V2 à Véronique*.

101 Warburg, E., *Zeiten und Gezeiten*, p. 270.

102 See Richardi, *SS Geiseln*.

103 www.stiftung-20-juli-1944.de/reden/die-toten-der-mordaktion-in-der-nacht-vom-23-auf-den-24-april-1945-prof-dr-johannes-tuchel-21042016.

104 Doerries, *Individualist and Diplomat*, p. 35.

105 Chernow, *Die Warburgs*, p. 650.

106 Lorenz, 'Heim', p. 348.

107 Ibid., p. 347.

108 Dönhoff, 'Leben heißt, sich verpfichtet wissen'. In: *Die Zeit*, No. 16, 11.4.1980.

109 Warburg E., *Zeiten und Gezeiten*, p. 249.

110 Greiner, *Morgenthau-Legende*, p. 35.

111 Quoted in Streb, 'Wissenstransfer', p. 289.

112 Heinrich Kronstein's Documents and Publications. Preface to Report on Conditions in Germany, ca. 1945. International Law Institute.

Chapter 6

1 Kleßmann, *M. M. Warburg*, p.115.

2 Ibid., p. 117.

3 Lillteicher, *Rückerstattung*, p. 78

4 Dan Diner, 'Im Zeichen des Banns'. In: *Die Welt*, 15.9.2012. Dan Diner 'Vorwort'. In: Goschler, *Kriegsverbrechen*, p. 11; Ibid., p. 31.

5 Lorenz, 'Heim', p. 352.

6 Stelzl-Gallian, 'Alfons Thorsch'.

7 Chernow, *Die Warburgs*, p. 680.

8 Warburg, E., *Zeiten und Gezeiten*, p. 215.

9 Zetsche, *The Quest for Atlanticism*, p. 50f.

10 Ibid.

11 Whereas in 1933 Emmet was still forming Christian committees to boycott the Nazis, by 1947 he was most often to be found sitting on CIA committees, for instance the International Rescue Commitee and the American Friends of the Captive Natons.

12 Zetsche, *The Quest for Atlanticism*, p. 57.

13 Heideking, *Politisches Kalkül*, p. 242f.

14 Quoted in Sebestyen, *Das Jahr*.

15 Mauer, *Brückenbauer*, p. 58.

16 Heideking, *Politisches Kalkül*, p. 246.

17 Ibid.

18 List of the Surviving Dependants of Murdered Resistance Fighters, 189 pages. F–10589, Stiftung Warburg Archiv.

19　'List of German Families involved in the Plot to Kill Hitler'.
　　F–10580, Stiftung Warburg Archiv.

20　Jenss, *Israelitisches Krankenhaus.*

21　Lorenz, 'Heim', p. 358.

22　See Pöppmann, 'Im Amt geblieben', p. 251.

23　'Im Gespräch: Richard von Weizsäcker. Es geht hier nicht um
　　meinen Vater', in *Frankfurter Allgemeine Zeitung*, 25.10.2010.

24　Boveri, *Diplomat.*

25　Hofmann, *Marion Dönhoff.*

26　Boveri, *Diplomat.*

27　Quoted in Hofmann, *Marion Dönhoff.*

28　On Ernst von Weizsäcker and the Wilhelmstraße trial, see:
　　Döscher, *Seilschaften*; Conze, 'Kein Hort des Widerstands';
　　Conze, *Amt*; Conze, 'Es wurde ganz wacker Widerstand
　　geleistet'; Pöppmann, 'Im Amt geblieben'; Weinke, *Nürnberger
　　Prozesse.*

29　Malinowski, Stephan, 'Vom König zum Führer', quoted in
　　Döscher, *Seilschaften.*

30　Dönhoff, De Nobilitate; Marion Dönhoff described the
　　circumstances of this first meeting in a volume of memoirs,
　　which Bernstorff's friend Elly Reventlow published at the
　　suggestion of Eric Warburg.

31　Cabinet minutes of the German Federal government online: The
　　Allied security and control system.

32　*The New York Times* 21.5.1949 quoted in Bird, Deutschlands
　　Prokonsul, p. 128.

33　Hellmut Becker to Marion Dönhoff 19.12.1949. F–10580,
　　Stiftung Warburg Archiv.

34　Wilmes, 'Wilhelmstraßenprozess'.

35　Ibid.

36　Frei, *Vergangenheitspolitik*, p. 140.

37　Asmussen, *Studnitz*, p. 97.

38　Letter from Reinhold Niebuhr to John McCloy, 15.6.1949;
　　Letter from George F. Kennan to John McCloy, 2.6.1949; Box
　　30 Folder No. 24. John J. McCloy Papers. Amherst College

Archives. Henry M. Andrews (Victor Gollancz): 'To The Editor Of *The Times*'. In: *The Times*, 19.12.1949.

39   Lillteicher, *Rückerstattung*, p. 89.

40   Lutz, 'Fälschungen'.

41   http://www.ifz-muenchen.de/archiv/zs/zs-2319.pdf.

42   Chernow, *Die Warburgs*, p. 713.

43   See the correspondence with Heinrich Kronstein in F–10580, Stiftung Warburg Archiv. See also Warburg 2013: 255.

44   *The New York Times*, 14.12.1949: 'Weizsaecker gets Porter, Arnold Aid; U.S. Lawyers to Fight 7-Year Sentence Imposed on Nazi by American Tribunal'.

45   This programme involved reducing the industrial capacity of Germany, whose heavy industrial sector had grown massively as a result of four-year plans and a war economy, to prewar levels once more and at the same time demilitarizing production. The dismantled machine tools and fabrication plants would also serve as reparations goods (Benz 2005).

46   Kramer, *Die britische Demontagepolitik*, p. 429.

47   Ibid., p. 431f. Süddeutsche Zeitung Foto: *Dossier Demontage und Reparationen, 1945–1949*. 53 images; Foerster, *Praktischer Stahlschiffbau*, p. 539.

48   Kramer, *Die britische Demontagepolitik*, p. 430; Warburg, E., *Zeiten und Gezeiten*, p. 265.

49   Chernow, *Die Warburgs*, p. 645.

50   Quoted in Ibid., p. 644.

51   Diaries – HICOG 1949, July – Dec 31; Box 3, Folder No. 6. John J. McCloy Papers. Amherst College Archives.

52   Lehmann, *Marshall Plan*, p. 223.

53   Ibid.

54   Warburg, E., *Zeiten und Gezeiten*, p. 265.

55   This account of events at the time has been taken from Peters' Salzgitter Speech 5./6.3.2010.

56   Letter from Eric Warburg to John McCloy, 'at present Hamburg, 75 Ferdinandstraße, August 27th, 1949.' F–10580, Stiftung Warburg Archiv.

57 Letter from John McCloy to US Secretary of State Dean
    Acheson. 14.9.1949. Box 3; Folder No. 6. John J. McCloy Papers.
    Amherst College Archives.

58 Schwarzer, *Marion Dönhoff*; *Die Zeit*: 'Marion Dönhoff wird
    75 Jahre alt: Widersprüche aushalten, Spannungen leben.'
    30.11.1984; *Stern*: 'Neuanfang: Von Schuld und Sühne.' 5.2.2001.

59 See *Hearings Before The Committee of . . .*, pp. III–15.

60 Ibid.

61 Schwartz, Begnadigung, p. 384.

62 Henry M. Andrews (Victor Gollancz): 'To The Editor Of *The
    Times*'. In: *The Times*, 19.12.1949.

63 Ibid.

64 Letter from Hellmut Becker to Marion Dönhoff. 19.12.1949.
    F-10580. Stiftung Warburg Archiv. Letter from Marion Dönhoff
    to Eric Warburg. 21.12.1949. F-10580. Stiftung Warburg Archiv.

65 Eric Warburg to John 'Jack' McCloy, 28.12.1949. F–10580,
    Stiftung Warburg Archiv. 'Brought down to its simplest form it
    is the knowledge that we are dealing in Nuremberg now with
    two distinct types of defendants, namely Nazi gangsters, who
    should be strictly punished, and the other type, whom you
    might refer to in the plural as the "Weizsäckers", (for he is a
    prototype of them), who – looking at the wrong Hindenburg
    example – perhaps wrongly stayed on with the erroneous hope
    that they could prevent worse and who, in their subsequent
    efforts, were often too timid and too weak.'

66 Frei, *Vergangenheitspolitik*, p. 193.

67 Letters to the editor of *The New York Times*. McCloy's Speech.
    Status of War Criminals Discussed in Democratizing of
    Germany. Robert S. Marcus, Political Director, World Jewish
    Congress, New York, 7 February 1950.

68 Carl Friedrich v. Weizsäcker to Eric Warburg, 12.2.50. F–10580,
    Stiftung Warburg Archiv.

69 Memorandum. General Statements. F–10580, Stiftung Warburg
    Archiv. Carl Friedrich v. Weizsäcker to Eric Warburg, 12.2.50.
    F–10580, Stiftung Warburg Archiv.

70 See Conze, *Amt.*

71 Carl Friedrich v. Weizsäcker to Eric Warburg, 12.2.50. F–10580, Stiftung Warburg Archiv.

72 Chernow, *Die Warburgs*, p. 645.

73 Carl Melchior, 1933, quoted in Döscher, *Seilschaften.*

74 Eric Warburg to John 'Jack' McCloy, 28.12.1949. F–10580, Stiftung Warburg Archiv.

75 Carl Friedrich v. Weizsäcker to Eric Warburg, 12.2.50. F–10580, Stiftung Warburg Archiv.

76 Cf. Conze, Aufstand; cf. Dönhoff, Marion: 'Leben heißt, sich verpfichtet wissen. Zum 80. Geburtstag von Eric Warburg'. In: *Die Zeit* No. 16/1980.

77 Eric Warburg to John 'Jack' McCloy, 28.12.1949. F–10580, Stiftung Warburg Archiv. '... the fact that some infamous documents carry their signature is, for these type of men to whom I refer, a great weight on their consciences, which, with imprisonment and ordeal of trial they have already suffered seems to me punishment enough.'

78 Eric Warburg to John 'Jack' McCloy, 28.12.1949. F–10580, Stiftung Warburg Archiv.

79 Chernow, *Die Warburgs*, p. 784.

80 Eric Warburg to John 'Jack' McCloy, 28.12.1949. F–10580, Stiftung Warburg Archiv.

81 Cf. Schwartz, *America's Germany*, p. 175.

82 Lillteicher, 'Rückerstattung'.

83 For an extensive account of this, see Lillteicher, *Die Ruckerstattung jüdischen Eigentums*, p. 244f.

84 See Goschler, *Kriegsverbrechen*, p. 30f.

85 Hofmann, *Marion Dönhoff*; Adam von Trott zu Solz, who in order to cloak his activities joined the NSDAP in 1940, was an active resistance fighter in the German Foreign Office, and secretly worked on plans to overthrow the Nazi regime. Yet Adam von Trott zu Solz had never signed documents that consigned Jews to the extermination camps.

86 Quoted in 'Warum Hitler die Bombe nicht baute', *Die Zeit* No. 18, 1992.
87 Jungk, Robert quoted in Ibid.
88 Quoted in Ibid.
89 Schirach, Richard v.: *Die Nacht der Physiker*.
90 Reus, 'A Plea of Humanity'.
91 Wentling, 'The Engineer'.
92 Berger, *AJC and Germany*.
93 Berger, Ibid., p. 8.
94 Ibid.
95 *Hearings before The Committee of ….* p. 65.
96 Ibid., p. 75.
97 Berger, *AJC and Germany*, p. 10.
98 Warburg, J., *Deutschland*, p. 269.
99 Chernow, *Die Warburgs*, p. 708; JTA: $3,000,000 left to charity.
100 Kleßmann, *M. M. Warburg*.
101 See Shafir, *Ambiguous Relations*.
102 Warburg, E., *Zeiten und Gezeiten*, p. 275.
103 Ibid., p. 270.
104 See Chernow, *Die Warburgs*, p. 706 f.

Chapter 7

1 Stimson/Bundy: *On Active Service*.
2 Letter from McCloy to Eric Warburg. 24 June 1983. Box 51, Folder No. 89. John J. McCloy Papers. Amherst College Archives.
3 Maurice Matloff and Goldberg Alfred: WWII and General Interview with John McCloy. S. 27. Box 51, Folder No. 69. John J. McCloy Papers. Amherst College Archives; Letter from McCloy to Eric Warburg. 24 June 1983. Box 51, Folder No. 89. John J. McCloy Papers. Amherst College Archives.
4 Ibid.
5 Quoted in Mintz: 'Why Didn't We Bomb Auschwitz?' In: *The Washington Post*, 17.4.1983.

6   Geyelin, Philip: 'John McCloy's Good Name'. In: *The Washington Post*, 29.6.1983.

7   Letter from McCloy to Eric Warburg. 24 June 1983. Box 51, Folder No. 89. John J. McCloy Papers. Amherst College Archives.

8   Geyelin, Philip: 'John McCloy's Good Name'. In: *The Washington Post*, 29.6.1983.

9   Letter from John McCloy to Eric Warburg, 7 November 1983. Box 51, Folder No. 83. John J. McCloy Papers. Amherst College Archives.

10   Correspondence with the BBC: 23 April 1981; 13 May 1981; 26 May 1981; 23 July 1981; 25 July 1981; 4 August 1981; Box 48, Folder No. 10. Request by Claude Lanzmann Box 50, Folder No. 27. John J. McCloy Papers. Amherst College Archives.

11   Goschler, *Kriegsverbrechen,* Document 14. Benjamin B. Ferencz and John J. McCloy. New York, 24.4.1984. Typewritten transcript, pp. 180–218.

12   Bird, *Chairman*, p.41f.

13   Czempiel, *Sicherheitssystem*, p.243

14   WWII and General interview with Herbert Okun. 6 May 1983. p. 2. Box 51, Folder No. 68. John J. McCloy Papers. Amherst College Archives.

15   Ibid.

16   Wyman, *Das unerwünschte Volk*, p. 366.

17   Quoted in Ibid., p. 366.

18   '... And there are these things like Auschwitz and these other things, maybe they constitute as little footnotes to history, but they are not the things that I'm interested in. I'm interested in trying to perpetuate something that's worthwhile perpetuating for the future security of the country, the sound decision-making aspect.' WWII and general interview with Herbert Okun. 6 May 1983. p. 11. Box 51, Folder No. 68. John J. McCloy Papers. Amherst College Archives.

19   Ibid.

20   Maurice Matloff and Goldberg Alfred: WWII and General

Interview with John McCloy. S. 20. Box 51, Folder No. 69. John J. McCloy Papers. Amherst College Archives.

21 Goschler, *Kriegsverbrechen*, Document 13. Benjamin B. Ferencz to John J. McCloy. New Rochelle, N.Y., 10 August 1983. Typewritten letter, 2 pages: pp. 178–80.

22 Chernow, *Die Warburgs*, pp. 63, 707.

23 The same year that Eric Warburg died.

24 Warburg Spinelli, *Erinnerungen*, p. 282.

25 Letter from Eric Warburg to John McCloy, 10.9.1981. Box 51, Folder No. 35. John J. McCloy Papers. Amherst College Archives.

Index

Erzberger, Matthias 30

F

Fein, Otto 67
Ferencz, Benjamin (Ben)
    186, 203, 216, 217
Finland
    Dalsbruk steelworks 97–8,
        115–16, 124
    Finnish–American trading
        company 123, 125–7, 130
    Finnish–Soviet Winter
        War 115, 118–20, 130
    guerilla warfare 123
    Jews 129–30
    military equipment
        125–7
    US aid 119, 120–21, 123–5
First World War
    Bethlehem Steel sabotage
        claims 94–6
    German reparations 18–19,
        21–2, 30, 35–6, 45
    US 11–12
    Warburg family
        experiences 12–15
Flexner, Abraham 64–5
Flick, Friedrich 96
Friedlaender, Ernst 208

G

Gaus, Friedrich 185, 188

German Communist Party
    (KPD) 189
German Democratic Party
    (DDP) 17, 26, 31
German Jewish Benevolent
    Society 60, 110
German Jews
    anti-Semitism 12–16, 31,
        206–7
    Benevolent Society for
        German Jews 60, 110
    exclusion from
        commercial life 60–61
    Hamburg 172–3
    Nuremburg Laws (1935)
        83, 84
    pogrom (1938) 110
    property expropriations
        104, 159, 173–4, 179–80
    repression 52–5
    self-help organisations 60
    see also emigration;
        reparations; war crimes
        trials
German Popular Party 13
Germany
    atomic bomb 204
    banking loans 42–4
    German–Soviet Non-
        Aggression Pact 116,
        118
    hyperinflation 32, 33–4